SAINT LENNY . . .

a merchant seaman, a borscht belt comic,
a night club superstar, a culture hero, a
victim of persecution from the courts and
the cops, a dead junkie, a legend!

THE ESSENTIAL
LENNY BRUCE

takes you into a vivid, insanely original,
devastatingly funny world—a comic pan-
orama of contemporary society created by
a tragic genius!

THE
ESSENTIAL
LENNY BRUCE

*compiled and edited
by John Cohen*

A Douglas/Ballantine Book
BALLANTINE BOOKS • NEW YORK

This book published with the cooperation of
Douglas International Corporation.

First U.S. Printing: December, 1967
Second U.S. Printing: January, 1968
Third U.S. Printing: March, 1968
Fourth U.S. Printing: June, 1968
Fifth U.S. Printing: March, 1970
Sixth U.S. Printing: April, 1971
Seventh U.S. Printing: July, 1971
Eighth U.S. Printing: February, 1973
Ninth U.S. Printing: August, 1974

First Canadian Printing: March, 1968
Second Printing: April, 1971

Cover photo © 1974 Time-Life Inc.

Printed in the United States of America

BALLANTINE BOOKS
A Division of Random House, Inc.
201 East 50th Street, New York, N.Y. 10022
Simultaneously published by
Ballantine Books, Ltd., Toronto, Canada

People should be taught what is,
not what should be. All my humor
is based on destruction and despair.
If the whole world were tranquil, without
disease and violence, I'd be standing in the
breadline—right back of J. Edgar Hoover.

—Lenny Bruce

"He was a sweet, peaceful and beautiful man.
We used to go sailing on the bay and Lenny
would sit and write poetry about love and
beauty—and about his own frustrations. I don't
think he was a comedian, really, I think he was
a preacher."

—Enrico Banducci, the hungry i, quoted in
the *Los Angeles Times*, August 5, 1966.

CONTENTS

EDITOR'S FOREWORD

Dead, Lenny Bruce has been lauded as a great satirist "in the tradition of Swift," as a great parodist, a moralist, a preacher, even as a shaman exorcizing the demons of our modern society. Whatever Bruce was—and above all he was incredibly funny—two basic characteristics were responsible for the effectiveness of his work: he was a fine poet and a fine dramatist. He had a fantastic ability to catch the perfect image at the perfect moment and to phrase it exactly and uniquely; and he had a beautiful sense of form and structure.

I have tried to make sure that Bruce's poetry and structure were not lost in the transformation of his material from the spoken work to the printed page. Something had to be lost, of course, if only his intonations, his accents, his rhythms, speeds, pauses and gestures; but wherever possible I have described the type of accent Bruce was using, and when speed or speech quality was extreme, I have suggested the effect by running words together, through spacing, or through punctuation.

Essentially, Bruce's material has been left uncut and uncensored. Fear of libel has forced the deletion of a name or phrase perhaps a half a dozen times in the whole book, and occasionally, when Bruce began a sentence but then crossed it out himself—verbally—I have left it out too. The only other deletion that has been made occurred when Bruce fell into a "you know" fit—when every sentence began and ended with "you know." This did not happen too frequently, and even when it did happen I have removed only a few of the "you knows" in the interests of easier reading; most I left in in order to preserve the feel of Bruce's language. In the text, dots between phrases or sentences do not mean that material was deleted; they mean that Bruce paused momentarily in his speech.

When Bruce was performing at his best, he sometimes gave an entire show a beautifully effective structure and form, and the whole show works as a well-organized argument skillfully dedicated to the proof of Bruce's point. These shows are so beautiful, they move so smoothly, logically and effectively from one bit to another, so artfully and absorbingly from beginning to end, that it seems a mistake not to organize the book as a series of complete shows.

But suppose that on one night Bruce did a beautiful show including six bits, in this order: a, b, c, d, e, and f. The next night in another beautiful show Bruce used bits a, g, b, h, c, i, and x in this order. If one were to preserve both beautiful shows, bits a, b, c and d would be duplicated. Even if space had permitted it, such duplication, as far as the reader's experience is concerned, would itself have ruined the beauty of the second show: few, if any, would read the bits a second (or third or fourth) time, and even those who did would not appreciate them fully in repetition. Thus the feeling of the beauty of the second show's form, even printed complete and unadulterated, would effectively have been ruined for the reader.

In any case, Bruce seldom produced a show where the entirety had such exquisite structure. Generally, Bruce's shows did hang together, and beautifully, but this was less because of the structure of the entire show than because all of Bruce's material was permeated by Bruce's own philosophy, a well-developed set of ideas and ideals which molded all his material. Each of Bruce's bits expressed a part of this whole outlook and was consistent (generally) with the whole. And Bruce did not organize his shows in advance . When he performed, he had at his command a tremendous amount of material he had already worked into shape, a brilliant mind and an amazing imagination, and a fantastic memory. With these tools, spontaneously, Bruce put his shows together. Never did he do a whole show exactly as he had any time before, just as he never redid any single bit exactly as he had before.

So instead of organizing this book around complete shows, I have tried a different method. Many of Bruce's shows concentrated on one dominant point or emphasized a certain topic: integration and segregation; the law; obscenity; Jews; show business; the good-good culture. Seldom if ever did Bruce concentrate exclusively on any such topic; but frequently he did spend almost all of a show's time on just one such topic.

It is into topics of this sort that I have reorganized Bruce's material, and I do not think that the organization is too arbitrary. In many cases, it has been possible to hook together a long string of bits exactly as Bruce himself hooked them together at one time or another, and for the most part the topics are ones which Bruce himself liked to concentrate his shows on. Also, this organization has made it possible to arrange the material so that Bruce's thoughts and preoccupations are unveiled and explained progressively. This is not crucial to the early sections, which could stand and explain themselves independently; but the sections on the dirty-word concept, busts and trials, heat, judges and lawyers, the law, obscenity, and the good-good culture are closely interrelated. They have been organized and arranged in a way which I hope will make both the individual bits and Bruce's over-all thinking as clear and meaningful as possible. And here, too, this has not caused any severe disruption of Bruce's own typical organization. For the most part, the bits follow each other as they did in one or another of Bruce's shows.

Above all, Lenny Bruce was a dramatist: the interplay of character and voice in a dramatic dialogue was his natural mode of expression. Again and again he tried to express ideas through analytic or descriptive phrases, stumbled, started again, stumbled, and then moved into a skit, a little play between voices, in order to grasp and express exactly what he meant. Usually, the plays worked beautifully. Plays, of course, are meant to be performed, and the text of Bruce's plays will never be as good as Lenny Bruce himself. But plays do make good reading, especially Bruce's plays—because they are not total scenes with entire characters and complex interrelationships between many persons; they are simple interchanges between exaggerated voices meant to express only one or two particular characteristics.

This is the "essential" Lenny Bruce—the dramatist and poet creating his fantastically funny, beautifully structured, delightfully phrased and very important little plays. If the reader opens up his imagination and hears the words printed on these pages, as he does when he reads poetry or anything that is made of lovely language, the "essential" Lenny Bruce will come back to life. And without Bruce around to do his material for us, I think it is better for him to live this way, for us to read his material exactly as he created it, than for it to be forgotten completely, or for us to watch some imitator's second-rate attempt to recreate the magical effects that Bruce himself had.

THE ESSENTIAL
LENNY BRUCE

Blacks

The reason I don't get hung up with, well, say, integration, is that by the time Bob Newhart is integrated, I'm bigoted. And anyway, Martin Luther King, Bayard Rustin are geniuses, the battle's won. By the way, are there any niggers here tonight?

> [*Outraged whisper*] *"What did he say?* 'Are there any *niggers* here tonight'? Jesus Christ! Is that *cruel.* Does he have to get that low for laughs? Wow! Have I ever talked about the *schwarzes* when the *schwarzes* had gone home? Or spoken about the Moulonjohns when they'd left? Or placated some Southerner by absence of voice when he ranted and raved about *nigger nigger nigger?"*

Are there any niggers here tonight? I know that one nigger who works here, I see him back there. Oh, there's two niggers, customers, and, ah, *aha!* Between those two niggers sits one kike—man, thank God for the kike!

Uh, two kikes. That's two kikes, and three niggers, and one spic. One spic—two, three spics. One mick. One mick, one spic, one hick, thick, funcky, spunky boogey. And there's another kike. Three kikes. Three kikes, one guinea, one greaseball. Three greaseballs, two guineas. Two guineas, one hunky funky lace-curtain Irish mick. That mick spic hunky funky boogey.

Two guineas plus three greaseballs and four boogies makes usually three spics. Minus two Yid spic Polack funky spunky Polacks.

AUCTIONEER: Five more niggers! Five more niggers!

GAMBLER: I pass with six niggers and eight micks and four spics.

The point? That the word's suppression gives it the power, the violence, the viciousness. If President Kennedy got on television and said, "Tonight I'd like to introduce the niggers in my cabinet," and he yelled "niggerniggerniggerniggerniggerniggernigger" at every nigger he saw, "boogeyboogeyboogeyboogeyboogey, niggerniggerniggernigger" till nigger didn't mean anything any more, till nigger lost its meaning—you'd never make any four-year-old nigger cry when he came home from school.

Screw "Negro!" Oh, it's so good to say, "Nigger!" Boy!

"Hello, Mr. Nigger, how're you?"

People remember. They'll remember specific people who broke their balls. That's the way people are, and they will be shitting for those people. You know, if you're thinking about the world, how the world looks to the Negro—here's how the world looks to the American Negro: he's a convict rioting in a corrupt prison, and if they do kill Pat O'Brien, so what? The conditions are bad, and sloppy, and that'll be the scene.

Dick Gregory said to me, "You wanna make the

16

marches?" and I said I was going through a lot of litigation, and I probably would bring down some heat, you know?

He said, "No, man," he said, "make 'em."

"Well," I said, "I'm reticent about making the marches, because I think people would assume it's a Joe Louis-Hoffa move—exploiting the issue for my own dues, you know? Anyway, the marches are sloppy, people shoving back and forth, Al Hibler and Ray Charles walking into people —"

But he said, "No, really make it."

Then he told me about his old lady being pregnant, getting thrown in the joint, and his getting in jail—the whole scene, all the hassles. Then he said something to me, really whipped me around.

He said, "It doesn't matter, you get thrown in the joint," he said, "as long as we trick Whitey."

I said, "What?"

He said, "It doesn't matter, the end result, as long as we trick Whitey, fuck up Boss Charley."

I said, "Trick Whitey, fuck up Boss Charley . . . I've never heard that before. That's an underground phrase."

Then I started thinking: I've never heard *any* hostility from any American Negroes. I did hear that from Jews and Christians, but never from any American Negroes. I've never heard any outward hostility, no spoken word. If you hear in traffic,

TOUGH VOICE: Hey, asshole, move it over dere! That's never a colored driver, Mack.

Isn't that a little strange? I don't think you've heard it either. And they're pissed off, and justifiably so. But yet I've never heard that. Then I realized I'm going to hear it. Oh, yeah. There's going to be a vote, and a change.

You see, there are a few more Negroes than you know

about. Oh, yeah. Because census-takers, I assume, have been remiss in their duties, and passed a few Negro houses:

> CENSUS TAKER: Ah, frig it, I'm not going in those houses—dogs, dirt—I don't wanna go in there. Ask that kid on the lawn. How many live on this block, sonny?
>
> KID: Ah, well, ah . . .
>
> CENSUS TAKER: O.K., write it down.

You'd shit if you saw a half a million from one town alone?

> "Two billion, taken from Alabama; the vote's still coming in!"
>
> "Two billion? Are you kidding? Two billion?"
>
> "Where're those votes coming from? Where've all these people been?"
>
> "They've been in the houses, man. Sixteen thousand to a house—bunks, tiers—they've been living there."

So the vote's going to bring a change. In a year you'll see an all-black jury and a black judge, and *shit!*

> OUTRAGED VOICE: *They're all black! How'm I gonna get a fair shake when they're all black?*

And you're not. Haha, haha. That's how it is.

And all the people'll be screaming.

> "Are you *kidding?* I was *before* those marches, I was *before* Bayard Rustin. Me? Me? I was so liberal—I'll show you cancelled checks, for Chrissakes! I've been since 1939 with that integration shit. Are you kidding with that?"
>
> NEGRO: You are? *You're full of shit, you liberal!* I'm tired of talking to you people. Every German you talk to loved the Jews, and they're all dead. So you're full of shit, Jim. That's it.

Liberal schmiberal. Um, hm.

18

Now, I don't think Barry Goldwater knows anything about that phrase, "Trick Whitey, fuck up boss Charley." I mean, he's from Arizona; their god is the auto club. They're cut off from everything. Will he be ready? Will he understand the language? Will he understand that huge block of—

> NEGROES: Look here, Mr. Goldwater, tell us what's happening. Don't shuck us, you dig?
>
> GOLDWATER: *What was that?* What are they talking about? This a trick or something?
>
> NEGRO: Now don't jive us, tell us what's happening, be straight.
>
> GOLDWATER: *What is this, a trick?* What are they . . . what does that *mean*, 'Be straight'?
>
> NEGRO: You jive, motherfucker, you jive!
>
> GOLDWATER: You *what?* 'You jive, motherfucker, you jive!'
>
> AIDE: Now Mr. Goldwater, *please*, before you make any decisions, that term may be a term of endearment with these people. It doesn't always relate to hostility.

Which is the truth.

> NEGRO: Hey, motherfucker, you're something else, Jim! That's it!

How about that? I mean, we piss away a million dollars on Radio Free Europe, and don't know anything about the country within the country—don't know *anything* about these people.

We got to stop pissing away all the money on Radio Free Europe. Mississippi is like the Amazon, with those missionaries down there. Let's face it—you'd be afraid to go to Mississippi—you'd be afraid to walk there alone down the street. It doesn't say that on your visa—"stamp O." We never give one nickel to Radio Free South—

ever. And I haven't seen one newspaper report that understood anything about those people, it's just *rank rank rank rank rank*.

The geography in this bit is unimportant, but I'm always searching for new areas, so I'll change it tonite to, ummm, Watertown, N.Y. That's a little ways from Buffalo and Niagara Falls.

Actually, its eighty tract homes, and we are now in the "Medallion Model Home," with a formica ceiling. I'm a construction boss. I built all these pads. This pad I built for about eighteen thousand five hundred dollars, I dumped it for sixty thousand—lotta built-ins.

Now, they have a party—when I sell the pad, the people hold a big house-warming party, right? And who do they invite? They invite the guy who built the house, and the neighbors. Eric,* being colored, he would be a musician, which does not make the people who have the party bigoted in the least. Because many people do not know colored people, though to invite them to a party as a prop is Crow Jim. And there's a good book on Crow Jim: Ralph Ellison, *The Invisible Man,* man, which really lays it on the stick, man.

Now, the party is swinging, and the humor emanates from the now-becoming-obscure white person's concept of "Just How Do You Relax Colored People at Parties?" And in the bit, I play the white guy:

> WHITE MAN [*rasping, aggressive voice*]: Oh, boy, what a hell of a party, eh?
> NEGRO [*clear, well-educated*]: Yeah, I'm enjoying myself, having a wonderful time.
> WHITE: I really stuffed myself, boy, and I'm pissed to the ears, too, on top of it. Oh, boy . . . Before

---

* Eric Miller, a Negro guitarist who helped Bruce occasionally by taking The Negro's part in this bit.

you drink you should take a tablespoonful of olive
oil.

NEGRO: Is that right?

WHITE: Thass the best . . .

NEGRO: Oh.

WHITE: I didn't get your name.

NEGRO: Miller.

WHITE: Miller, my name is Mr. Anderson.

NEGRO: Mr. Anderson, glad to know you.

WHITE: Pleasure to know you indeed, sir.

[*Pause. Neither knows what to say next.*]

WHITE: You know, that Joe Louis was a hell of a
fighter.

NEGRO: Yeah, you can say that again. Joe Louis
was a hell of a fighter.

WHITE: What a man, boy.

NEGRO: Yeah, got right in there, right out.

WHITE: He's a credit to your race. Don't you ever
forget that, you sonofagun.

NEGRO: Well, thank you very much.

WHITE: Thass awright, perfectly awright.

[*Pause*]

WHITE: Well, here's to Henry Armstrong.

NEGRO: Yeah, here's to Henry Armstrong.

WHITE: Awright . . .

[*Pause*]

WHITE: You know, I did all the construction here,
you know?

NEGRO: Oh, you did?

WHITE: I did all except the painting, and these
Hebes—[*whispers*] you're not Jewish, are you?

NEGRO: No, man, I'm not.

WHITE: You know what I mean?

NEGRO: Yeah, I understand.

WHITE: Someone calls me a Sheeney I'll knock em
right on their ass . . . I wanna tell you sometin. I

21

don't care what the hell a guy is so long as they keep in their place, you know?

NEGRO: Right.

WHITE: So anyway, I tell all these Mochs—Jewish people, you know—I say, I'm gonna put up the lath. You know how they talk you know, "Vut tchou doink, dahlink"? You know? I'll tell you some Aby-and-Becky jokes later. So anyway, they say, "Vut tchou doink vit de paint," you know? That's Chinese—I do all the dialects. And, ah, then they pick out this color—themselves—isn't that a crappy color for ya?

NEGRO: No, I don't think so. I think that's very interesting, how they use the Dufy Blue with so many other pastels.

WHITE: That sounds like alotta Commie horseshit to me—Du-fee blue.

NEGRO: Yeah, that's what it is, a Dufy blue.

WHITE: Whatthehellissat?

NEGRO: Some French painter derived that color. I dunno.

WHITE: Yeah? Du-Fee blue! I like that. That's pretty good. Du-fee blue. You didn't learn that in the back of the bus, you sonufagun! You're awright! Du-fee blue. How 'bout that. You know, you're a white Jew, you're O.K. You're really a good guy,

NEGRO: Thank you, thank you.

[*Pause*]

WHITE: Well, here's to Stephen Fetcher.

NEGRO: Yeah, here's to Stephen Fetcher.

[*Pause*]

WHITE: I guess you know alotta people in the show business, eh?

NEGRO: Yeah, I've met quite a few in my travels.

22

WHITE: Aaaah, I'm bad on names, what the hell is that, aaaaah . . . You know Aunt Jemimah?

NEGRO: No, I don't know Aunt Jemimah. I'm sorry, I don't know her.

WHITE: That guy on the—on the Cream of Wheat box?

NEGRO: No, I don't know him either.

[*Pause*]

WHITE: Well, here's to Paul Robinson.

NEGRO: Yeah, here's to Paul Robinson.

WHITE: Yeah, boy . . . . You get anything to eat yet?

NEGRO: No, I'm kinda hungry. I wish a had a sandwich or something.

WHITE: I haven't got any fried chicken or watermelon, ahhh . . . raisins, or rice, whatever you people eat, but, aaahhhh, we'll get sometin up for you there . . .

You know sometin, you're awright, you know that? And I'm a good guy too—you see what I just did? *I touched ya.* Yeah! You're awright. Come over here. I like you, you sonofagun, you're awright.

NEGRO: Well, thank you . . .

WHITE: I'd like to have you over the house.

NEGRO: Well, thank you very much. I'd like to come over.

WHITE: Wouldja like that?

NEGRO: Umhum.

WHITE: It'll be dark soon, aaahhh . . . I mean, what the hell, you know, aaahhh . . . . You gotta be careful they're all movin' in . . . you know? I mean, what the hell, I read some jerk overn the paper, *The Howard Star,* there, they're jus bein smart, you know—that first, the Indians were here, then when the white people came they said "Oh Christ the white people are moving in," you know,

and they're gonna be all over, you know—but
that's dangerous, that kinda talk, you know?
[*Pause*]
WHITE: Here's to all colored people.
NEGRO: O.K.
WHITE: Awright . . . Now, I wanya to comover
the house, but I gotta tell ya somtin cause I know
you people get touchy once in a while.
NEGRO: Oh, umhm?
WHITE: Yeah, ahhh, I gotta sister, ya see?
NEGRO: Yeah?
WHITE: Well now cummere. [*Whispers*] You
wouldn't wanna Jew doin it to your sister, wouldja?
NEGRO: It doesn't make any difference to me, just
as long as he's a nice guy.
WHITE: *Whattayou, on the weed or somtin?* Look,
nobody wants a Sheeney plowin' their sister, an
I don't want no coon doin' it to my sister. What the
hell, that makes sense. You can come over my
house if you promise you don't do it to my sister.
Promise?
NEGRO: O.K.
WHITE: Awright.
NEGRO: Here's to the Mau Mau.
WHITE: Awright.

The guy in this bit, we assume—see, that's the funny
thing about indictment—we assume that this cat is all
bad, then, and we destroy him. But you can't, man. He's
bad in this sense, cause he has not matured, he has not
been in a proper environment, cause if he were, to learn
and to listen, he would swing, cause there are sensitive
parts to him also, man. Cause the weird part we get hung
up with, "I am pure and I am good, and those people
are dirty and those murderers are bad and I am so pure,
I'm so good that I have to murder those murderers."
And then *you* end up getting screwed up. That's right.

WHITE: How d'ya like this color they picked out here? Isn't this ridiculous color?

NEGRO: Hm,mm, interesting, the Dufy blues and pastels here . . . Margaret Sanger Clinic . . . We never knock 'em up, that's the, uh, thing about it.

WHITE: And you really like to do it to everybody's sister?

NEGRO: Well, no, you missed the vernacular, it's not everybody's sister—I do it to sisters.

WHITE: Waddaya mean, "sisters"?

NEGRO: Just that—sisters.

WHITE: Why, you don't mean *sister* sisters!

NEGRO: Yeah.

WHITE: Ah, that's *impossible*. Oh, I never knew *that!* Ah, that's alotta horseshit, you can't do that to the—to the *sisters* . . . No kidding! Do they put out, those sisters?

NEGRO: Well, I mean, if you're built the way we are, you know, we're, ah, we're built abnormally large, you know that, don't you?

WHITE: I heard you guys got a wang on ya, ya sonofagun, ya!

NEGRO: Yes, uh, to use the vernacular, uh, it's sort of like a baby's arm with an apple in its fist, I think that's what, ah, Tennessee Williams said.

WHITE: Well, uh, ya mind if I see it?

NEGRO: No, I couldn't do that. I'm just playing guitar at this party.

WHITE: Whatthehell, just whip it out there. Let's see that roll of tarpaper you got there, Johnny, yeah?

NEGRO: No, I, uh, I couldn't show it. . . .

I wonder if Tom McCann was originally Uncle Tom?

That would really be some strange things. Uncle Tom. Turn him upside down and we'll piss on his head and drink beer. Sand—you know those dopey things that stand on one side and you turn them over and the sand runs out.

Now, here is a good summation on the cliche "Would You Want One of Them to Marry Your Sister?" Yeah. I would like to do this even though it's no *tour de force* to do integration in Los Angeles—because we assume you are integrationists, you know, because of *economics*. Alright.

So I say, where can I really do it where it'll count? *Mobile, Alabama*. If I got any balls I'll do it there. Right? O.K. I'm gonna do it in Mobile.

Then, I wanna do it for the Ku Klux Klan—and I am being objective—the Ku Klux Klan. Again there's no good or bad. They are part of their environment, and they think one way because they've been educated a certain way. You take those same cats out of that environment, and you educate them—and you *can* teach an old dog new tricks—that's why you go from Republican to Democrat, like that! [*snaps fingers*] It's that simple.

O.K. So now I wanna tell him, "I'll leave the sister aspect, I'll get closer to home. You are a white, the Imperial Wizard, a man forty years old, and now you have a choice—and if you don't think this is logic you can burn me on the fiery cross. This is the logic: you have the choice of spending fifteen years married to a woman—a black woman or a white woman. Fifteen years kissing and hugging and sleeping real close on hot nights, watching her take off her garter belt, taking her makeup off, seeing every facet of her—fifteen years —with a *black black* woman, or fifteen years with a *white white* woman. And these two women are about

26

the same age bracket, so it's not an unfair comparison. Fifteen years with a black woman or fifteen years with a white woman.

The white woman is Kate Smith . . . and the black woman is Lena Horne!

So you're not concerned with black or white any more, are you? You are concerned with how cute, how pretty. And if you are concerned with how cute or how pretty, then let's *really* get basic and persecute *ugly* people. Not black or white, cause you see, its a facade, man.

And now, as far as your sister is concerned, you can assume that your sister, boy, when she searches her soul, she will jump over fifty Charles Laughtons to get next to one Harry Belafonte. And ball him in front of the fifty Laughtons. It's gonna be a fifteen-year span, man.

Did you ever think about minority groups? You know who was the most persecuted group ever? In my generation, the Irish. The Irish got *schpritzed* and *schpritzed* and *schpritzed*. It's a subtle persecution, but it's there, and the most vicious. When a Jew says a *schicka* is a *goy,* he doesn't mean the Greek. That's it. You agree. When the Italian says

"*Manage, Irlandesi!*"

When the Negro says

"That Paddy motherfucker!"

that's it, Jim. It's the Irish. *Zing zing zing,* continually *schpritzed.* Now that's the worst kind of persecution— when it's unspoken. It's like this:

[*Whisper*] "They're moving in. They're moving in. They're moving in."

Who said that? The American Indians.

INDIAN: Oh, Christ! The white people are moving in—you let in *one* white family, and the whole *neighborhood* will be white.

27

How come they're not worried about the real fifth column—the Seminoles? The American Indian is waiting, just waiting to turn on us.

This is a satire on a film that you might recognize—but I'm not gonna tell you what it's from. Give me some full music—anything, barrelhouse, something full. O.K.? Blackout!

WHITE [*Heavy Southern white accent*]: Come on, Jane! Come on, Jane.

NEGRO: Whaddayou keep callin me Jane for?

WHITE: You don' wanna be called "boy," do ya?

NEGRO: No.

WHITE: You know, I tell ya sumthin. Come over here Randy. You know, buddy, when us broke outta here, I jus couldn't stand to look at you, I jus hated you. Boy, if my Daddy ever heard me say this he'd sure whup me good—but Randy, I wanna tell you one thing, buddy [*almost crying*], since we broke out, I really can't believe it, buddy. Randy, come heah. Randy, you know what I tell ya, when we fust broke outta here, as I toldja, I hated ya, but standin next to ya like this, an being chained to ya an runnin away from all them hounds, well, it's, it's taught me a lesson, it's, it's opened up mah *eyes,* Randy, standing nex to ya like this has really shown me somethin.

RANDY: What's that?

WHITE: I'm taller than you . . . An Randy, being taller than you is a lesson in equality itself.

RANDY: Speakin of equality, I wonder, will there ever be any equality?

WHITE: Well, it is, Randy—don't forget: To Play The Star Spangled Banner It Takes Both The White Keys And The Darkeys. Randy, in fact, Randy, if you jus think about it, jus a little while, all talk about equality—thats jus alotta nonsense. Why, evvruthin's equal, jus, them people's tryina cause trouble. I'll tellya why, Randy. Look: You ready for some xamples? On equality?

Now, at income tax time, don't you getta chance to pay income tax same as evvribuddy else?

RANDY: Yeah.

WHITE: Thass equal, ain't it? Awright. Now, you gonna hol up a store—don't you get the same time as ennybuddy else does?

RANDY: Yeah.

WHITE: Thass equal. Awright. Ready for the third one heah? When it comes time for getting drafted in the army, don't you get drafted along with evvribuddy else?

RANDY: Yeah.

WHITE: Well that's equal.

RANDY: Yeah, but, but—but what about the schools and segregated housing?

WHITE: Well those things take a little *time*. Ya cain't shove *evvruthin* down people's throats there, Randy.

Now I wanna tell ya, heah, heah? Heah heah heah? N'luk heah. Someday, Randy, up theah, up theah in Equality Heaven, they'll all be theah Randy, the people who believe in it—Zanuck, and Kramer. Thass why they make them pictures, [*voice trembling with emotion*] cause, they *believe* in equality, Randy, an up theah, it's gonna happ'n, cause they caused it, an, an, an then you gonna be livin in Zanuck's house with all yo colored friends, and next dore to Kramer on his property in Malibu, you be helpin them people, Randy— polishin dem cahs. . . . Yeah, you—yessir, I'm gonna tell you buddy it's gonna be a, it's gonna be a Message World, Randy, that's what it'll be,

Randy, a Message World, and now, speakin of messages, a message from our sponsuh:

SPONSOR: Hello out there. Are you tired and run down? Do you lack the strength to throw that rope up over a limb and put in a full day of lynching? If so, try high-potency Lynch-em-all. And now, back to our film.

WHITE: You know what's rotten, Randy?

RANDY: What?

WHITE: With all this screamin heah we haven't said a damn thing in this picture yet.

RANDY: Wait a minute. When you say "yet," remember you're off to a good start, because "yet" has only three letters.

WHITE [*pensively*]: I never thought of it that way. Maybe if evvryone in the world knew that "yet" only had three letters it would be a different world, Randy. If they knew that "yet" only had three letters an "knish" had five letters, it would be a world of three-letter and five-lettuh "yet-knishes." [*Passionately*] You'd like to say it, wouldnya, Randy?

RANDY [*whispers*]: Yeah.

WHITE: *Say* it, buddy.

RANDY [*Pauses. This means so much to him. Finally . . .*]: Yet-knish!

WHITE: Lemme say it withya. Say it togethuh:

BOTH: Yet-knish, yet-knish! [*begin to sing "Yet-knish" to the tune of a hymn*]

WHITE: Kugel. Say it, Randy: Kugel.

RANDY: Kugel.

WHITE: Goddamn, you say that good Randy. Yet-knish-kugel.

RANDY: Yet, yet-knish-kugel.

WHITE [*screaming*]: *Jus yell it out, Randy! Say it, Randy!*

RANDY [*screams*]: *Yet-knish-kugel!*

WHITE [*screams*]: GODDAMN IT MAKES YA FEEL CLEAN, DON'T IT? Boy, Randy, think of jus runnin round the whole world, and yelling that. We just run over to Rooshia, then tell all them Eyetalians about it an jus scream at evvryone and jus run over theah and jus yell, "Yet-knish-kugel, Mr. Khrushchev!" Boy, they'd really know it then, wouldn't they, buddy? An then, Randy, it won't mattuh, it won't mattuh any more even if you are colored and I'm Jewish, and even if Fritz is Japanese, and Wong is Greek, because then, Randy, we're all gonna stick togethuh—and beat up the Polacks!

I got white shoes now. I really like them. This is the first present I ever got. The guy said to me, he said, "I really dug your work and I wanna give you a pair of shoes."

I felt colored. Cause that's what they gave colored people—shoes. Shoes, or, "I'll give you a jacket."

Dig. Oh boy, I really thought of a good bit. Paul Krassner, he's editor of a newspaper, and he's married to this chick and she says to me, they're talking about help, you know, like domestic help, and the wife says to me, "You know, every time we have a girl in cleaning, he's always—he *placates* them, very obsequiously. He lifts up the vacuum cleaner, and he does as much work as the chick does." And I wondered, Why? I wondered if—not that he's a good guy—but if he had guilt for his mother and father, who exploited the shit out of those people. Those *schnorer* bits: "Oh you'll do this and this, and here's a bit of *schnapps* for this and this."

But there's no more "help" help. Negroes knew that, that you were considered *schwarzes,* second-rate help.

31

The Negro's gone now. Puerto Ricans? Too much garbage to get them to help us. So there's nobody left. Would any contemporary Negro serve you fried chicken and watermelon? I doubt it. Nor would they send their children to tap-dancing school to entertain Boss Charley. It's possible that in ten years the Negro will be out of the entertainment industry. And the replacement? Perhaps that's why Pat O'Brien is at Basin Street East.

How the Negro got into show business—here's how I figure it. The Negro had a boss that worked him twenty hours a day. So he wanted to get off for a couple of hours:

NEGRO: How'm I gonna just cool this guy out? How'm I gonna stop for about eight hours a day? . . . I don't feel good!

BOSS: Bullshit! Back to work.

NEGRO: My kid's sick!

BOSS: Bullshit! Back to work.

NEGRO [*sings*]: Hmm hmm, yessuh, my Lord, yessuh . . .

BOSS: Hey, I didn't know you guys could sing! What the hell is that? Come over here.

NEGRO [*sings*]: Hmm, yessuh, my Lord . . .

BOSS: Hey, these guys are O.K.! Come on, put that hoe down. Let's see. Lemme hear that again. Get some more in.

NEGRO [*sings*]: Yessuh, my Lo-o-o-ord . . .

He kept singing, singing—a party, right? And the weeds are growing up over the people. . . .

NEGRO [*singing*]: Yessuh, my lord.

And they split.

O.K. We're gonna do a tune now. Lovely tune. We're gonna do all these bits on the Art Linkletter show, by

32

the way. Ah, Perry Como, they'll let us—Jack Paar'll let us do these bits, sure . . .

FIRST WEST INDIES NEGRO VOICE: Well Buck, we gwine to Hebben, on de boat an de lebby. What is de fust ting dot you gwine—

dats getting some West Indian talk too, man, some high class dere. That's good really in-out, in-out—

What's de fust ting you gwine do when you gwine up dere to Hebbin?

SECOND WEST INDIAN VOICE: Well mister, the fust ting I gwine do when I gwine get to Hebbin, is fine out what a "gwine" is.

FIRST VOICE: Fine out what a "gwine" is?

SECOND VOICE: Yeah.

FIRST VOICE: Whaddaya gwine do when you get that gwine?

SECOND VOICE: I'm gonna *schtup* dat gwine.

FIRST VOICE: You gwine *schtup* a gwine?

SECOND VOICE: Yup. I'm gonna *schtup* a gwine.

FIRST VOICE: You gonna tote dat barge and *schtup* dat gwine.

[*both voices sing*]

You gonna tote that barge and *schtup* that gwine,
Yes, Lord, yes.
Gonna tote that barge and *schtup* that gwine,
Yes, Lord, yes.
Gonna tote that barge and *schtup* that gwine,
Yes, Lord, yes.

SOUTHERN WHITE TRASH VOICE: Now we gonna sing a song, folks. It's a patriotic song. And it tells a stawry.

BOTH VOICES: Don't forget, folks, To Play The Star Spangled Banner, It Takes Both The White Keys And The Darkeys.

Poor Richard's Almanac.

[*both voices*]:
   Damn your ass, Mr. Stalin,
   Don't come foolin' round over here,
   Cause iffin you come foolin' round over here,
   We're gonna come foolin round over there.

   And Texas is the best state in the Union.
   Now Adolph Hitler, and Hirohito,
   They tried it too, and Mussolini,
   And then Eyetalians—damn their asses too.
   Damn their asses too.

   Damn your ass, Mr. Stalin—
   Keep America free, for democracy,
   Keep America free, for democracy,
   Keep America free, for democracy;
   And keep the Jews and the niggersssss—
   Outta Tennessee!
   Keep the Jews and the niggers outta Tennessee,
   Keep the Jews and the niggers outta Tennessee,
   Keep the Jews and the niggers outta Tennessee!

Jews

Eichmann really figured, you know, "The Jews—the most liberal people in the world—they'll give me a fair shake." Fair? *Certainly.* "Rabbi" means lawyer. He'll get the best trial in the world, Eichmann. *Ha!* They were shaving his leg while he was giving his appeal! That's the last bit of insanity, man.

Come on down, Christ and Moses, come on down!
   I bet you, when Christ and Moses return, the *shules* have had it first.
   Saturday they would make every kind of *shule*—a drive-in *shule,* Frank Lloyd Wright *shule,* West Coast *shule.* West Coast? Santa Monica—there is that A-frame *shule* that they just put the statues in:
      "Are you putting a *madonna* in the *shule?*"
      "Yes, it's contemporary, that's all."
      "Whew! Don't figure out, man . . . that's, uh, they *supposed* to have one?"
West Coast reform *shule.* Reform rabbi. So reformed they're ashamed they're Jewish. Rabbis that had this kind of sound:
      "Heyyy, mein Liebe, heyyyyy . . ."

These rabbis have turned into doctors of law. And
they've lost their beards, because they were called beatniks. And now they have this sound:

> REFORMED RABBI [*Clipped, hearty, good-fellow
> British articulation*]: Ha ha! This sabbath we dis-
> cuss Is-roy-el. Where is Is-roy-el? Quench yon
> flaming yortsite candle! Alas, alas, poor Yossel
> . . . Deah deah deah! Today, on Chin-ukka, with
> Rose-o-shonah approaching, do you know, some-
> one had the chutz-pah to ask me,
>> "Tell me something, doctor of law, is there a
>> god, or not?"
> What cheek! To ask this in a temple! We're not
> here to talk of God—we're here to sell bonds for
> Israel! Remember that! A pox upon you, Christ
> and Moses! Go among them and kiss your empty
> *mezuzahs.*
> JEW: Rabbi, that was a beautiful speech!
> RABBI [*Jewish accent*]: Danksalot. Ya like dot? Vat
> de hell, tossetoff de top mine head, dot's all. *Und
> tsi gurnischt."*

So Moses is depressed. The *shules* are gone. No more
shules. He breaks open a *mezuzah*—nothing inside!
> *"GEVULT!"*
But a piece of paper that says
> "Made in Japan."

It's weird. I met a guy the other night, I wanted to, you
know, relax him. He was very *La Boheme,* he had the
beard, you know. So, I used to talk in a hip idiom, so
I started talking.

I said, "What's shakin, man?"

And he started talking Jewish! He was a rabbi! Said,
"Gurnischt, health!" And he gave me a couple of pills.

Now the Jews celebrate this holiday, Rose-o-shonah and

Yom-Ky-Poor, where they, actually, they celebrate the killing of Christ. Underground. You know, when they all get loaded, and you know, they just

> "Oh ho ho! We killed him! Ho ho! More Chicken
> soup! Oh ho ho ho!"

You know, kids running around with wooden sticks in the backyard:

> "C'mon. Come up the hill! Come up the hill to
> Gethsemane!"

You know.

I think that's the challenge—that the Jews want to sit for Jehovah. They're wrestling for the position all the time. They want to be the right-hand man, sitting at the gate.

But Filipinos know this for sure: that as beautifully liberal as any Jewish mother is—she'll march in every parade—yet, let the daughter bring home a nice, respectable Filipino son-in-law, with a nice, long, black foreskin and a gold tooth—

> "Ma, this is my new husband. I met him at college."
> *"Ahhhhhhhh! Ahhhhhhhh!"*
> "He's a very sensitive man, and he's Phi Beta
> Kappa."
> *"Ahhhhhhhh! Ahhhhhhhh!"*

That's all. Yeah.

I got this tattoo in Malta, in the Mediterranean, in 1942. So my aunt, she looks at it, you know, and there's a thing, you know—Orthodox Jews, you can't be buried in a Jewish cemetery with a tattoo. That's the truth. You have to go out of the world just the way you came in, with no changes—which certainly, the Rabbi, I dunno how that figures in there; they keep philosophizing and say, "It's not ours to question."

So she sees this, you know, so she looks—I dunno

37

what it was, I was washing—so she looks, you know, she goes

"*Vaghhhh! Vaghhhhh!*"

It's a Jewish seagull—

"Look vat you did!

You got aunts who talk that way, like parakeets—

"*Hah! Hah! Lenny! Vat you did! You ruined your arm! Vy'd you do that? You can't be buried in a Jewish cemetery.*"

I said,

"So what are you buggin me? They'll cut this arm off, they'll bury it in a Gentile cemetery. Don't nudge me any more."

She was really weird. You know, the mole with hair in it, her breath always smelled from onion rolls, you know?

"Don't kiss me, Mema, I don't like to kiss people. Lemme alone."

Look at that [*shows a painting*]. Do you like that? I painted it. I did it.

LITTLE BOY: Do you like it Ma?

JEWISH MOTHER: *Eh,* it's nice.

BOY: Whaddaya mean it's nice, Ma? Do you, do you really *like* it?

MOTHER: I like it, I like it.

BOY: But I mean, don't just say you like it, Ma. Do you get any feeling from it?

MOTHER: It's very nice.

BOY: No. Don't just tell me it's nice. Whaddaya *dig* about the painting?

MOTHER: I like it because—*I like it because you stay home* when you paint, that's why!

Ha ha! A real momma's hearts kind of scene.

Faye Bainter, Andy Hardy's mother, screwed up every

mother in the world. She really did, man. Dig, who can be like Faye Bainter, man? Faye Bainter was always in the kitchen sweeping with an apron. And Anglo-Saxon—and my mother was sweating and Jewish and hollering, man. Why couldn't she be like Faye Bainter? And that's what everyone wants their mother to be. And she was a virgin. Yeah, she never balled anyone because old Louis Stone would say, *"Andrew,"* and that was all, man. Unless there was some kind of pollination that way—through dates or some esoteric, mystical thing, yeah. So that's some heavy propaganda, man.

Now we take you to a young boy who's returning home from Fort Loeb. But first we dissolve to the interior of the home, on Second Avenue.

> JEWISH MOTHER: Vell, jus' tink. Soon, he'll be home. Our boy's cominck home from military school. I saved every penny vot ve had to bring him der success dot der outside vorld vud neffer gif him. Ah, soon our boy vill be home, from overseas in Delaware.

Now dissolve to the kid, on the steps, going through the trauma of going home:

> KID [*Ivy League voice*]: I don't wanna be there with those Mockies! I don't wanna look at them anymore, with their onion-roll breaths. I found something new at Fort Loeb, and a girl who doesn't know anything about the Lower East Side.

Cut to parting scene by the cannon on the hilltop:

> KID: I'm going now, darling, but I'll be back.

Now back at the apartment:

> KID: Hello, Mom.
> MOM [*overpoweringly*]: *Hello dollink!*
> KID: *Aaaaggh!*
> MOM: What's da matta vit chew?

39

KID: Nothing, Mother. I'm just so excited about seeing Bellevue and Zeder, I just don't know how to say . . .

MOM: Avvright, you'll siddown, you'll have some soup get into.

KID: It's not like that Philadelphia scrapnet school. Bronx mockie! *Aaagghh!* [*briskly*] Well, Taddy, I have to run back now to school and I hope that you and your people . . .

Now that's another thing that you sense—a street Arab. I am of a Semetic background—I *assume* I'm Jewish. A lot of Jews who think they're Jewish are not—they're switched babies.

Now, a Jew, in the dictionary, is one who is descended from the ancient tribes of Judea, or one who is regarded as descended from that tribe. That's what it says in the dictionary; but you and I know what a Jew is—*One Who Killed Our Lord*. I don't know if we got much press on that in Illinois—we did this about two thousand years ago—two thousand years of Polack kids whacking the shit out of us coming home from school. Dear, dear. And although there should be a statute of limitations for that crime, it seems that those who neither have the actions nor the gait of Christians, pagan or not, will bust us out, unrelenting dues, for another deuce.

And I really searched it out, why we pay the dues. Why do you keep breaking our balls for this crime?

"Why, Jew, because you skirt the issue. You blame it on Roman soldiers."

Alright. I'll clear the air once and for all, and confess. Yes, we did it. I did it, my family. I found a note in my basement. It said:

"We killed him.

signed,

Morty."

40

And a lot of people say to me,
"Why did you kill Christ?"
"I dunno . . . it was one of those parties, got out of hand, you know."
We killed him because he didn't want to become a doctor, that's why we killed him.

Or maybe it would shock some people, some people who are involved with the dogma, to say that we killed him at his own request, because he knew that people would exploit him. In his name they would do all sorts of bust-out things, and bust out people. In Christ's name they would exploit the flag, the Bible, and—*whew!* Boy, the things they've done in his name!

This routine always goes good in Minnesota, with about two Jews in the audience.

But he's going to get it if he comes back. Definitely. He's going to get killed again, because he made us pay so many dues. So he's going to get whacked out. And you can tell that to the Jehovah's Witnesses, who have all those dates. As soon as he comes back, whacked out again.

Now, a lot of people say, "Well, that's certainly not a very nice attitude, you know. You'll bring back the racial hatred." But I'm going to tell you something about that. See, I neologize Jewish and *goyish.* There's like, the literal meaning—first I'll start with *goyish,* cause it'll really knock you out. Dig this. *Goy*—"one who is not civilized, one who is not Mormon, one who is not Jewish." It's "heathen," that's what *goyish* means. Now, a Jew—dictionary style—"one who is descended from the ancient tribes of Judea, or one who is regarded to have descended from that tribe."

Now I neologize Jewish and *goyish.* Dig: I'm Jewish. Count Basie's Jewish. Ray Charles is Jewish. Eddie Cantor's *goyish.* B'Nai Brith is *goyish;* Hadassah, Jewish.

Marine corps—heavy *goyim,* dangerous. Koolaid is *goyish.* All Drake's Cakes are *goyish.* Pumpernickel is Jewish, and, as you know, white bread is very *goyish.* Instant potatoes—*goyish.* Black cherry soda's very Jewish, Macaroons are *very* Jewish—very Jewish cake. Fruit salad is Jewish. Lime jello is *goyish.* Lime soda is *very goyish.* Trailer parks are so *goyish* that Jews won't go near them. Jack Paar Show is very *goyish.* Underwear is definitely *goyish.* Balls are *goyish.* Titties are Jewish. Mouths are Jewish. All Italians are Jewish. Greeks are *goyish*—bad sauce. Eugene O'Neill—Jewish; Dylan Thomas, Jewish. Steve is *goyish,* though. It's the hair. He combs his hair in the boys' room with that soap all the time.

Louis. That's my name in Jewish. Louis Schneider.
"Why havn't ya got Louis Schneider up on the marquee?"
"Well, cause it's not show business. It doesn't fit."
"No, no, I don't wanna hear that. You Jewish?"
"Yeah."
"You ashamed of it?"
"Yeah."
"Why you ashamed you're Jewish?"
"I'm not any more! But it used to be a problem. Until *Playboy Magazine* came out."
Yeah. That's right. IN—OUT. You just can't be that urbane bachelor and drive down the street driving a Jag or a Lotus yelling "nigger" and "kike." It don't fit. That's what's really happened.

Up to about six or seven years ago, there was such a difference between Christians and Jews, that—maybe you did know—but, forget about it! Just a line there that would, *whew!* And the 'Brotherhood of Christians

42

and Jews' was like some fifth column bullshit. I don't know, it was like a phony dumb board.

No, I don't think so—I don't think Christians did know it. Because only the group that's involved—it's like: the defense counsel knows it because he has a narrow view, where the D.A., he's hung up with a bigger practice. So it's the same: the Jew is hung up with his shit and maybe the Christian—because, when the Christians say, like, "Oh, is he Jewish? I didn't know. I can't tell when somebody's Jewish."

I always thought, "That's bullshit."

But he can't. Cause he never got hung up with that shit, man. And Jews are very hung up with that, all the time.

I always try to search out the meaning of any cliches that attach to any ethnic group. And I've always heard that stupid *bubeh miseh* about Jews and all the smut books, and all. But here's where all that must come from —and in part it's true. Dig. But I have to tell you by way of a complaint report.

At the Troubadour Theatre in Los Angeles I was arrested for putting on an allegedly obscene show. Now the report said, he did a routine that related to his ex-wife, and he said that his ex-wife was the type of person who became upset when he walked into the bathroom while she was "*fressing* the maid." "*Fressing*" is Yiddish; it means eating. Eating is an act of oral copulation. So I'm putting on an obscene show. How's that for from Tinker to Evans to Chance?

But it ought to continue with, an act of oral copulation is *goyish*. Because there's no word in Yiddish that describes oral copulation. In fact, there are no gutter phrases in Yiddish—it's amazing. Homosexuality is known as "the English disease." *Emmis*. There are no

43

words in Jewish that describe any sexual act—*emmis*—or parts, or lusts.

Dig: "schmuck" is a German word. In Yiddish (this is the official Yiddish dictionary) *"schmuck*: a yard, a fool." So dig what happens, a weird thing happens. The Jews take it humorously, make a colloquialism out of a literal word—and some *putz* who doesn't understand what we're talking about busts you for obscenity.

Dig this. Doesn't it seem strange to you that Jewish judges, when it comes to obscenity cases, they're never the dissent? They're never swinging for the guy being not guilty. But Jewish *attorneys defend* alleged pornographers. Roth was Jewish. You should think about that. Why is that? Are Jews pornographers?

Or is it that the Jew has no concept? To a Jew f-u-c-k and s-h-i-t have the same value on the dirty-word graph. A Jew has no concept that f-u-c-k is worth 90 points, and s-h-i-t 10. And the reason for that is that—well, see, rabbis and priests both s-h-i-t, but only one f-u-c-ks.

You see, in the Jewish culture, there's no merit badge for not doing that. And Jewish attorneys better get hip to that.

And since the leaders of my tribe, rabbis, are *schtuppers,* perhaps that's why words come freer to me.

Now, the reason, perhaps, for my irreverence is that I have no knowledge of the god, because the Jews lost their god. Really. Before I was born the god was going away.

Because to have a god you have to know something about him, and as a child I didn't speak the same language as the Jewish god.

To have a god you have to love him and know about him as kids—early instruction—and I didn't know what he looked like. Our god has no mother, no father, no manger in the five and ten, on cereal boxes and on television shows. The Jewish god—what's his face? Moses? Ah, he's a friend of god's:

"I dunno. Moses, he's, I dunno, his uncle, I dunno . . ."

He has no true identity. Is he a strong God? Are there little stories? Are there Bible tales about god, that one god, our faceless god?

The Christian god, you're lucky in that way, because you've got Mary, a mother, a father, a beginning, the five-and-ten little mangers—identity. Your god, the Christian god, is all over. He's on rocks, he saves you, he's dying on bank buildings—he's been in three films. He's on crucifixes all over. It's a story you can follow. Constant identification.

The Jewish god—where's the Jewish god? He's on a little box nailed to the door jamb. In a *mezuzah*. There he is, in there. He's standing on a slant, god. And all the Jews are looking at him, and kissing him on the way into the house:

"I told the super *don't paint god!* Hey, Super! C'mere. What the hell's the matter with you? I told you twenty times, that's *god* there. What're you painting god for? My old lady kissed the doorbell three times this week. You paint here, here, but don't paint there, alright? Never mind it's dirty, we'll take care of it. Alright.

Wait a minute . . . Maybe he's not in there any more . . . maybe the Puerto Ricans stole him—they probably would, to make more garbage. That's it . . . I dunno what to do . . . You wanna open it up? . . . Yeah? . . . We'll pry it open, if he's in there . . . *Gevult!* They stashed a joint!"

Now there's a curtain line for great Jewish theatre.

This would be a capper on Broadway. The old Jewish couple, there they are, they open up the *mezuzah,* and the guy goes:

"*Gevult!* They stashed a joint!"
Boom! Curtain.

That's vernacular for a marijuana cigarette. You'd make a bad vice officer, for Chrissake:

"They what? They what? What?"

"Ah, *putzo,* shut up! Just forget about it. Just get hot, and that's it."

A *mezuzah* is a Jewish chapstick. That's why they're always kissing it when they go out.

The Puerto Ricans, their dues—what's their eccentricity? They love garbage, oh yeah.

"They love garbage! Are you kidding? Puerto Ricans, they bring it from Puerto Rico! And they take the garbage and they have it on a string— they won't let people throw it away. They put it on the street like flowers. Puerto Rican garbage. There it is. They disperse it. Ya think they throw it away? No, change it around, different neighborhoods. Nice garbage. Puerto Rico, garbage. Roll in it, and love it, and hug it and kiss it."

Actually, the Collier brothers were Puerto Rican.

The Puerto Ricans are bad, bad, bad. We were bad, once, too, the Jews. Bad Jews once. Our bad label was that we were capable of screwing everyone.

You know why Jews are the smartest people in the world? Cause everybody told them that, for years:

"*They'll screw ya,* you can't trust em, they'll screw *everybody!*"

And the *schmucks* really believed it:

"That's right. We're the smartest people—screw

46

anybody! Goddamn right, we're smart! We'll screw everybody. Boy, we'll screw them all. We're so smart."

"Dave Brubeck—he gets ten grand a night! Isn't that amazing?"
"Jewish—they all do that, you know."

It's all in the *goyish mezuzah,* the white plastic statue. Break the head off and you open it up and there it is.

A *schicka* is a *goy.* That's right. That was the concept in the late thirties, that was the Jewish phrase. It meant, literally, a Christian is a drunk. That was the concept of all Jews that I knew then, that Christians were drunks. And that Jewish mothers were the only mothers, and Christian mothers sold their children for bottles of whisky. And all their kids had grape jelly on their underwear and rotten teeth. They even had rotten teeth on their underwear. That was the badge of all Christians—they had rotten teeth.

I'll bet you that if I got a chance to listen at the Christian window I would have heard some *"schicka* is a *goy"* in reverse. But I never got a chance to pass, cause you never catch them without the mask on.

That's weird. You never do catch the people—once Belli got caught with the mask off. That's a drag. Melvin Belli. Yeah. Every once in a while, you know, if some guy's whacking out his old lady, or just some dumb scene, he does get caught: like you drop peaches on the floor and you're eating them and somebody comes in the room. Just that, kind of, caught with the mask off.

Once in a while you hear, "You *mockie* bastard!" Or, "The *goyim!*" But just once in a while.

You know, Ruby did it, and why he did it was because

47

he was Jewish—and the villain was his grandmother.
I really want to tell you that. I want to tell Christians
that, you know. I can tell it to you because it's all over
now. I wouldn't cop out when it was going on; but it is
all over now.

Why Ruby did it. You see, when I was a kid I had
tremendous hostility for Christians my age. The reason
I had the hostility is that I had no balls for fighting, and
they could duke. So I disliked them for it, but I admired
them for it—it was a tremendous ambivalence all the
time: admiring somebody who could do that, you know,
and then disliking them for it. Now the neighborhood I
came from there were a lot of Jews, so there was no
big problem with a balls-virility complex.

But *Ruby* came from *Texas*. They're *really* concerned
with "bawls"—they got ninety-year-old men biting rat-
tlesnakes' heads off! And shooting guns! And a Jew in
Texas is a tailor. So what went on in Ruby's mind, I'm
sure, is that

> "Well, if *I* kill the guy that killed the *president*,
> the Christians'll go:
>
> > '*Whew!* What bawls he had, hey? We always
> > thought the Jews were chickenshit, but look at
> > that! See, a Jew at the end, saved everybody!'"

And the Christians'll kiss him and hug him and they'll
lift him on high. A JEWISH BILLY THE KID RODE
OUT OF THE WEST!

But he didn't know that was just a fantasy from his
grandmother, the villain, telling him about the Christians
who punch everybody.

Yeah. Even the shot was Jewish—the way he held
the gun. It was a doney Jewish way. He probably went
"*Nach!*", too—that means "There!" in Jewish. *Nach!*

Italians and Jews—I can report that culture best—they
don't hit their old ladies. They don't punch them; but

they're *pinchers,* and they grab their arms as though they won't hurt them, and squeeze a little extra. But Anglo-Saxons are rifle people—they *shoot* their old ladies.

Now, Italians are really tough to get away from. Oh yeah. If you're married for ten years, chick has a lotta dues. You got to start maybe, oh, three years before, just getting ready to split. You start out with things like

> "Listen, Rocko, there's nobody else. I want you to know that. But I just, someday I just want to get away . . . and think. *There's nobody else!* Nobody else, I just want to get away, I just want a little, maybe a convent! Maybe a nun'll come and pick me up and take me in a car, and I'll be watched, and examined every day by a doctor . . . and I'll just think. . . . *But there's nobody else!"*

And *maybe, maybe* the chick will get away. Maybe, and escape the spitting on the windows and clothes getting cut up.

Alright. Now, the first thing that Italians and Jews do, they malign the old lady's reputation:

> "That piece of *shit!* I didn't tell ya about her. She was a lesbian—I didn't tell ya that either. And she screwed Paul Robeson's nephew, too. And, ah, you better have paper cups over here, too—you know what else she does, I didn't tell ya that either."

And he calls up her mother, the final touch:

> "You wanna hear what a *cunt* your daughter is?"

Vicious poison, poison, poison, and more poison.

Chutzpah: I'll show you pictorially what it means: *Life Magazine* did a recap of what they consider the grooviest-looking chicks of the last twenty-five years. They started here with Katy Stevens, Gina Lolabrigida, Rita Hayworth. Then they keep building—Janet Leigh, Grace

Kelly, to Marilyn Monroe, Audrey Hepburn, just really groovy-looking chicks. And they build and build in a crescendo, to the end chick—they give her a full page, True Beauty, and this is it, man—Jackie Kennedy! *Now that's what chutzpah means.* A chick like that could hitchhike from coast to coast and not be molested.

How The Jew Got Into Show Business.

The Jew had a hip boss, the Egyptian, oh yeah. Couldn't bullshit the Egyptian, you know. No, he was pretty slick. But the Jew kept working at it, working at being charming.

> EGYPTIAN: Never mind the horseshit, thank you. We got the pyramids to build, and that's where it's at. Gonna get it up, takes your generation, next generation, do a nice workmanlike job here."
>
> JEW: Oh thank you, thank you."
>
> EGYPTIAN: Get outta here with that horseshit! Now stop it now!"

But the Jew kept working at it, working at being charming. And he got so slick at it—he never carried it off—but he honed his arguments so good, he got so good at it, that that was his expertise:

> EGYPTIAN: These Jews got bullshit that don't quit! I mean, it's an *art* with them. C'mon. Let's go watch a Jew be charming. Hey! Jew! Do that charming bit for us, there. We know you're bullshitting, but you do it so good we get a kick out of it. Do it for us, will ya please?"

See? That was it, and he was on his way.

Now dig the switch-around. Now the Jew gets into show business. And, he writes motion pictures, he's making the images—he has the film industry knocked up—he controls it! And the Jew naturally writes what he thinks is pretty, what he thinks is ugly—and it's *amazing,* but you never see one Jewish bad guy in the movies.

Not ever a Jewish villain, man. Gregory Peck, Paul Muni—haha! It's wonderful! Who's the bad guy? *The goyim!* The Irish!

And you see a lot of pictures about Christ—a ton of religious pictures, in the most respectful position. And the reason that is, I'm sure, it's the way the Jew's saying, "I'm sorry." That's where it's at.

Religions Inc.; Catholicism; Christ and Moses; and the Lone Ranger

Who wants to hear first? See, walk, and everything like that?

I really am Father Flotsky. Yeah, I was a Catholic priest for about two and a half years. *Emmis.* And I really dug it. The only hangup is that—well, the religion is consistent, but the confessions are really a bore. *Whew! Ridiculous,* man. It's the same scene again and again.

I've talked to a lot of ex-priests, and I'll say, "How come you quit the gig?"

And they'll all tell you the same reason: it's confessions. One out of fifty is sexually stimulating, but the rest—*whew!* It's the same trite crap over and over, week after week:

> "Look, why don't you come up with a new story already? Were you here two months ago? Are you the bloomers-smeller?"
>
> "Yeah."
>
> "What's wrong? Look, there's nothing wrong with smelling bloomers. But you like to tell me that story, you *meschugenah.* That don't get me hot.

You always come in here,

'Oh God, I smelled bloomuhs.'

They're *bloomers!* Whatsa matter? They're your *own* bloomers, we found out. You wash them out and they're clean bloomers. And if you wanna smell 'em it's up to you. But don't confess it to me, and then say to me at the end of the story,

'How'd ya like dat?'

I don't like it. It's not disgusting, it's silly. And I got a lot of people waiting outside with some real good stories for me. If you could come up with one horny story, maybe. But it's always the same bit: you choked a chicken, you did it to a horse, you smelled bloomers. You're a *weirdo!* I dunno."

These bastards come in like they think they've got new stories all the time. And a lot of them make it up, too. A lot of horseshit:

"Weren't you here last month?"

"Yeah."

"What do you do, every month you come back here? Just come to the horny part and get outta here! That's all, man."

And I got busted, cause I taped one of them. Yeah. Made an album, *Horny Sounds From A Booth*.

Cardinal Spellman in Denver said that the sin of pornography—this really just whipped me right up out of my chair—the sin of pornography is that it ends in self-gratification. *Pssshheeeew!* That's a definition of prurient? Something that ends up in self-gratification!

Now here's another case where we're innocent, ignorant. Jews don't know about that because most Jewish psychiatrists have been justifying masturbation. So these are the two different cultures. So how am I going to ever know that pornography, something that leads to self-gratification, is—? Then I did some thinking. That people bullshit him—Spellman—in their confessions. How would he know about the people, but from what the people tell him? Would they lie to him? In truth, they would lie. I don't think they would confess the *real* sins that are laying heavy on the heart:

> SINNER: Father, father I want to confess that I punch my eight-year-old son with the same force that I'd punch a drunk. The reason I punched him that hard is he was cruel to the cat—the cat that I put in a burlap bag and drowned. But I wanna say that I gave him a good home. I also exploit the church and crippled people and blind people, and screw the income tax people too.

No, I would surely confess the childhood sins.

The only *the* religion, actually, is Catholicism. I mean, as far as strength—Patamonza Yogananda's cute, but The Church, that's it. Catholic Church is really power power power.

I've been really interested in Catholicism lately. I figured out what it is. It's like, there's more churches and people that work for the church than I think there are courthouses and judges. So actually, what it is, Catholicism is like Howard Johnson, and what they have are these franchises and they give all these people different franchises in the different countries but they have one government, and when you buy the Howard Johnson franchise you can apply it to the geography—whatever's cool for that area—and then you, you know, pay the bread to the main office. And you have to, you know, keep a certain standard. Which is cool. But it is definitely a government by itself.

And I think that's what we're doing in Vietnam. Because the Communists are a threat to those jobs. That's where it's at, man, you know? And I think that's what it's always been—that those two factions are always bitching and fighting with each other, and so actually we have the Catholic government inside our government, and they have this bitch with the Communists, because they're always fighting over the work, you know, and they take over and do them out of their gig.

Ha! Dig. Now, I know, just from the reaction, that a good sixty per cent of this audience is Catholic. Isn't that strange? I know that you're Catholic—this gentleman here. This lady probably.

I don't indict Catholicism anymore, cause I suddenly woke up one day and said, "Well, Christ, I can't knock Catholicism because I'm not an ex-Catholic, I don't *know* it. The same as Communism. I can't say I'd rather be dead than Red unless I was an ex-Commie. Unless I know what's happening with it.

The thing with Catholicism, the same as all religions, is that it teaches what *should* be, which seems rather incorrect. This is "what should be." Now, if you're taught to live up to a "what should be" that never existed—only an occult superstition, no proof of this "should be"—then you can sit on a jury and indict easily, you can cast the first stone, you can burn Adolf Eichmann, like that!

There's no right or wrong. Wrong means, Lost.

The Ecumenical Council has given the Pope permission to become a nun. Just on Fridays, though.

The Pope is too much. Looks like the Birdman of Alcatraz and Eichmann combined. He's really cute. He's like a little bird. Spellman looks like Shirley Temple—that's what I got in trouble for in New York, for saying

55

that; but a *priest* told me that, that's what burns me up. That's what really pisses me off.

I feel the Pope is devout. He's a good man, and I believe he is sincere. But what's the job of religion? To relate to mother, father, family; and he can do it in The Vatican and around that area, but he can't run his business six thousand miles away.

The Pope cannot help American Catholics, cause to help you he has to know you. No brain surgeon can pick up a book and just do it—he's gotta have flying time. The Pope does not know about American Catholics. He doesn't know how to gear down a Porsche, he can't work a cigarette machine, doesn't know about Bank Americard—doesn't know about any of your problems.

And the *big* issue, contraceptives—he never *makes* it with anybody! He lives in a state of celibacy, and I respect him for this, but he cannot relate to a problem about it, then, if he is that far removed from it, man.

I always wonder if he's gonna come in and see me one night. He could, and nobody would know it, man:

"I want to see this boy"

You know, he comes in:

"Well, you're not gonna go in *that* outfit!"

Dig. They give him a Howard's suit. Comes in, sits down—cause he is a sweet man, a humble man, like all prophets and teachers, right? And he would cool it and watch me, too.

Angelo, the maître 'd, would give it all away, though, kneeling there.

What if I was one of those comics who involve the audience?

"And what's your name, sir? And your name? Your name?"

And he's a man of truth:

    "Pope Pius."

I'd figure that was another Henry Wilson bit, like Rock Hudson, Rip Torn—Pope Pius.

You know, my attorney in Chicago told me, "Don't have a priest, because *they'll* get two bishops, and *you'll* have to get three monseigneurs"—and that's my last case ace:

> LEGAL VOICE: Who's that little guy over there? I seen him somewhere.
>
> DEFENSE ATTORNEY: Paul, don't wear the hat, just put that away.
>
> LEGAL VOICE: Alright, swear in your name.
>
> POPE: GOWANUS VOBISCUM SPIRITUM [*begins blessing everyone*]
>
> DEFENSE ATTORNEY: Paul, are you gonna be sworn in and stop that!

He owes me a favor, and that's all. Would that be weird? Would they flip out?

Every day people are straying away from the church and going back to God. Really.

But I know that Christ and Moses are in heaven, and they're saying,

> "What the hell are they doing with The Book? They're shoving it in motel drawers? Let's make Earth!"

Come on down, Christ and Moses, Come on down! Come on down.

And they're *going* to come down. They're going to come down, and they're going to make you pay some dues, you people who believe:

> "This is Chet Huntley with Christ and Moses in New York. And Mike Wallace. Tell me something: the fellow throwing up on the waitress's

tits over there—ah, it's getting a little ridiculous working in this shithouse! You wanna break it up? . . ."

Christ and Moses standing in the back of St. Pat's, looking around. Confused, Christ is, at the grandeur of the interior, the baroque interior, the rococque baroque interior. Because his route took him through Spanish Harlem, and he was wondering what the hell fifty Puerto Ricans were doing living in one room when that stained glass window is worth ten G's a square foot? And this guy had a ring worth eight grand. Why weren't the Puerto Ricans living here? That was the purpose of church—for the people.

Spellman is up on the lectern—played by Ed Begley —telling about giving to the people and loving, Love, Christian love, that is nothing but forgiveness and no hostility. Bishop Sheen—played by Hugh Herbert— spots Christ and Moses standing in the back arguing back and forth, and runs up to Spellman on the lectern:

> SHEEN [*whispers*]: *Pssst!* Spellman! C'mon down here, I gotta talk to you! They're here!
>
> SPELLMAN [*whispering*]: Get back to the blackboard, dum-dum, and stop bugging me.
>
> SHEEN: Dum-dum your ass! You better get down here.

O.K. Put the choir on for ten minutes.

> SPELLMAN: Hey, *putzo,* whaddaya mean, running up in the middle of a bit like that?
>
> SHEEN: Oh, it's terrible terrible terrible. They're here! They're here! Ohhh, owwwww! They're here they're here they're really here!
>
> SPELLMAN: Who's here?
>
> SHEEN: Who's here? I'm here, you're here.
>
> SPELLMAN: You're not all there.
>
> SHEEN: Hoo-hoo! It's here, it's here.
>
> SPELLMAN: *Who's* here?

SHEEN: You better sit down, you're gonna faint. Ready for a shocker? *Christ and Moses, schmuck,* that's who's here.

SPELLMAN: Oh bullshit! Are you putting me on, now? Where?

SHEEN: They're standing in the back—don't look now, you idiot! They can see us.

SPELLMAN: Which ones are they?

SHEEN: The one's that're glowing. *Hoo! Glowing!* Terrible.

SPELLMAN: Are you sure it's them?

SHEEN: I've just seen 'em in pictures, but I'm pretty sure—Moses is a ringer for Charlton Heston.

SPELLMAN: Are they armed?

SHEEN: I dunno.

SPELLMAN: Poor box locked?

SHEEN: Yeah. I'll grab the box and meet you round the back!

SPELLMAN: No, we better just cool it. You better get me Rome, quickly. Now what the hell do they want here?

SHEEN: Maybe they want to audit the books?

SPELLMAN: No, I don't think so. Well, we're in for it now, Goddamnit! Did Christ bring the family with him? What's the mother's name? . . . Hurry up with Rome! . . . If we just cool it, maybe we can talk to them. . . . Don't tell anyone they're here . . . Oh, *shit!* Who copped out they're here?

SHEEN: Why?

SPELLMAN: Why? *Schmuck,* look at the front door!

SHEEN: What's the matter?

SPELLMAN: What's the matter? *Putz!* Here come the lepers!

SHEEN: Where the hell do *they* live around here? Oh, Christ!

SPELLMAN: Phew! Alright. Get me Rome. Hurry up. . . .

[*Cheerful loud voice*] Hello, lepers! How are you? Hello lepers, hello lepers. [*Sings*] *Hello, young lepers wherever you are.* . . . Howareya? Look, ah, nuttin personal, but, ah, don't touch anything, O.K.? Heh heh. That's right. No offense, but, what the hell, you can pick up anything—you might get something from us! Heh heh. Right? So, ah, why don't you all get outside and get some air? O.K.? Pick up your nose, your foot and your arm, and split. That's right . . . Now look, whatta you doing? You waiting for St. Francis? Look, I'm gonna level with you right now—that's a bullshit story. He never kissed any lepers. He just danced with two merchant marines and we kicked him the hell outta the parish. That's all. What the hell you wanna kiss a leper for? Put yourself in our place. Would you kiss a leper? What the hell are ya gonna get outta that? Awright? That's alotta bullshit—you try to kiss 'em and they fall apart. Kissing lepers—you know how Ben Hur's mother and sister got leprosy, don't ya? They didn't put paper on the seats, that's all. Now come on, haul ass! Can't you be nice, you people? Just get the hell outta here!

[*Talking into phone*] Hullo, John? . . . Fran, New York. Listen, a coupla the kids dropped in. . . . You bet your ass you know them. . . . Ah, well, I can't really talk now, there's alotta people. It's really filling up here. . . . Well, one kid is like [*sings*] "With the cross of blank blank . . ." No, *not* Zorro! . . . Yes, *him.* Yeah. . . . I'm *not* kidding you. . . . Yes, he brought a very attractive Jewish boy with him—excuse me. [*Off phone*] What is it?

REPORTERS: Ah, we're from *Life Magazine,* and we want to know if that's really them.

SPELLMAN: Ah, just a moment—Sonny, will you get off my hem here?—Yes, that is them. . . . No, I don't know if they're gonna do any tricks.

[*Back to phone*] Hullo? . . . They're standing in back, way in the back. . . . *Course they're white!* Look, this is New York City, mister, Puerto Ricans stand in the back . . . Look, I don't wanna hear that. This place is filling up. What're we paying protection for? . . . I dunno . . . Look, all I know's that I'm up to my ass in crutches and wheelchairs here!"

We take you now to the headquarters of Religions Incorporated. And, seated around the desk on Madison Avenue, sit the new religious leaders of our country: Oral Roberts, Olin Jaggers, Billy Graham, Patamunzo Yogananda, Herb Jeffries, Danny Thomas and Eddie Cantor, Jane Russell, Frances Farmer, Pat O'Brien, and General Sarnoff and the other people who feel insecure in industry.

As we listen closely, the Dodge-Plymouth dealers have just had their annual raffle, and they've just given away a 1958 Catholic church.

Religion, big business. We hear H. A. Allen addressing the tight little group on Madison Avenue:

[*Southern accent*]: Good evening, gentlemen. Nice to see so many boys heah tonight. Most of yew religious leaders ah haven't seen in many yeuhs. Ah jus wus tawkin ta Billi this aftuhnoon. Ah said, "Billi yew come a lawng way, sweetie, lawng way." Who woulda thawt back in '31—we were hustlin baby pittures then, an shingles an siding. We're swingin, yew know—we didn't know what-thehell we doin. The c.c. camps were stahtina

61

move, yeah. Ah didn't know mahself, yew know? An' jus lahk *that!* we came on it, yew know? The Gideon, an *Bop!* an theah we were. Hah!

Ah, the greyaph heah tells the stawry. That's about it. Faw the fust time in twelve yeuhs, Catholicism is up nine points. Judaism is up fifteen. The Big P., the Pentecostal, is stahtina move, finally, and ah . . . . [*aside*] yew faggot! You're a Jehovah's Witness! Got that five & ten franchise weah tryna break up.

Now, gentlemen, we got mistuh Necktyuh, from our religious novelty house in Chicago, who's got a beautiful selluh—the gen-yew-ine Jewish-star-lucky-cross-cigarette-lighter combined; an we got the kiss-me-in-the-dahk *mezuzah*; an the wawk-me-tawk-me camel; an these wunnerful lil cocktail napkins with some hel!uva sayings theah—"Anuthuh mahtini faw Mu;huh Cabrini"—an some pretty fah out things. Some real winnahs. Now. As yew know theahs alotta religious leaduhs that we've seen heah, boys we don't know, this the first time we've really yew-nited lahk this—theahs about six thousand boys out heah from all ovuh the country—an little favuhs, yew knew the commissionuh promised that theah'd be no individual hustlin, yew know. Ah mean, less make the scene tugethuh, because lahk if we burn ourselves, wheah we gonna end up, yew dig me? O.K. NOW! I wanna introduce—Oh! We got Mr. Acton, heah, a great man, our Seventh-Day Adventist who on a leading tour of the lepuh colonies took some beautiful coluh slides, that we're doing for the Mahaliah Jackson covuh. She's doing a helluva numbuh, "Are You Tellin Yo Beads More Than Yo're Tellin To Me?" Sure sell. On the flip side of "Little Richard Goes Home."

An now, ah, heah is the greatest holy rolluh in America today, a man who has talked from the crisp, cool shores of Montauk Point to the shady groves of Oregon, a great man an a great holy rolluh, the wunnaful Mistah Oral Roberts! Oral?
ROBERTS [*Shouting*]: *WELL THANKYAVERY MUCH, A.A.!* HEAH! Heah boy, have a snake. Oh yeah, it is good, good to see faces, faces [*voice dies to trembling sentiment*] I haven't seen in many yeuhs . . . faces that set awf a good time. Oh boy, ah'll tell yew, ah wuz tawking tonight to some wunnerful people, an they said, Oral, tonight you're going to be facing a different awdience, [*shouting*] TONIGHT! TONIGHT YOU'RE NOT GOIN' TO BE FACING THE PEOPLE THAT STEINBECK WROTE ABOUT! You're not going to be facing God's Little Acre, tonight yo're not going to be looking into the face of a factory workuh, tonight you're not going to be looking at the sawdust. TONIGHT! You're not gonna feel that heat of a gas-burner on your neck. NO! Tonight [*voice hushes to a whisper*] you're going to be speaking to men that are hip! that ah know, that *He* knows, that ah know, [*begins to sing*] that ah know, that yew know, . . .

NOW! GENTLEMEN! Ah have jus retuhned from San Francisco, Sin Town—that BAGHDAD by the beach, and when ah SAT in a San Franciscan restaurant ah looked out o'er the icy watuhs of San Francisco Bay [*whispers*], and ah looked at Alcatraz . . . ALCATRAZ! THIRTEEN ACRES OF GREY GRANITE LIKE AN ANGRY FIST THRUSTING THROUGH THE WATER GENTLEMEN, AND I REFLECTED ALCATRAZ! Ah tol the men ah was speaking to ah sayd Look into your hahts gentlemen and suddenly gentle-

men, a voice, from THIRTEEN THOUSAND
PEOPLE THAT SAT IN THE COW PALACE
outside of San Francisco, a voice boomed up an
yelled at me, "DUMBBELL!"

Ah stopped, gentlemen, an ah looked, an they
looked, [*whispers*] and ah said, There is one of
Satan's armies, do not pounce upon him, AND
AGAIN THE VOICE REITERATED "DUMB-
BELL DUMBBELL!"

Ah said, Well, mah friend, you may have a
point. Maybe ah am a dumbbell, maybe that's it,
maybe the man standing up heah is a dumbbell.
Why don't you laugh at me, mah friends? Hah hah
hah! Theah's the dumbbell. Ah'm dumb, ah tol
them, ah'm very dumb, AH'VE GOT TWO LIN-
COLN CONTINENTALS! THAT'S HOW GOD-
DAMN DUMB AH AM! Well, they all laughed
their asses off with that, ah can tell yew.

NOW. The point to bring, gentlemen, is,
WHERE IS THE HEAVENLY LAND? Did you
think about that gentlemen? Does it sink innnnn?
Ah'll tellyouonething, the Heavenly Land is not on
Wall Street, the Heavenly Land is not in the neigh-
borhood bar, and the Heavenly land is not [*cre-
scendo*] in the burlesque house! You might say
to me, All right! [*screaming*] YEW SAYAD IT'S
NOT IN THE BURLESQUE HOUSE AN YEW
SAYAD IT'S NOT IN WALL STREET, THEN
WHY DON'T YEW TELL US WHERE IT IS!!!?
[*Still screaming*] WELL MAYBE GENTLEMEN
[*voice drops to puckish whisper*], that's what ah'll
dew.

It's in the Bay area. In the Bay Area that has
three times the suicides and three times the alcohol
consumed [*screaming again*] AND SIX TIMES
THE MARRIAGES DO YOU KNOW WHAT

64

THAT MEANS THREE THREE AND SIX?
WELL AH KNOW! IT MEANS TWELVE!!

Yes. Now, it's theah, gentlemen, theah in the
Bay area, WHEAH IS IT? HUNTER'S POINT!
AND THEM SONS-A-BITCHES ARE TRYNA
TAKE IT AWAY FROM US! WRITE IN
EVERY DAY! Now, gentlemen—[*aside*] What's
that?—

AIDE: 'Scuse me sir, your long-distance call just
came in from overseas.

ROBERTS: Justa moment heah. We gotta nuthuh
man, a great man, who can tell us the message,
GIVE US THE MESSAGE! TELL US WHAT
TO DO WITH HEAVENLY LAND WHEN WE
GET IT! Tell us pleeeese, now! [*singing again*]
Tell us, now, why don'tja tell us now, what to do
with the heavenly land. We don know cause
'sgrand at the heavenly land . . . TELL US NOW,
what to do with the HEAVENLY LAND. . . .
RABBI STEVEN H. WEISS!

RABBI WEISS [*British accent*]: Well, thankyou
veddy moch. I think we should subdivide.

ROBERTS: NOW. Before I go any futhuh gentlemen, we got some—

AIDE: Sir, the call is still waiting—

ROBERTS: Alright . . . . Ah got a lawng distance
cawl in heah from headquarters, the Vatican—ah'll
tawk to yew boys latuh ¯ . . . . Yes opuratuh, this
is Oral Roberts . . . . Yes, yes, alright, ah'll take
the chahges . . . yeah . . . yeah . . . HELLO
JOHNNY! WHAT'S SHAKIN BABY? . . . yeah
. . . Meant to congratulate you on the election . . .
yeah . . . That puff of white smoke was a genius
stroke. Was in the papuhs faw six days heah . . .
Great! . . . We got an eight-page layout with
Viceroy—"The New Pope Is A Thinking Man."

Ah'll send ya a tear sheet on it . . . yeah . . . yeah
. . . Same old jazz . . . How's your Old Lady? . . .
No, nobody's onna phone . . . Listen, Ah hate
to bug ya, but they're buggin us again with that
dumb integration . . . NO, AH DUNNO why the
hell they wanna go to school eithuh . . . yeah that
school bus scene . . . Well, we hadda givem the
bus, but theah's two toilets on each bus . . . that's
what's spending awl the money. We got awl toilets
for evvribuddi. An we got some mo advances—
we gotta new bus that drives from the back . . .
yeah . . . yeah . . . BUT THAT'S IT! . . . Yeas
. . . They keep saying, Integration, make the religious leaduhs tawk about it . . . No . . . Yes . . .
No they donwannany quaotations from the Bahble.
They wannus to come out an *say* things. Say Let
Them Go To School With Them . . . No you *dunno*
whatthehell is goin on heah! . . . Ah, ah *did* Walkin
Across The Watuh! . . . Yeah, an the Stop The
War Scene. He said, "Thou shalt not kill means
just that, it doesn't mean 'Amend section A, it
means stop war" . . . Ah *did* Snake inna Cane
too. Ah did em *awl* ah'm tellin yew . . . . BUT
THEY'RE BUGGIN US! . . . STEVENSON!
THAT BAWLBUSTUH! . . . Yeah, ah know it.
. . . No ah ain't gettin snotty but we gotta *dew*
somethin! . . . WELL WHATTHEHELL YEW
THINK AH CAWLED YA FAW? . . . YEAH!
POPE: *Dominus vobiscum populus succubus* . . .
ROBERTS: SURE, THAT'S EASY FAW YEW TO
SAY, YOU'RE OVUH THEAH! . . . Yeah . . .
Yeah we got the deal with Langendorff, the daily
bread scene . . . Yeah . . . Yeah . . . Don lie to
me! . . . Yeah . . . Yeah . . . Yeah . . . Listen.
Listen, hold on a minute, heah?

[*Aside*] Hey, Billi! Yew wanna say somethin to em? . . .

[*Back on phone*] Billi wants to know if yew can get him a deal on one o those Dago spawts cahs . . . Ferali or some dumb thing . . . yeah . . . yeah . . . Willie Mays threw up on the Alcazar? Ha ha! That syrup! Really freaked awf! . . . Yeah . . . yeah . . . yeah, sweetie . . . O.K. . . . yeah . . . [*lowers voice*] Oh, lissen heah: ah'm sendin ovuh a real winnuh—kid bout twenny-three from Rodondo Beach. Greatest showman you've evuh seen. We grossed seventi-three thousand dollahs in four days in Oakland. Great boy . . . . Well, he does Throwin Away the Crutches and See Again. Good timing, knows when to quit. He can really knot up them dayyim legs . . . yeah . . . A real Lon Chaney . . . Yeah . . . Ten percent of the house . . . But watch the W2 forms, though . . . He's cool, yeah . . . yeah, uh huh, . . . yeah . . . When ya comin to the coast? I can get ya the Steve Allen Show the nineteenth . . . Matinee Theatre dropped. . . . Jus wave, thass awl. Wear the big ring . . . yeah . . . yeah . . . yeah . . . yeah . . . O.K., Sweetie . . . yeah . . . Yew cool it tew . . . NO, NOBODY KNOWS YOU'RE JEWISH!

Dig. Not the people, necessarily, who are involved with the religion, but the religion itself, Catholicism, is a genius religion. Four years ago I used to do a bit, you know, Religions Incorporated, so my view at that time was, "Here's a rich church, and next door's poverty—so it's hypocracy." Obvious view. Then I started digging, digging, reading, reading, getting into it, and I realized the reason for the baroque church, the grand church in the poverty neighborhood, is that what the church is, is a school. It's a method of instruction.

And people who have no understanding, who need instruction, don't know about philosophy, they can only understand material things. So a raggedy-ass guy won't go into a raggedy-ass temple:

> "I *live* in a shithouse—whadda I gotta go in one faw?"

I wanted to do a film showing—because I'm sure that day in the cell, it's just like in the tank, like four, five, six people in the cell there, and there was Cestus, Distus, and this guy who was probably crapped out in the corner:

GUARD: O.K.—you two.

GOOD THIEF: What?

GUARD: You get crucified today.

GOOD THIEF: Get my file down here. That's bullshit.

GUARD: O.K. Get ready all you guys. You're all getting crucified in this cell.

GOOD THIEF: I'm the good thief. Whaddayou bullshittin me for? I'm in here for checks!

GUARD: Come on, you. Get ready. You're gettin crucified.

GOOD THIEF: Heh heh. I'm *not* getting crucified. Get my file down here. I'm the good thief. I'm here for petty theft. Understand? *Checks.* How can I get crucified now? I dunno what the hell that guy's doing, but. . . .

O.K. Now he sees they're getting him all ready and they're moving him:

GOOD THIEF: *Hey!* What the hell, are you kidding with this shit? I'm not getting cruc—hey mister! Do me a favor? There's a mistake here. They think that I'm with you, for some reason here.

And Christ says

CHRIST: Don't worry—you'll be with me.

68

GOOD THIEF: Come *on* with that! I'm *not* with you. Tell them. Come on, it's no joke now. We're goin up the hill.

But he's praying, everybody's pushing,

GOOD THIEF: Well come on! Hey! Get the public defender. Come on, this is bullshit now, ahh . . .

O.K. Now. Up on the cross.

GOOD THIEF: Hey mistuh! Please, before it's too late. Do me a favuh, O.K.? Tell them?

CHRIST: Don't worry, you're with me . . .

GOOD THIEF: STOP SAYIN THAT! Will ya? I'M *not with you,* O.K.? I mean, I'm with you, I like you, but stop telling these assholes I'm *with* you. They think "I'm with you" means that I'm *with* you, I conspired with you, I dunno . . . Look. Don't be pushy. I like you, O.K.? I dunno what you're talking about, I woke up, all I know I'm getting crucified—I'm here for checks, I *can't* get crucified. I'm being denied due process, I'm entitled to do my time for checks first. And I don-wanna get crucified. I *can't* go now. O.K.? I'll meet you later. . . . Come on. Don't be pushy now, O.K?

O.K. *Mop.* They all went. And then when the guy came back,

"*Hey* . . . you were *right* . . . I knew you weren't bullshitting, but, uh, heh, heh, I had alotta faith in you, but you get to meet alotta weird people in the joint, you know? . . . You relax; I'll talk to the press. That's all."

Remember this: I'm dying for your sins. For your sins and your kids' sins. I'm dying, so—well, just *shape up!* That's all. I'm dying so that, in the future, things will be right, so you just realize what the values are. Good things—remember the good: remember that being born is an original sin. And once we scrub that dirt off you with lye, a few of you will stray and do it again. Try to fight it. Try to fight it, and remember that the physical is not the most desirable. The spiritual—that's the thing to look for, since spiritual trim—I'm getting off here now, cause I see that dying for you does no good. You don't appreciate I'm dying for you. That's what I've done, I've suffered my whole life for you, and whaddaya do, ya run away with some cheap *shicksa*. Go be nice to people! Go get crucified! Look at my hands: I'm Helena Rubenstein. That's who she really is—*corpus christi*.

There was only one guy—I just thought of a man now —Selflessness—a guy who did it *all* for *you,* and wanted nothing in return. Ohhhh [*sigh*], what a *good* man, a man that never waited for "thankyou." Who was that good man?

The Lone Ranger.

He was truly that Corpus Christi image projected, a man that never waited for "thankyou." Cleaned up towns of five thousand people. Always did the same bit: The Silver Bullet; nod; and split—HHHHHYYYYYUU, SSSLLLLLLLVVVVVVAAA. . . .

JEWISH VOICE [*High, whiny*]: Hey! What's with that *schmuck*? He didn't wait for "thankyou," nuttin. We made coffee and cake . . .

NEGRO VOICE: You don't know 'bout him, man? Thass the Lone Ranger.

JEWISH VOICE: What's his story? A *feystich*? Takes the bullet and *"nach!"* and he runs. He don't want anything?

NEGRO VOICE: Nothing, man. He's a *verbissener*. He goes "gruuuuuhhhhh," and runs off.

JEWISH VOICE [*Whistles*]: That's amazing, man. Has anyone ever clocked him? But how come he rides off? He never—not a thankyou! How come he left us a bullet?

70

NEGRO VOICE: I dunno . . . That's weird . . . After he does his *schtuck* about, you know, "Why do you wear a mask?" "I'm not an outlaw, *nach*," and he runs. But a bullet . . . that sort of takes the good out of it.

JEWISH VOICE: Yeah?

NEGRO VOICE: You know what he meant by that bullet, don't you?

JEWISH VOICE: *Vas?*

NEGRO VOICE: Doctor Erlich.

JEWISH VOICE: Whaddaya mean, Doctor Erlich?

NEGRO VOICE: You dunno, *schmuck?* Doctor Erlich—the magic bullet!

JEWISH VOICE: I still don't get it.

NEGRO VOICE: He's telling you the whole world has *syphilis!*

JEWISH VOICE: Get the hell outta here with that! Are you kidding me? What a slap in the face that is, man. [*Whistles*] Syphilis?

NEGRO VOICE: *Schmuck,* that's why he rides away: "HHHHHMMMMMOOOOOSSSPPHHLS" . . .

JEWISH VOICE: That's too much, man. *Emmis.* Well, we'll ambush him and find out. . . .

[*Voices change. The next scene opens with the slow drawl of a Southwestern rural hick*]

HICK: Don' you move, you psychotic bastard! [*Aside*] Hold this gun, Maw. Hey, massed man, what the hell is yo sto-ree? How come you never wait for thankyous? You know these kids here made up a *homentash?* And they made up a sawng, Thank You Lone Ranger. And look at you—you're jus too damn good for evvribuddy. You jus gotta run awff an never assept any love. You know thass Anti-Christian in spirit—not to assept a thankyou, some love?

LONE RANGER [*in the oratorical, upright, deep*

71

voice of an early American demagogue or poli-
tician]: Well, I'll explain—if you'll get your goddamn hands off me. You see, the reason I never
wait for thankyous, I figure, supposing one day I
wait for a thankyou:

> HEARTY VOICE: Thank you, Lone Ranger!
> LONE RANGER: Whassat?
> HEARTY VOICE: I said, "Thank you."
> LONE RANGER: Hmmmmmmm . . . I sort of
> like thankyous. I've never had one before; can
> I have one more?
> HEARTY VOICE: Wright. Thank You.
> LONE RANGER: Just one more.
> HEARTY VOICE: What the hell, I'm not goin ta
> kiss your ass all day. Thankyouthankyou.

LONE RANGER [*back into explanation to hick*]: Now
I've had my first thankyou, and I dig it, and I'm
riding all around: "Thank you!" "Don't mention
it, donmentionit." "Thank you, thankyouthank-
you." But the real reason is [*voice changes, becomes an old Jewish man*], I sent two boice to
collich.

HICK: Whassat?

LONE RANGER: Dots right.

HICK: Well, goddamn, maw, the massed man's
Jewish!

LONE RANGER: Of course, *schmuck*! Dots vy, ven
I tuk on the radio, dots all you hear, is
HHHHHHHHHHHAAAAAA, SSSSSSUUUUU.
You vanna svitch it ova from sefenty-eight to toity-
tree-und-a-toid? You'll hear [*imitating slowed-
down record*], HIGHH YOOOSILLL BERRRR.
I sent two boice to collich. You tink dey even sent
me a pustul cud? Hmmm. I got tebble bucitis of
my yarm. Alotta *tsuris* I have, mine friend. *Zug-
nicht* and *goyim.* [*returns to original oratorical*

voice, strong conman] So one week, when I've had all the thankyous I need, and they say:

> FIRST VOICE [*desperate*]: Hey, get the Lone Ranger!
>
> SECOND VOICE: Can't get *him*—he's too busy getting thankyous. He wouldn't get off his ass without a thankyou.
>
> FIRST VOICE: Really mean that? We're screwed! We're deaf mutes!
>
> LONE RANGER [*Original deep voice*]: Oh, I see.
>
> SECOND VOICE: Well, I tell you what—givim a present.
>
> FIRST VOICE [*turning Jewish*]: He wouldn't take.
>
> SECOND VOICE [*Jewish*]: He'll take. They'll all take.
>
> FIRST VOICE: The Lone Ranger'll take?
>
> SECOND VOICE: He'll take.
>
> FIRST VOICE: He'll take?
>
> SECOND VOICE: He'll take. They'll all take. Givim an Esterbrook Pen.
>
> LONE RANGER: No, I have it . . . An Esterbrook pen . . . I'll save it for Bert. You see, I take my stuff an I hang it up. I put it away, and then when I look for it, I know where to find it. My brother Alfred takes his stuff and throws it all around the room. Then he says, "Where's my stuff?" Ha ha ha. [*singsong*] He hasn't nothing left; I have mine, all hung up . . . They call me a *schmuck,* hanging up a pen, but I, I . . . Yessuh, an Esterbrook pen . . .

And now, that's the way it goes: I'm running around getting thankyous and pens, and I love it. Now a week goes by. The week has passed. No

73

presents. No thankyous. What happened to them all?

NEW VOICE [*impersonal commentator*]: What happened? There's no more *tsuris*.

LONE RANGER: What?

COMMENTATOR: Yes. You see, you and J. Edgar Hoover and Lenny Bruce and Jonas Salk thrive upon unrest, violence and disease. If there were none—and there is none now—no more presents.

LONE RANGER [*in his old man's Jewish voice*]: You mean? That's how I got my presents? Because of *tsuris*?

COMMENTATOR: That's right.

LONE RANGER: Hm, hm, hm. *Nach.* I got one left. Another bullet. [*Changes back to deep oratorical voice*] This way, what I don't have, I don't miss.

HICK: Wall, goddam, massed man, that was a sorta nice speech, but the kids still got the *homentasch,* hear? And they wanna give you some. Can't you take, bend, jus assept love one time?

LONE RANGER [*voice strong and demanding*]: Awright. Gimme that Indian over there!

HICK: Tonto?

LONE RANGER: Whatever the Spic-halfbreed his name is. Yes, Tonto.

HICK: Goddamn, massed man, we can't give ya a hooman beeeeng!

LONE RANGER: *Bull Shit* you can't give me a human being! What did you think I was going to ask for, *schmuck,* a dish? I knew it was going to be this way: "Waddaya want? *Vas? Forbis, schmuck, oder yeda* I'll help you widda windows." No. "Can't give ya a human being." Well, I'm gonna take you to the labor commission. I want that Indian!

HICK: Awright. What the hell you wannim faw?

LONE RANGER: To perform an unnatural act.

HICK: Whassat?

LONE RANGER: You heard me: to perform an unnatural act.

HICK: Goddamn. *Blagh! Agh! The massed man's
a fag.* Blagh, blagh, blaghaghaghagh! Dja hear that?
Wall, goddamn, massed man, I never knew you
were that way.

LONE RANGER: I'm not, but I've heard so much
about it an how bad it is, the repression sorta has
me horny, you know, I . . . I'd like to try it just
once before I die. I like what they do with homosexuals in this country—they throw them in jail
with a lot of men. Good punishment. Quite correct. Hahahaha. Thasright. Washim up an getim
ready! And I tell you what: while you're at it, I
want that horse, too.

HICK: Fawwat?

LONE RANGER: For the act.

HICK: *Blagh!* Gawd, maw, djuhear that? Blagh-
blaghaghagh! The massed man wants a haws faw the
act, too, damn degenerate!

LONE RANGER: Oh, yes; this mask. I've made many
movies in Paris with a mustache and garters. You
didn't recognize me, did you?

It's like "Tilly, Mack and Tonto"—those would be really
good *schmutz* books.

I always wonder about the anonymous giver. Cause
the anonymous giver truly is the egomaniac: "I'm so
good—I'm not going to tell *any*body." That's sick, man.
I'm going to leave you with this, that the only anonymous giver is the guy that knocks up your daughter.

Politics

I can't get worked up about politics. I grew up in New York, and I was hip as a kid that I was corrupt and that the mayor was corrupt. I have no illusions.

You believe politicians, what they say? It's a device to get elected. If you were to follow Stevenson from New York to Alabama you would shit from the changes.

It's like two syndicates, man—the government syndicate, and the Maf. Or the labor syndicate. But morals don't enter into it.

A Hoffa, for example, I assume is a giant intellect. Intellect resolves into creativity, so if he doesn't have that—he doesn't have the resources of the government—they would've nailed him years ago, man. But, like, he's a *hais* mind and a mover.

So, where is the decadence? How can you say Anastasia lived in decadence when there was a Governor Long, who not only was whacked out *schtupping* strippers, but a bust-out thief, man, who had relatives who were thieves—which relates to a Mafia concept, then: Earl Long, and Huey Long.

Then New York with Jimmy Walker—a heavy *gonif*, a master *gonif*, man. The Seabury Investigation—the echoes faded away into a William O'Dwyer, who was the district attorney of the largest city in the world, man. He put guys in the joint who'll never see light again. As a kid, the D.A. was this concept:

DEEP, SELF-RIGHTEOUS VOICE: And it shall be my duty as the District Attorney—

to smoke pot on the Perry Mason show.

Now, he became mayor, and good image, the mayor; and *schlepping,* grabbing; and then they punished him, not the way they did Jimmy Walker (they *really* punished him—Bob Hope did his life), O'Dwyer they really gave it *hais* to—he moved to Mexico. As the ambassador.

And now he's back in New York. What's he doing? Just laying on the floor laughing his ass off. That's it. Jail is for poor people. Cause Sherman Adams and St. Bernard Goldfein never sat in the joint, man. Cause it's juice, man. That's it. The only rights that you got are knowing the right guy.

The epitome of juice would be this. Dig this. A card you get:

"He can do anything.

Jack."

From the president. Right? He can do anything. Forget it, man. Go to the toilet on the roof of the Astor, *schtup* president's wives from other countries. "He can do anything, Jack."

"What've you got on Kennedy?"

"*Zug nicht.* Enough. I got enough."

"Whaddaya know about him?"

"He's Moslem."

Would that be a twist-o? He's a Moslem. Sabu is his kid.

You going to vote any more? I mean—

"My father told me that all businessmen are son-ovabitches. But I never believed him till now."

You know who said that? You know? Do you? Who? *Kennedy*, that's right. And they're going to bust him this show. They're taking in Truman for saying

"Drew Pearson is a sonovabitch!"

and they're going to arrest Kennedy for saying that his father said that. They're going to *schlep* the father in too. It's going to be a big bust, and Birdie is going to take over the government.

That word is pretty popular in the White House, sonovabitch. Why do they say that? That some secret ritual they go through?

"Nyanyanyanyablahblah *sonovabitch!*"

You gotta just chuck it in there any way—just get sonov-abitch in. It's like an Alfred Hitchcock movie—they get sonovabitch in, somehow, in every administration. Be weird if he'd stub his toe at the inauguration,

"Ow, sonovabitch!"

What is that, onomatapoeia?

"You *sonovabitch!*"

"Ah, Mr., ah, Kennedy, we have the boy scouts here, and the Legion of Decency here, they're ah, giving you the, ah, plaque for the year, for the boy scouts-girl scouts of America. What would you like to say?"

"Ah, you sonovabitch! All businessmen are sonov-abitches!"

"Hey, heh . . . I know, Mr. Kennedy, but we've just got the boy scouts here, you know?"

"Well they'll be sonovabitches too; if you're a sonovabitch you're a sonovabitch!"

"Well, I guess you're the president, you know what you're talking about. . . . Heh heh . . . where'd you learn that?"

"Ah, from President Truman. He called Drew
Pearson a sonovabitch."
That's the White House word—sonovabitch!

Now. Lyndon Johnson. Good guy. Good American.
Brilliant craftsman, *brilliant* politician. But because
there's a lot of bigots in this country, Lyndon Johnson
never had a chance. Why? Bigotry, man, out-and-out.
His whole culture is into the shithouse. No matter how
profound Lyndon Johnson could ever be, as soon as he
opens up his mouth—
    "Folks, ah think new-cleer fishing—"
    "You think your *putz*, you dummy! Get that *schlub*
    outta here!"
    "But ah th—"
    "You don't think *anything, schmuck!*"
Cause bigots say that
    "Anybody tawks that way's a shitkickuh, Daddy.
    He cain't know a damn thing."

Because the liberals can understand everything but people who don't understand them. The liberal, the true
liberal:
    "I'm so understanding, I can't understand anyone
    not understanding me, as understanding as I am.
    I'm so liberal I've never had any *roch munas* for
    the white Southerner—'He tawks lahk that, he
    tawks lahk that'—"
The poor *schmuck* probably doesn't even talk like that,
but some *schmuck* in the Bronx wrote a screenplay with
him 'tawkin lahk that' so the *putz* ends up 'tawkin lahk
taht.'

Lyndon Johnson—they didn't even let him talk for the
first six months. It took him six months to learn how to
say Nee-Grow.

79

"Nig-ger-a-o . . ."

"O.K., ah, let's hear it one more time, Lyndon, now."

"Nig-ger-a-o . . ."

"No. Can't you say—look, say it quick—Negro!"

"O.K. Nigrao-o, Gigernao—ah cain't *help* it! Ah cain't say it! Thass awl; Ah cain't say niggera— cussin in bed 'n' evvrythin, stutterin—ah cain't! What the hell! Niggera, Naggra, Nee-graa—lemme show 'em my scar."

"No, no, no. Just say it. Say it, and that's it. Yeah." Yeah. He's completely confused.

But they're really—that family is so—*phew!* You know, there's a certain kind of *non*-Jewish look. They could pass any test—they are the biggest non-Jews in the world. No question, they'd walk right through the line.

The wife, with the white flannel socks, with the zipper up the front, with the nail polish—she's beautiful, man. She looks at home in a trailer park. Yeah.

Dig. The Catholic religion is a genius religion. And the Ecumenical Council really are geniuses, and they make some tremendous moves. But somebody talked Lyndon Johnson's daughter into converting; that set the religion back two thousand years. That dress she had on—she looked like a Guatemalan slave. A real Philomena at the wedding. National Geographic picture.

But showing his scar is beautiful. That's just where he's at. He's just a shitkicker.

I was just thinking of that picture of Oswald, you know, when he got shot? That's Lyndon Johnson's relation face —you know, that guy with the hat on, the big Texan.

We take you now to the home of Governor Faubus. The succulent smell of magnolias pervades the old

80

mansion, and as we listen closely we hear the governor, played by Fritz Kuen, talking to his daughter, Sheila Jordan. The daughter talks:

"Ah sweah, if yo'er dayaddy turned ovuh in his greyave as menni tieyums as yew sayid he deeyid, the whole—Dayaddy! Will yew tawk ta me? Ah'm tahd of freakin awf with mahself!"

"Well, what is it, Belle of the South?"

"Well, Dayaddy, yo'er daughtuh, Sheila Jordan, is goin ta get married!"

"Married! That certainly brings a warm spot to my old Southern heart! Jus cain't believe that mah Sheila's such a big girl—getting married! Are yew marrying local boy, Sugah?"

"No Dayaddy, he's a New York stayage actuh—Mom an ah met him last year at Lynbrook, Long Island."

"A stage actuh? Well, ah don't know tew much about stage people—what's his name, Sugah?"

"Harry Belafonte."

"Eyetalian boy, eh? Oh yeah. Sugah, that's adorable."

Cut to—the wedding:

"This is Vince Stevenson with the news here at the Faubus wedding. Certainly lovely. They're rubbing tar on the groom now . . ."

O.K. George Lincoln Rockwell, the head of the American Nazi Party. Friends of mine always come up, "That *putz!* Look at that paper!" And I'm reading, and I start to dig something: Who's always showing me these articles? *Liberals.* Who's interested in bigotry, reading everything they can on it? Liberals. Hm hm.

George Lincoln Rockwell is a very knowledgeable businessman with no political convictions whatsoever. He's just hip: he puts something *verbissener* in an article; they keep reading it and buying it; and they *support* it! George Lincoln Rockwell probably works to mass rallies of nothing but Jews shaking their fists at him.

Yeah. He's probably got about two followers, that are deaf, and they think the swastika is an Aztec symbol. That's what it could be, right?

That *schmuck* Ross Barnett had more *chutzpah* than Kennedy and that other *putz,* Stevenson. Because he had the *chutzpah* to tell the president, *gai schoin!* You realize what he did? This man, Ross Barnett, caused Lyndon Johnson to lay on the bathroom floor drunk.

I don't condone Ross Barnett, but still, he had more *chutzpah* than Stevenson. Chicago is the reason that Stevenson never made it; because Ross Barnett had the *chutzpah* to tell the president *screeve quanda rive,* where Stevenson never had the *chutzpah* to tell that to the Maf.

You know, I used to really pray that one guy would become president—Norman Thomas. I used to say, Why doesn't Norman Thomas make it? And just for one reason—just cause I knew he wouldn't be ready:

"You're *in,* Norm!"

"In where? *Bullshit!* What time is it? Get the hell outta here! What the hell are you guys doing here with all the cameras an' everything?"

"Norm, you're the *president!*"

"Bullshit! Get outta here now! Come on, get outta here! Damn pranksters."

"Norm, you're the President of the United States! Look at this."

"What? . . . Why, I didn't run this year, did I? . . . Am I really the president? . . . Damn! [*Shouts upstairs to his wife*] Min! I'm the president! . . . I said 'Bullshit' too, but they got a paper down here, it says 'Greetings I am' not 'From' . . . [*to reporter*] You wouldn't bullshit me, would you? I been waiting forty years to be president . . . Goddamn! I finally made it. . . . But I *can't* be president—haven't got any *clothes!* . . . How much does it pay?"

"Seventy-five thousand dollars a year."

"Goddamn! Isn't that a kick in the ass! Well, I better call Wilkie. . . . Oh, I forgot . . . and I got all these PMs I didn't read yet—small towns like this it's the A&P page and the editorial page . . . let's see, now . . . which platform did I run on? I don't know . . . I'll bring back Paul Robeson!"

"He donwanna come back, Norm. He's in alotta trouble."

"Awright. Let's see, now. Ummm . . . I'll integrate!"

"They've done it."

"Oh, crap! They really have? Dammit! I gotta read some papers . . . Let's see . . . I got it! I'll *discriminate!*"

"Discriminate! That's rather unique."

"You like that? O.K. Write it down. That's it— I'll discriminate."

"Against who?"

"I dunno. There's not many left . . . um . . . the Filipinos!"

"Filipinos, Norm?"

"They're *disgusting!* Make me sick to my stomach. Ugh!"

"Do you *know* any?"

"No. That's the trouble—they're standoffish. Here is the platform: 'If you're Filipino, watch your ass, because Norm's in!' You like it? Say it again. 'If you're Filipino, watch your ass, cause Noorrrmmmms'—no, you gotta do it this way, see? 'If your Filipino, watchyourassbecause Norrrrmmmms innnnn!' Get the 'Norrrmmmmss innnn' there—you can hum it—and then they'll *really* watch they're ass. Boy oh boy! I just get sick to my stomach every time I think of em! We'll just whack 'em out in one day. Pretty good, isn't it?"

"Yeah, it's pretty good, Norm, but—how'll we find 'em?"

"I dunno. But get 'em up here—oh, *goddamn it!* Forget about it."

"Why?"

"They're all in the Navy."

"Oh, that's right."

"That's all you can do if you're Filippino in this country: become a chief in the Navy, get a gold tooth, ball a hooker, come quick and giggle. That's it! . . . Let's see, then, we need another group to persecute. . . How do we qualify who deserves to be persecuted? . . . A group that doesn't join in with us, rejects us . . . I got it! *Midgets!*"

"Oh, *Christ!* He's whacked out. He's sick. He's weird. *Midgets!* Norm, whatthehell you got against midgets?"

"They're *snotty*. Always combing their hair in the boy's room, with soap. They're jus no damn good. They're *unnatural*. This is the platform: Smack A Midget For Norm! *Pow!* You like that?"

"Well, yeah. It's got a good ring to it. I never . . . Are there that many of them?"

"There's more than Negroes and Jews and any other minority group. There's thousands!"

"Where the hell are they?"

"That's the idea! They are really vicious. Just think about all the times you haven't been helped

84

by midgets. When you were a kid freezin your ass off hitchhiking in those corduroy knickers, did a midget ever stop once and pick you up?"

"No. . . ."

"And it just scares the crap outta ya—you don't see anybody driving. There's no head at the wheel —jus those little hands. No, they're no good. They're jus no good. They jus wanna get jacked off or picked up on your lap. They're *disgusting*. I wanna show you somethin. Look at this chair. Under every chair there's supposedly a tag, and the tag will say, 'Do not remove this tag under penalty of law.' Where is the tag? Who copped it? Those goddamn midgets! They're vandals. Every midget ring we've broken up, we find piles and piles of those tags:

   'Whaddayou steal those things for, you disgusting perverts? 'Whaddaya steal those for!'

   'It's all we can reach.'

   'You chewed the gum, too, didn't ya?'

Dirty slobs. They've always got the same bitch, too, you know?

   'When you're a midget, you have a very limited
   point of view—the whole world is a crotch!'

Very clever. Very nice. They're so little! And they hate to be called cute—they bite ya."

I don't like to go into politics, cause I know that belongs to Mort Sahl and Phyllis Kirk, the Vic and Sade of show business, but communism doesn't make it at all. Not for me. Cause it's complete government control. The capitalist system is the best, cause we can barter, we can go somewhere else. Communism is one big phone company. That's it, man. Can't go nowhere else, Jim. Tell the phone company,

   "I want a phone put in Monday at 9:30."

"You'll have it at the end of the week."

"I want it at 9:30!"

"Alright, *schmuck!* Go to the May Company for a phone."

That's right, I'm screwed. Where'm I going to go? There's one desk to go to. That's what communism is. But a capitalist system is beautiful, man, cause we can go here, there, and that's the barter system, you know. And I want to keep my system.

The system starts here: I got 90, and my mother and father hug and kiss me: "Did so good, he got 90! MMMM, kiss kiss." But that 90 don't mean anything unless you got a 20. And if I'm not a nut, and if 90 gets me loving and kissing, I hope you get 20, man. I'm gonna hope you fail.

But later on I really jive myself and say, "May the best man win." May the best man your ass! I'm going to win out and get my kissing and hugging!

Yeah. The competitive system.

The Russians blew it. Thank God. But they always tell the people those dummy bits—"The Russians are godless"—forget it, man. That doesn't work.

But this is the best system in the world. Do you realize that if this were communist controlled and I carried on like this, I'd have to pay a lot of dues. All government control. Forget it. Communism is like one big phone company—you're screwed. That's the only reason it doesn't make it. All those other things don't count, all those other *bubah miseh*.

Well, we are a second-rate power. And, it's weird, we *know* it, and we don't *believe* it. Because Walker really blew Africa for us completely. I travel a lot, man, and the anti-American feeling is just overwhelming. In Aus-

86

tralia—dig the headlines. They take everything out of context: KENNEDY WILL CRUSH CUBA! And they really have us as the villain over there. England, they are the hipsters, the greatest diplomats, the greatest bull-shit artists ever—so they're gonna cook and go with the wind, you know. Now we don't have anybody really cooking for us—you know how big Russia is? And China? India?

And I'm sure in the last days when Hitler was flipping out, there was a lot of guys must have said "Christ, they're madmen there!" But it's not that they were madmen. It's like, in the House of Representatives, when you see that there's a guy in there who says that he knows the people that are going to try and kill Mere-dith, and he's too smart—you *kidding* with that, man? You had a governor that was *schtupping* Blaze Starr; a governor who defies the president. And it just really bugs the shit out of me, cause I really do dig this coun-try.

Harold Gray—I'd like to bring him up before the House Unamerican Activities Committee. When *I* handle it, it'll be O.K. Heh heh. *I* know what bad guys to get:

> "Now, ah, Daddy Warbucks, ah, what we wanna ask you about is this, is your house and your activi-ties, acts, practices. You've got this little girl, this Annie . . ."

Warren Harding was a quadroon. D'you know that? Who *is* running, anyway? I've been in court so much this week—maybe that's sort of a barometer, because from the little that leaks in through the courts, I notice certain names. Goldwater's name, Scranton—and that's about all I heard. Who else is running?

Goldwater, how amazing. Having a Jewish president really knocks me out. Can't believe that there. Too much. And tell me, has there been much Jewish support? Singing in Jewish? Forget "Goldwater." "Barry?" *Barry!?* Are you kidding with that? Mogen David. Barry! Where is there one *goy* with the name of Barry? It's the most Jewishjewishjewish. You know Barry. Yeah. Barry is always the name of the one Jew that sings with an octilla, brandy wine, and a *farbish* finkle. And at Jewish theatres there's always one dopey Jew with the black hair—he sings American and Yiddish songs, Barry. He's a ventriloquist.

Not many Jews feel hostility towards Goldwater cause he is Jewish and changed his religion. See, *all* Jews did that. I'm Leonard Alfred Schneider, not Lenny Bruce. I'm Lenny Bruce, legally, but it was a pain in the ass, man. A lot of dues.

So dig. Goldwater lives in Arizona. He did a switch, man. He says *"Frig it.* I'll *keep* my name and I'll change my *religion."* That was his bit.

That's weird, you know? Finally we have a man in— that's going to be Goldwater's last step: gets in, gets before the T.V. cameras for the acceptance speech, and *he rips off the mask and you see the big nose and the semitic look and the spittle coming out* and

> [*Goldwater screaming vindictively*] *YAHAHAH-AAAAAA! WE'LL BURN ALL THE CHURCHES!"*

That's what we're planning, yes. Three days after the election—all of our smut factories have been working for years—hot books and swinging and everything. What's going to happen? Vere vill ve go vrom here? Maybe in a year—God! Think of it—we'll all be walking around naked! What a horrible thought! We'll all die immediately. That's worse than communism—to

88

walk around naked. Imagine that. All those naked women—nay-nays—*phah!*

The presidency is a young man's job. He rides herd on one hundred and eighty million people. That's it—physical gig. So big industry and educators continually have told me—especially big business—that a young president, even a thirty-year-old president, is better.

Because, here's the parallel: You want to take a chance on a man over fifty-five when Mutual of Omaha won't? That's just for a policy—this is the presidency. Rayburn is 78, and Allstate would kick him in the keester, man. So what a paradox that is. It's a young man's gig.

Now this is no slam against President Eisenhower—there was a great man and a great American, and I like him for that—but he's too old now for the job. And soon I'll be too old for my gig. That's no indictment of old age. I'm thirty-five, I'll be fifty soon, and I'll know I can't do the gig.

I would like Kennedy for president, cause he is a young man. That's the first thing in his favor. Second, he's got a pretty wife. Which is a plus factor. Cause you want your wife to be pretty. Everybody wants their wife to be pretty, so that's really groovy. And he's a bright man. He is healthy. He thinks good.

Now, to say, "Should a Roman Catholic be president?" is again, bigotry. Course he should. And boy, they really said what I've been saying these last few days, they said, "Let's stop talking about religion," because they realized, and they've said it, that religion is a disorganizer. That being Protestant and Catholic and Jewish is a big hangup. And they saw it defeated them. So they said, in essence, Don't be Catholic any more, don't

89

be Jewish any more—there's one Jehovah. Because if we break it up, we'll break up our campaign.

Now, he has no allegiance to the Pope—*I* don't.

Now here's something the guys will dig in the audience. I voted for Kennedy, too. What was the big winning factor? His *punim*. How many chicks have I talked to, man, that said, "He's a doll." What is that? Is that a voting concept? It's a good *schtup* image. Every chick digs him, man. He's a *hais* for them, which was a big winning factor.

That is one of the reasons why I voted for him. Because there's the first time that I actually could identify with a president that has some dimension. I'll see a child born in the White House, and I feel that the only one who can help me, as a leader, is a guy who knows my problems, who can really identify with me. And my grandfather can*not,* man. He can play with my kid, but he'll spoil him. He won't really know what is contemporary, what is happening today. And the Kennedy scene is right there—mother, father, family. It's a groovy thing with Kennedy—he's real. And I actually dig that.

Now President Eisenhower—I could never even fantasize him kissing his wife. Not on the mouth, anyway. No. He never took his clothes off; he never went to the toilet; he just stood there.

Eisenhower—no one listens to the war stories any more. Keeps trying on the uniform. He likes the one salute that he does—always does it wrong. Got an '06 rifle . . .

Did you watch the television yesterday? You must have all watched it yesterday. The thing that was really cute, you know, Kennedy's in the car with his old lady, driving along, and the thing that really knocked me out was that he puts the hat on, and then—you know, that far away, you can just see pantomime—the wife is looking the other way, then he puts the hat on, then she sort of turns to him and looks, you know, up at the hat, and you see the mouth move, then you see the hat come off, man.

And you just *know* she said, "You look like a *schmuck* with that hat on." I know that was what happened! It was really great.

Did you see when Jacqueline Kennedy *schlepped* the people around the house? I was praying for one quick shot—the door opens, the old man is standing there in his underwear, drunk.

Kennedy was just a genius at organization, and just a sophisticated man. I mean, sophistication just means knowledge, learning, a lot of background. And the other guys—I'd like to get some tapes of those people. Yeah. That would really be a treat to hear them.

Nixon? I like him, but he hung out with Eisenhower too long. Environment. You know. That's why he'll never make it. You know that. In your heart, he can't make it. He's a good cat, and I appreciate the fact that he went to South America, I really do. I wouldn't want to make that scene, I don't think that those students had any intellect or any heart or any *sympatico*. What kind of *kohach* is that, for two hundred thousand students to stone one poor *schmuck* in a sedan—no, those students don't make it at all, Jim.

That goes for the Japanese students, too, that bugged Hagerty. That's only one or two cats, man. That's a big mob. So they're not too nice either.

So I'm grateful for the dues that Nixon paid.

Nixon—Nixon is a megalomaniac, a complete nut. Ran to Argentina twelve times already—has a Hitler thing going. Let's see now. Any women you would like to know about in the White House? A lot of them stay there, the wives. They dig it and they just stay there and the old men split. Eisenhower and his wife are hydrocephalic cases, with that cap—their heads were cut.

We hear Ike talking to Sherm:

IKE [*drawling like a senile moron*]: Well, Sherm ya goofed, baby . . . that six iron . . . Let's see, I'll make that little putt there . . . Ah, Sherm, ah, I donwanna fire ya, baby, but, ah, I really have got my hands tied now. But maybe we can beat this if you tell me now. Now, let's see. Get it straight. You got a coat, right?"

SHERM [*shamefaced*]: Yeah.

IKE: And ya got the rug?

SHERM: Yeah.

IKE: And, ah . . . [*irritated*] Now what did you do in the hotel for two thousand dollars? What I wanna know is, did you get anything else?

SHERM: Well, no, I didn't take . . .

IKE: *Don't lie to me!* Cause, you know, I won't hit ya if you tell me the truth. Tell me the truth, get it off your chest now. You know I hate a liar. If I find out *later,* then I'll, you know, rap ya around a little.

SHERM: Well, I, I got one more thing.

IKE: What's that?

SHERM: Delaware.

IKE: Oh, how could you take *that?* You can't do things like that! What's the matter with you?

SHERM: I dunno.

IKE: Well, how're we gonna get outta this?

SHERM: I sorta got an idea. You're gonna laugh at me for saying this . . .

IKE: What?

SHERM: The newspapers are really bringing all the heat on us, so if we could think of a headline to sorta wipe it out, just for four or five days . . .

IKE: Well, what could we do?

SHERM: How about getting one of the cabinet members assassinated?

IKE: Well, I dunno. Some of those things backfire.

SHERM: Maybe if we could just get them—not in this country, somewhere else.

IKE: I got an idea! Switch on the intercom. Cel, send in Nixon! . . . Hello Nix, sweetie! Siddown, baby . . . Oh, isn't he cute? Howsa black curly-haired devil? Ah, get some of that twelve-year-old Scotch over there . . . Little Havana, huh baby? Huh sweetie?

NIXON: [*suspicious, like a delinquent kid*]: What's goin on here? Don't put me on, Ike.

IKE: Nobody's putting you on. I got the greatest idea for you—how'd ya like to go to Lebanon?

NIXON: Why don't you stop, Ike? I donwanna go on any more trips!

IKE: Why not? You kiddin? They'll *love* you over there.

NIXON: Na, they *won't* love me over there, an I donwanna go. Lemme stay for a *few* days, awright? What don't you send Dulles? He's been home for two days.

IKE: Oh, now, is that ridiculous, huh? Send my sweetie over there, huh? Come back with a Moroccan wallet? Wouldn't ya like that?

NIXON: I donwanna go, that's all! Lemme alone! I donwanna go *anywhere* any more. I just wanna stay [*wistful*] jus to see the cherry blossoms.

IKE: Oh, don't get maudlin now. I don't know why you donwanna go. You did *great* in Caracas!

NIXON: Are you kidding? They *hated* me there! They spit at me! Look at this suit—I never had it cleaned. That's just to remind you. They spit at me, they hate me, they threw rocks at me—

IKE: You gonna go by a few people, a few squares that didn't dig ya, a few rabblerousers? I got letters from people who really like you. I got a ton of mail on my desk now.

NIXON: I donwanna go anyway.

IKE: Is that a nice way to talk to me? Create a monster, is that what I did? The boy I helped? I capped your teeth . . .

NIXON: I donwanna be ungrateful or anything like that. I know ya been nice to me, I know, but, just, I don't, I don't—you know, if I did good in *one* place . . .

IKE: You did good in Biloxi.

NIXON: Ah, yeah, but I had alotta people on my side—Father Coughlan . . . I think it's about time that I took a stand: I just donwanna go anywhere any more!

IKE: Why?

NIXON: I just told you why—they just don't like me, that's all. I'm not gonna fool myself, I just haven't got it, I guess. Something about my hair, I think.

IKE: Want me to tell you the truth?

NIXON: What?

IKE: They like *you*—it's your old lady.

NIXON: Pat?

IKE: That's it. Everybody dug *you*—it's *her*. She overdresses. Besides, who brings their wife on a trip? You'll go! You're not even going to fly tourist this time!

Wait a minute, I'll stamp out the bomb! That went out too, like jazz. The bomb was another thing that everybody cherished and stamped out and students marched 17,000-strong. Kennedy had left, and there was Lyndon Johnson in the White House:

STUDENT: Mr. Johnson, I represent 17,000 students. We're here to stamp out the bomb. We wanna get some pictures of it, too.

LBJ: Son, ah dunno what ta hell ya think's goin on here. Ya see, this place is a *shithouse*—they steal linen, silverware here. Ah cain't find a damn thing. Whaddayou wanna, bomb? That's bullshit. They *pissed* all the money away—never was no bomb. Two Jew writers from Hollywood made up a story about a bomb and that was it. No bomb, not a bit, but there's this piece of shit inna garage, here.

STUDENT: I'm not gonna tell those kids that—that there's no bomb. They marched from Maryland! "Kids, there's no bomb." "Say it isn't so, Joe." Uh uh, I can't tell those kids that. Come on, you got a piece of a bomb, something that looks like a bomb.

LBJ: Son, ah ain't got a damn thing, I ain't got a popped piston—you see this place, there ain't even no groceries here. Now if I *had* a bomb, I'd give it ta ya.

STUDENT: Well, give us a button, then.

LBJ: What button izzat?

STUDENT: The madmen are always gonna push a button.

LBJ: Okay, son. Turn around. Here it is.

STUDENT: That's the button? "USN." Your pants are falling down! That's a button off your fly!

LBJ: That's right. I kept it there all during the war.

95

Mah wife was frigid and she never would touch it.

STUDENT: *That's* the bomb button, eh?

The bomb—it's dropped already. What they found out is—dig the bomb. When it went up there—the Russians sent theirs off, we sent ours off—and when it hit that stratacaposphere, something happened to change it, and it came down and hit only bomb shelters. Attracted to nothing but bomb shelters. *Phoomphoom*—just really on target. Anything that would have dirt around it and was a hole. Bomb shelters and cheap swimming pools in a valley.

I'm gonna leave you with a nice thought to depress you. I've been thinking about this, and I want to share it with you—the Bay of Pigs. See, Castro—see, I'm a little closer to him than you are. You know, propinquity: I used to go to Havana a lot—Havana was a delightful place for tourists. Tell you what a bad guy Castro is. Since Castro came, you can get no narcotics, no abortions, and there're no prostitutes there. He's really screwed it up for vacationers. That's right. He's really an asshole, this guy.

The Southern Sound

I wonder if we'll ever see that—if we'll ever see the Southerner get any acceptance at all. I mean, it's the fault of the motion pictures, that have made the Southerner "a shitkickuh, a dumb fuckhead." He can't be sensitive, he can't be liked, and he sounds disgusting to Italians:

> "Luk heah, Eyetalian, mah momma made me some pastafazoola—"

Bloaghhhh! The back goes up.

> "Gimme some scungilli! Hey, momma mia, momma mia—"

Haghhh!

But it's just his sound. That's why Lyndon Johnson is a fluke—because we've never had a president with a sound like that. Cause we know in our culture that "peeple who tawk lahk thayat"—they may be bright, articulate, wonderful people—but "people who tawk lahk thayat are shitkickuhs." As bright as any Southerner could be, if Albert Einstein "tawked lahk thayat, theah wouldn't be no bomb":

> "Folks, ah wanna tell ya bout new-cleer fishin—"
> *"Get outta here, schmuck!"*

97

"How come ah'm a *schmuck?*"

"Cause you 'tawk lahk thayat,' that's why."

"But ah'm tawkin some stuff, buddi."

"Will you stop, you nitwit, and get outta here? You're wasting our time."

They'll damn you for your sound—you and your damn sound.

You know, the singer that talks on the stage, I wonder if he knows the dues he has to pay, that his sound is not pleasant when he talks:

"Ah bin awl ovuh, buddi, an ah wanna tell yew thayat . . ."

Yeah.

Now, Ruby—anybody can second guess, naturally—but I figure that's why he did lose it. Ruby had an attorney that sounded like that in reverse. Marvin Belli handled a preliminary for me, and he's a groovy lawyer, except that he got caught with his mask off. In Texas, Belli sounded to those people like the reverse of a Southern attorney talking to Liebowitz and a Jewish and Italian jury. Yeah, cause they didn't like his sound, the Northern sound. He sounded

"Lahk a dayim New York Jew-lawyer, buddi, comin dressed to cawt lahk a dayim peeyimp, with awl thayat shit on his nayils and evvrithin."

And Belli, he forgot the geography. It's the same kind of law, but it really is in the words. You just have to speak them slower in that area, and there are a few changes, but they don't change the substance of the law.

It's like, as good a case as I could have with you, if I pick my nose, although it's not dishonest, it's just going to lose it, you know. So Belli didn't wear the right suit, because anybody whose suit fits him good in the South "luks lahk a dayim peeyimp." And he should have known that, but he was offended with the judge chewing tobacco—and that's a natural thing down there.

There was like a dopey picture I saw going around, and it said, "This is your local police department," and it showed some kind of cops in this Southern place and they were laughing and one guy was smoking a cigar. That was it. But that's just the behavior in the Southern court. And the fact that everyone was laughing—Southerners are just, they're childlike in that area, they're not sophisticated. I mean, picture-taking: they see

"Picture?"

"Smile!"

That's why they're always smiling in the pictures— they're not arrogant, they just think they're supposed to smile when you take their picture. And the Northerners are just hip—they do the cool.

So Belli trying to sell those jurors anything, the idea of it must have just broke their balls! That qualifying must have really got them good and crazy. Any attorneys here, forget that. If I was an attorney, here's what would be my pitch. First place, no qualifying. No challenges at all. First jurors come up, they're the jurors:

"You jurors, you're people who think alot of the community, cause you vote. That's why you're jurors."

And give them all a hundred bucks apiece and get 'em laid and that's it. I'd be a terrible law professor, eh?

STUDENT: What'd he say at the end there? "Just give em a hundred bucks and get em laid?" . . . Ah, professor, can we talk to you, ah . . . the conclusion that you made there, the hundred dollars to get em laid?

PROF: Yeah, yeah, get em laid, that's all that counts.

STUDENT: But that don't fit with the beginning of the conversation.

PROF: That's all bullshit, gotta figure around it . . .

STUDENT: Ah, he's bottled out, get him . . .

99

Yeah, Belli talking to those people, he sounded to that jury like a Southern attorney would sound to Greek, Irish, Italian, Jewish, Northern jurors:

"Luk heah, now, jurors, ah lahk Eyetalian peeple, at's fust off. Ah see we got some Eyetalian peeple heah by the. . . . Ah'm gonna tell you a little stowrey now. This ol buck nigger and this Jew-boy—"

"*Aggghhhhhh!*"

"What the hell evvribuddy get so hot faw?"

"Just shut up, don't say any more!"

"What ah say? At's a cute stowrey, evvribuddy getsa kick outta it."

"No they don't! Just shut up. I can't explain it to you. You look South, your hair's wet, I don't know what it is—just dummy up, that's all."

Yeah. If I had handled Ruby I certainly would have given him an attorney that wore a suit three sizes too big, that was blue and shiny, and who would've stepped on his dick the whole time:

"Duh, Mr., duh, uh, wha? . . ."

And the jurors would've done what all jurors do—their job—to forgive. Yeah, The Forgivers, man.

On Performing and the Art of Comedy

And more people are coming into the little theatre off
Times Square . . .
USHER: Seating in the outer aisle only!
Your cab is ready, Mister First-Nighter, at the little
theatre off Times Square . . .
TOUGH VOICE: Never mind the theatre, driver—
I've got a few hookers waiting for me in Sausolito!

What'll I do? What'll I show you? That's weird. I can
tell you this cause I like you. It's such a problem for
me, you know. I'm the only comic I think that has this
sickness.

First place, I don't write. I create everything that I do,
you know. I never actually sit down and write before;
but I'll *ad lib* things on the floor, and then they'll become
bits, right? So—like the airplane bit—now I've done that
for about a year, right? Now I go to a new town, you
know. It swings, you know. But like I did that the last
time I was here, and I really get alot of guilt about doing
it, and I feel dishonest, and it gets to be a real bug, you
know?

I continually create things, but even though they're

good things, I just feel a dishonesty, you know? It's really a terrible thing.

That's why I'm studying hairdressing.

Here's how I work. I never sit down and write anything out. I've never sat down and typed out a satire. What I will do, is I will *ad lib* a line on the stage. It'll be funny. Then the next night I'll do another line, or I'll be thinking about it, like in a cab, and it'll get some form, and it'll work into a bit.

Everything I do on the stage I create myself. If I do an hour show, if I'm extremely fertile, there will be about fifteen minutes of pure *ad lib*. But on an average it's about four or five minutes. But the fact that I've created it in *ad lib* seems to give it a complete feeling of free form. And the new stuff pushes the other—old —out.

But I'm not original. The only way I could truly say I was original is if I created the English language. I did, man, but they don't believe me.

The reason I don't get hung up usually with doing anything I've done on records is that—well, the reason I'm in this business, I assume all performers are—it's "Look at me, Ma!" It's acceptance, you know—"Look at me Ma, look at me Ma, look at me Ma." And if your mother watches, you'll show off till you're exhausted; but if your mother goes, *Ptshew!* . . .

So I knew if I ever do everything you want record-wise:

"What do you want me to do?"

"Do Religious Incorporated, and do the Hitler bit, and do the Pope bit, and do this bit, and the prison bit—"

and I do all the bits you want me to, you walk out,

"How do you like him?"

"Ah, alright. But every time you see him it's the same shit, man."

I never want that, Jim, so I got to be one step this way, this way this way, all the time with you.

But I'm going to do one bit for you. It's a bit about a comedian, a comedian that thinks there's such a thing as a "class room," that rooms have identity. And he's got a manager, and the scene opens up in Sherman Oaks, California. The pool isn't in yet, but the patio's dry.

Now the comedian is bugged, cause he thinks that what's wrong with his career is he's never worked these class rooms, and he talks to the agent:

"Hey, Bullets. Wanna talk to ya for a minute, awright? Listen, I'm tired of working these craphouses, man. You know, everybody started with me, they moved—Joey Bishop, Alan King, Frank Marlow, Frank Fonteyn—they're all movin'. Me, I never went nowhere. Ya know why? Never worked the class room. And you know what I want? I want the Palladium Theatre in London."

"The Palladium! You *putz,* you. Whaddaya you, the Palladium? It's a *vaudeville* house."

"It's a vaudeville house? Well, I wanna tell you something about vaudeville houses. Alan King played it—look, I don't want no horseshit. I don't want to start going back to Montreal, that's *it!* You're not going to get the commissions from Vegas, and we've had it!"

Alright. Two weeks later, the agent:

"Awright, ya creep, ya got it. Ya don't belong there. You open up the nineteenth with [star singer], Bobby Breen and Bruno Hauptmann's son, But you don't belong there, you creep, you. It's a class room."

103

"Look, I'm gonna fool you. You dunno my act. I've got it *down* now. I work to Jewish people—I've learned how to say 'toe-kiss.' I work to the Italian people—I've got the *mamma mia* bit—I got it all down. I got a Jolson finish, I'll *murder* them now! You kiddin? I got so many bits now—you didn't see me work in a year, that's why."

All right—the show. [*Star singer*] is on now, she's been on about two hours. She's now into her Tribute-to-Sophie-Tucker-Hello-God number. The comic, waiting to go on; and —— has got that kind of empathy going. That show —— has this kind of magic, that she breaks her straps and she's getting screams on her nay-nays. Three hours, finally gets off:

"Ladies and gentlemen, a nice warm reception now for America's fastest-rising young comedian, the dean of satire, Mr. Frank Dell!"

"Well, good evening ladies and gentlemen, I just got back from a funny little place in Nevada called Lost Wages!"

"Ahhhhhhhhhhh."

"You know folks, funny thing about working Lost Wages, you meet alotta weird people out there."

"Ahhhhhhhhh."

"Folks, I—"

Alright, into the toilet. Nothing. Into the shithouse. People are staring at him, complete blank-out. Now, after fifteen minutes he's starting to sweat, he's doing — —'s numbers from out of left field. And in his inadequacy he vents his hostility on the audience:

"Ah, squares—*bullshit!*"

It's embarrassing. The band's reading *Punch*.

"Folks, um, I tell you what, here's a bit that everybody likes. But I'm not going to do it for you—gonna fool you, right? Ha ha . . . Joly, I'm not doing too good this afternoon, buddy, but you're

104

up there in show-business heaven, sweetheart.
Folks, I'm gonna do a tune now for Al Jolson.
Now you can knock me, but don't knock a guy
that's dead, awright? Don't knock a guy that helped
alotta servicemen, awright? O.K. Joly, I dunno
how they're gonna like ya, but, it's up to them.
They can rap ya, send ya away; but I'm on your
side. The hell with them! Rock-a-bye—"

Rock your *putz*, Daddy, he's had it. That exploitation
of the dead didn't work, and it's *verfallen*, and he's back
to the dressing room, the comedian:

[*Vomiting sounds, then a knock at the door*]:
"Come in."

[*British accent*]: "Oh, you're getting it all over!
Here's some kleenex. Here, son . . . hahaha . . .
and we just had the rugs done. Hahaha . . . Get
it on the dog, at least . . . However, my name is
Val Parnell, and I'm the house booker here. This
is Hadden Swaffle, the critic from the London
Times, and, ah, *goddamn* they were grim, weren't
they son? I don't know what went on out there, we
were in the box office, you know, when all of a
sudden I heard that unnatural silence. And we
walked out, and there you were, you poor bugger.
You were on there for about three hours, weren't
you? I really wonder what it was? You're quite
good—that reefer bit was quite unique. My wife
loved you—she's been to the Catskyull Mountains,
she got all those esoteric references about Grass-
hangers and the Concoward, and all those places,
but I, ah—what do you think, son? I mean, you're
a clever chap, you've been around, ah, ah, I don't
think it went over, did you? You're too damn *good*
for them, that's what it is. Too clever. Fact I got
some ideas. I said, Hadden, this boy here's going
over their heads, he's got all that hip stuff, ah, we

got one idea, think you're going to get a kick out of it. Look, ah, ah, about leaving Thursday, now, I wonder if you'd mind signing this release here—"

"*Hey!* Sign what? Sign your *chooch!* Whaddayou, kiddin? Whaddayou, kiddin, sign a release? Look, you had alotta kids out there, how you gonna make kids laugh, huh? I didn't do my fag-at-the-ballgame bit yet!"

"Thank God, son! Ah, ah, look, ah, I'm only the manager here, but it would seem to me that—son, this is no reflection on your talent, you're damn clever! Here, sign it, you're too good for them! You'll laugh at *them* years from now, Here, sign it, here."

"Now look, I dunno if your kiddin me or what, but, ah, I gotta hot temper, you know what I mean? I wanna tell you somethin, now, c'mere. C'mere! Where you going? [*very angry*] C'MERE! I wanna talk to ya now! Now look, I'm not horseshittin you, now, now, ah, I dunno if you think you're dealin with some Johnny-come-lately here, I worked alotta good rooms, now, and I wanta tell you somethin. You can't cancel me after one show! I got union here, and, ah . . . [*Collapses*] Look, man, I'm sorry I got hot with ya, but ah, ah . . . look man, you don't . . . you see . . . I donwanna hafta work in shithouses my whole life, man . . . My wife didn't want me to have this date, and my, ah, manager didn't want me to have it . . . I hate to cop it to ya like this, man, but, ah, *ya can't let me go like this,* you unnerstan what I mean? . . . You *gotta* let me do the nighttime show. I gotta lotta bits, I'll change around, but, ah, you know —they gave me a party an everything . . . I'll tell you how much this date means to me—*I'll kill you!* Really would, man. You think I'm horseshit-

106

tin? I'll *kill* you! . . . You gonna let me do the nighttime show. I don't give a shit about the money, man. Look. I tell you what . . . I'll give you my guitar, man. I got two hundred dollars that I brought over with me—you can have it, man. Just don't junk me after the first show. Whaddaya want me to do, awright? Gimme a break, or I'm gonna kill ya. I'm not horseshittin ya, I'm telling ya the truth."

". . . You're obsessed! You'd really do me bodily harm? Dear, dear! Well, if you think one show'll do it, well, ah, . . . Son, ah, isn't comedy, ah, it is a bit or a joke, isn't it rather the totality? I know it's rather an amorphous craft, son—"

"Look, never mind widdat Commie horseshit! Lemme do the show, awright? Don't break my chops. You said it's o.k., its o.k."

That night, the show. Now, for some cats this would really be good trauma, a scar that you'd never forget. This cat is very light. Delicatessin; pastrami; and he's on his way. Now, —— —— is on; he's waiting to go on. —— —— is now into her tribute to anyone in show business that may ever die. She's doing the bond drive and she's really got it wrapped up, and he's waiting to go on, the comic:

"Whatthehell is she doin, that talk out there. Go ahead, *talk,* ya fat-ass broad! *I'll* sing when I get out there. Hey Bobby, she supposed to do all that talk? Ahhh, sing some of *this,* awright? 'At cunt, what is she, kiddin with that horseshit? Hey, toot-sie! Hey, what's she gonna do, ten hours out there? . . . I'll do my Peter Lorre . . . no, I'll do my army bit first . . . [*sings*] Racing with the moon . . ."

Meanwhile she took a bow—he didn't know that—bow, and now, dig what she does for an encore, an encore before the comedian comes on:

"Oh, thankyou very much. Oh, God bless you. Oh,

you've been so good to an ugly American. You know, I'm going to ask for a favor now: a moment of silence. How do you like that? You'd never expect that from a ham like me, a moment of silence for the poor boys who went to Dunkirk and never came back, a moment of silence for the poor boys . . ."

Go follow that. You can follow that with Art Baker whacking it in Bert Parks' face, but, you know, forget it! So the whole audience is crying their eyes out, jumping from the balconies, sobbing, Rachmaninoff out of the dead—bows, alright:

"Ladies and gentlemen, it's comedy time! C'mon, cry-babies! We all lost a boy or two in the service! Now here's Frank Dell!"

"Well, good evening ladies and gentlemen! You know, I just got back from a place in Nevada called Lost Wages. A funny thing about working Lost Wages . . ."

Into the shithouse. Forget-it city. Now the manager's watching him in the wings:

"Hey, Hey, why don't you go up on the roof, there, hey? Hey, tootsie?

He's a whack-out—it's the manager:

"Racing with the moon—"

It's granite. Mt. Rushmore's out there:

"Hey, come on, you Limey assholes, what are you, kiddin? I was in the service too, you jack-offs, what are you provin, or sometin, eh? I can tell you got a kick outta it—ya gotta dry sense of humor. Haha. You're awright."

Now it's ridiculous—fifteen hundred people, an oil painting out there. Manager's still watching him:

"O.K. folks, ah, before we have the movie, ah, we gotta nother bit, everybody gets a kick outta here. How about this, ah, SCREW IRELAND! How

108

bout that, eh? They really bum-rapped ya, the I.R.A. Screw the Irish, awright?"

A heckler in the balcony:

"Well that's the funniest thing you've said all night, boy! That's right. SCREW IRELAND!"

"Now take it easy, buster, that's just a joke, ya know."

"NOT HERE. SCREW THE IRISH!"

The manager:

"What's going on out there?"

"SCREW THE IRISH!"

"Get him off stage! Go to the newsreel, Johnny!"

"BLAST THE IRISH!"

"Get the newsreel! Wind it up!"

"SCREW THE IRISH!"

"Get the bobbies!"

"RIP THE SEATS OFF!"

Alright. Back to the dressing room:

[*Vomiting. Knock on the door.*]

In comes the house booker.

"Oh, *goddamn,* son, you're a bloody Mau-mau! Oh, dear! Bar the door, Freddy! Oh, dear! *Whew!* I don't *believe* what's going on out there. You've destroyed the second balcony. Go ahead, you leper, get in there, do it up right! I've never seen anything like that! God *damn* son, do you know what's going on out there? You've changed the architecture of the oldest theatre in London! Oh, well, we'll get you out of the country some way—here, sign this release right over here—I believe someone left a wig in the closet many years ago. Damn! Here. Sign it right here."

"Now, just a minute."

"What? Did I hear 'Just a minute'? Just a minute for what? To return to the crusades? Look, Bomb-o, you stunk it up out there, you know that,

109

don't you? Son, you don't use narcotics, do you? Cause that's the only rationalization I could have —you could be oblivious to the cacophony of sound that went on out there. Son, well, why . . . what are you *looking* at me for, you psychotic bastard, you? You're not funny, you sonovabitch! Get up! When I came out this afternoon I thought that—you're not funny. Everyone in the whole world is funny and *you're not* funny. That's crude, you see. But, I mean, the world is filled with unfunny people, and you're one of them, you *leper!* Now, you sign this or I'll black your eye right now! And I'm not a violent man. You sign this right now."

"Now, just a minute."

"Just a minute for what?"

"I didn't do my spicey-blue-risqué number yet."

"Get my digitalis—my face is becoming paralyzed! Your spicey-blue-risqué number? What did you call that, ah, what did you call that bit of classic mime you did? What was that for the women and children out there? Hm? What was that? HM? What was that? A new writer? Hahaha! What would that mean to everyone? What was that? Table for one, mister, Hm?"

That's the bit. The bit is, ah, naturally, part me.

See, it's a weird thing, some performers are that naïve that they think there's such a thing as a good audience and a bad audience. A good audience would mean an audience that agrees with the comic's point of view or the singer's selection of tunes. This means that the whole audience has the same mother and father, same upbringing, same ethnic, whole *schtuck*. Impossible. It's the ringside, Jim, and how *he* reflects and feels that night.

The only way I can at least justify in my own mind the prejudices I have—it manifests itself with fear, rather than hostility. I'm frightened, I'll get inhibited.

If I have old people sitting ringside, it really, *whew!* You give me an audience over sixty, then you'll see an entirely different show. I feel, all I can tell people over sixty is,

"Thank you, I've had enough to eat."
Cause I always figure, Oh, they'll get offended.

All performers, I think, work to ringside. Cause the whole thing is "Look at me. Ma! Can you see me Ma? Watch me, Ma." And if your mother watches, you'll show off till you're exhausted; but if your Ma goes, pass, then forget it. So actually, eight people do it. That's why the *schtarkers* are a deterrent to the show.

It was absurd, obviously absurd, but people got upset when I said, "Bobby Franks was a snotty kid, anyway." Today's comedian has a cross to bear that he built himself. A comedian of the older generation did an "act" and he told the audience, "This is my act." Today's comic is not doing an act. The audience assumes he's telling the truth. What is truth today may be a damn lie next week.

The truth. When I'm interested in a truth, it's really a *truth* truth, one hundred per cent. And that's a terrible kind of truth to be interested in.

It's like, any comedian, see, all comedians—it's "To thine own self be true." The guy, he paints a certain way, he's consistent. That's the only way he can paint, and he's painting, and then people who like that go to see him. It's like Stravinsky, you put Stravinsky on concert in The Bronx, and the same people dig him there as in Toocomecatrol, as in Biloxi, Mississippi. Presley will *schlep* out the same people at Loc Shodric as he will here, Jim.

With an art form, there's no right or wrong, man.

Dig. The only honest art form is laughter, comedy. You can't fake it, Jim. Try to fake three laughs in an hour— ha ha ha ha ha—they'll take you away, man. You can't.

Talk about my mother for a minute. And I really love her, and the reason I dig her is I realize—I'm not doing Don Rickles, who killed his father for a finish—because I got a lot of humor from her. She exposed me to many areas that I never would have been hip to.

Sometimes I look at life in the fun mirror at a carnival. I see myself as a profound, incisive wit, concerned with man's inhumanity to man. Then I stroll to the next mirror and I see a pompous, subjective ass whose humor is hardly spiritual.

I see traces of Mephistopheles. All my humor is based upon destruction and despair. If the whole world were tranquil, without disease and violence, I'd be standing on the breadline right in back of J. Edgar Hoover and —who's another real heavyweight?—Dr. Jonas Salk.

The kind of comedy I do isn't, like, going to change the world; but certain areas of society make me unhappy, and satirizing them—aside from being lucrative—provides a release for me.

Last night I was very bad, you know, like you sort of *revolt,* you know, just, all of a sudden you're working and—I do that—and all of a sudden you say, *"Aghhh!"* And then you start really getting vicious with the audience. But sometimes they hit back. So I decided with this size crowd I was really going to do a nice *haimish* kind

of show. And to open it up I've got an audience partici-
pation thing, a thing I worked out here with the sprinkler
system with gasoline. It's nice. You'll go quick. It'll be
enjoyable.

Yes, I'm tired. I'm very lethargic. This is the second
show tonight. The first show I met alot of hostility to
my left, if you call throwing up on my suit a bit of
rejection, as I walked off. And the second show—I'm
a little apprehensive.

No. Saturday night I feel insecure. I'm always a little
apprehensive of Saturday night audiences. It's sort of
like people who come to nightclubs on New Years Eve
at eight-thirty, you know? They sit there with a hat and
a horn, waiting, you know? For what? For something
to happen there. But I feel good. I feel alotta love for
all of you.

I keep getting a different kind of audience every year.
Three years ago my audience was comprised of—nobody drank in my audience three years ago. And my
audience was thirty per cent Negro. Then after that I
got sort of a doctor audience—that's when I was going
through the narcotics trial. Yeah. Then when I first got
started with the obscenity scene there, I got just lawyers.
Then I got a little esoteric, and then I got the appellate
court. Really. And then I got the teacher crowd.

Now I forgot what the fuck I was talking about. That's
very good. I blew it completely. Where was I? Once in a
while if I lose it, you know, and then try to bullshit, but
then when it's really gone it's gone.

You see, that's the problem of being a performer. A
judge can get away with that shit, you know:

"Ummmmmmm, wellll. . . . ."
Completely dunced out, you know?

"Ahhhhhhh . . . I'll take that under consideration, ahhhh . . ."

Oh, by the way, how about the decor here? They just re-did the place. In Early Gangster.

The way I figure it out is that the owner here must have been captured in the Phillippines, and this was a high school gym, and he rebuilt it, you know, he's one of those kind of nuts, you know—

"I want every brick!"

What could they do with this place, finally? Except pour kerosene on it.

First place, it's not functional from an artistic stand-point. This area—I don't know what it's for—they give you like little challenges, you know. I don't want any proscenium there, but at least, you know, you feel a closeness with the audience.

I'm not going to do anything offensive, you know, I'm not that Rickles type—audience attack. But if I were this close—that's what it is! That's the success of a stage. That's the success of a club that's *intime,* that you're this close to the audience. I just realized why it's a success. It's not that there's that rapport with the audience-performer, but they're *embarrassed* not to laugh. That's what it must be, right? So you get all that fake approval.

Sometimes I lapse into complete fantasy. I'm doing a bit now which I thought about on the way over in the cab. I'm going to do it for the first time for you. I started thinking about, comics are the only ones, as performers —you know how they're always getting bugged with reviewers, you know, they say "This guy bum rapped me, and this and that?" Well, if they could band to-gether, they could have a Celebrity Killing Service, where they could, you know, maybe knock a few guys

114

off—as other big organizations do, you know. They send out a little warning, like a bag of cement. So dig. It could work both ways. You know, get this organization together, you figure, "Who's a threat to me?" In the cafe industry. All right, we'll say Mort Sahl. Who by the way I think is a genius, I love him. All right. Say I wanna get rid of Mort. Celebrity Killing Service.

> "All right. Now, let's see. Now, whaddawe do with Mort Sahl? Well, it'll cost you about fifteen grand. What we'll do is, we will buy up all of the newsstands within a fifteen-mile radius of the club. Then we will hire a newsboy and we'll start delivering nothing but old newspapers.

Understand? So Mort will come out,

> "Well, folks, a funny thing happened tonight—the Von Hindenburg exploded."

And he'll get completely whacked out.

Now, suppose we want to assassinate—I haven't thought of this figure yet, that we're going to assassinate—but this guy is eccentric. He's very well guarded. You can't get at him. You know, they've tried all devious methods to get at him. And he has one eccentricity—he likes to watch Civil War veterans' parades.

> "Alright. O.K. Now, whaddawe gonna do? He's a freak for watching those parades. O.K. We gotta get in an old assassin. O.K. Look in the files. Lessee. Here's a guy, he's over a hundred years old, and he's, yes, a pretty good assassin. O.K. Get him over here."

They get him over.

> "O.K. What's the name there?"

> "Booth."

> "Awright, ah, come in, Mr. Booth."

> "Pleased to see you, child."

> "Awright, never mind the acting bit, we've got a wonderful job. Listen, Mr. Booth, I don't like to

bring it up, maybe you're a little touchy about it, but, ah, you're the one who gave it to Abe?"

"Yes. That was my job. Course, when I jumped—I can't dance any more. My leg jiggles."

Now, for me to satirize the assassination of Abraham Lincoln, which—I don't know if he's done it or not—but Sid Caesar, that's his type of humor or, Steve Allen, would satirize, you know? And it's like, they'd plan the satire out, and it'd have form, you know. It isn't just sort of *ad lib*. Everybody would laugh at it. I definitely know that I could do a satire on the assassination of Abraham Lincoln and really get screams with it on television. Although Abraham Lincoln was a wonderful man.

But, here's the thing on comedy. If I were to do a satire on the assassination of John Foster Dulles, it would shock people. They'd say, "That is in heinous taste." Why? Because it's fresh. And that's what my contention is: that satire is tragedy plus time. You give it enough time, the public, the reviewers will allow you to satirize it. Which is rather ridiculous, when you think about it. And I know, probably 500 years from today, someone will do a satire on Adolf Hitler, maybe even showing him as a hero, and everyone will laugh. There'll be good fellowship. Hitler'll be just a figure. And yet if you did it today it would be bad. Yet today I could satirize Napoleon Bonaparte. Because, you know, he's gone.

I'm doing a new bit that you'll just flip out with. It's social commentary. I do it with a colored guitarist, Eric Miller. The bit is on integration.

So anyway, we do the bit together. Halfway through the bit—there is a party of four to my right, and they're really bugging me, you know, saying "I don't unnerstan it."

So I give the woman a quick stab: "You *schlub,* you wouldn't understand anything"—you know.

So her husband says, "What'd he say to her?"

The other guy says, "He said something dirty in Jewish."

So I said, "There is nothing dirty in Jewish."

So dig, she takes this old-fashioned glass, and starts winging it, man, *vvvooom!* Right past me, man. I'm shocked. It crashes behind me.

So I say, "You've got a bad sense of humor, and bad aim."

So she gets bugged again, throws a second glass.

I said, "Well, assuming I'm the most vulgar, irreverent comedian you've ever seen, you've capped it with violence. You realize what a terrible thing—you threw a glass at me!"

So dig what the husband says: "What else would a lady have done?"

I said, "Faint!"

I satirize many subjects that are particular sacred cows. In other words, I am a satirist basically. I am irreverent politically, religiously, or any things that I think need discussing and satirizing. And some people who are involved emotionally with the subject I'm satirizing just get bugged, get verbal, and some get physically violent. That's what happens.

"Ah, he's not funny, he's *disgusting*.
That's what I always got in school. Every time.
"Up to a point he's funny, but then he just get's downright disgusting. I mean, there's certain things that's funny, and there's certain things that are downright disgusting. I mean, he starts talking about snot—that's not funny. Anybody can get a laugh on snot. Ya slob, ya! Ya disgusting creature!"

It's a comedian's duty to maintain a level of good taste and this to me is a semantic beartrap. I've been accused of bad taste and I'll go down to my grave accused of it and always by the same people—the ones who eat in restaurants that reserve the right to refuse service to anyone.

If you can tell me Christ or Moses, for instance, would say to some kid,

>"Hey, kid! That's a *white* fountain—you can't drink out of there!"

You're out of your skull. No one can tell me Christ or Moses would do *that*. And people who do aren't even agnostics. They're atheists. That's where the bad taste jazz comes from.

Is this comedy, or what? Now you know it's not comedy—I'm pissing on the velvet, that's what I'm doing. It's comedy. It's comedy that gets laughs. It's not funny. It's the same question: Is this painting?

>"That a painting? I mean, that may be painting, alotta horseshit to me, man. Maybe, maybe I don't understand it."

Yeah. Humility is the worst form of the ego, man, that's it.

>"I mean, maybe I am jerky, or somethin, for Chrissakes, I dunno—"

No you don't know, that's right.

Here's what comedy is. Now, all these people that you saw leave, did not. They were all beat up at the head of the stairs. I used to let them get away with it, but now, they're all coming back now, apologizing at the door, with a note, "I'll be good."

[*People walk out*]

More friends . . . Well, no one really enjoys rejection. Certainly, I abhor any cat who does the wounded bird, but it's, the whole motivation for every performer is "Look at me, Ma." . . . You know, the only thing that confuses me, I lay in bed at night and I think, What the hell did that guy come in for. . . . Does he, is that the lowest form of entrapment? Does he come to bust me? What kind of humor is his humor? Is his humor the Joe E. Lewis, the Sophie Tucker, the *double-entendre,* the naughty-but-nice, the spicey-haha-you-know-what-that-means wedding-night jokes, motel jokes, Rusty Warren, Johnny got a zero, Dwight Fisk, Mr. Yo-Yo can't get his yo-yo up, he's got the biggest dingy in the navy?

God, don't have a stroke, that's all I need. That'll be about the end press for me.

Remember the old bit, Religions Incorporated? Right? I'm in New York, and I start out with a stream of consciousness with this bit, at Basin Street, a third show, and I had about one hundred and twenty Grey Line Tourers there, you know? And I had forgot that they were there, see? I went into the bit and all of a sudden I see about ninety people—*vvvooom!*—an exodus! I dump another sixty five minutes later, and the *maitre d's* are flippin, man. A sixty-party walkout is a big taste, you know.

And then about an hour later I realized how much I did offend these people—they left without the bus and the drivers! That's a heavy kind of move, you know. Definitely. That's a real *schtark* kind of move.

But I didn't feel any hostility towards them. Cause I wasn't right, and they weren't right. A right-or-wrong concept isn't involved there. Of course they gotta do that! That's only right.

Now. One thing I'd like to tell the people leaving, is, that you're very genteel. This is the first time I've had an audience that, they walk out, but they're very nice about it.

In Milwaukee, *Phew!* They used to walk out and walk *towards* me. Milwaukee I had such grief, man—Milwaukee, that's like Grey Line *en mass*. Yeah. Really got rank, the people there, with me, you know. Oh, it was really grim in Milwaukee. The club was right next to the river, and even *that* started to look good.

Dig what happened in Milwaukee:

First place, the reason that I worked there is that I'm ashamed of the prejudice that I have within me. I pre-judge a town right away, say "Ah, they're squares." Downright bigotry.

But this guy hits on me, he sees me at the Crescendo in Hollywood.

"You'll do very good there!"

"*I* don't think I'll do good there."

"You'll do *great!* Have alotta fun—do ya bowl?"

"*Uh oh. . . .*"

Conflict, back and forth. Then I think, "What the hell, I'm not going to prejudge people; frig it, I'll make it, I'll work the town."

Now, I get there, and the first thing that scares me to death, they've got a six-thirty dinner show. Six-thirty at night, people go to a nightclub?

CHILD'S VOICE: It's not dark out yet, I donwanna go in the house!

There's *bikes* outside the club—it's a neighborhood movie matinee. *Kids* there. I go into the men's room, and I see *kids* in the men's room. Kids four years old, six years old.

Now I see some poetry, it's really beautiful. I see these kids in the men's room, they're looking, and these kids are in awe of this men's room—this is the first time they've ever been in a place their mother isn't allowed in. It's amazing to them; they can't figure it out:

120

FIRST KID: Your mother isn't allowed in here?

SECOND KID: Nope. Not even for a minute. Not even to get something. She's not allowed in here.

And they stay in there for hours:

MOTHER: Come outta there!

KID: Na! Hahaha!

MOTHER: I'm gonna come an get you!

KIDS: No you're not—you're not allowed in here, cause everybody's doing, and making wet in here.

O.K. Curtain. *Christ!* These people look *familiar!* But I've never been to Milwaukee before. Where the hell did I see—these are the *Grey Line tourers,* before they leave! This is where they *live. Sic semper* Tom McCann.

All right. As soon as I ever have to think of what I'm gonna do when I get out here, then I'm dead. Then it's a lie. You know, if I say I'll do this bit and that bit, then it becomes a bit, and its terrible.

I'm out there for about fifteen minutes and people are staring at me in disbelief. Then the shock wears off, and I start to hear:

"What's 'poots' mean?"

"I dunno."

"What is he supposed to be talking about?"

"I dunno."

"What is he? What's 'schmuck'? He keeps saying 'schmuck' and 'pootz,' "pout," 'poots,' 'parts,' . . . and, and 'bread,' 'cool,' 'dig,' "schmooz,' 'grap,' 'pup' 'schluph,' 'murgh'—"

It sounds like garble to them—these are *Jews* asking this now.

"I dunno whatthehell he's talking about."

"I dunno, it's a bunch of silliness."

"It's doubletalk, I think. That's what he's doing, doubletalk."

"Well, I dunno, it's, ah, its, ah, good . . . I guess."

121

"You like him?"

"I wanna go to the toilet."

"Awright . . . I'll go with ya."

"I donwanna walk in front of him."

"Yeah, but everybody's walking out. And he's still up there—'poots,' 'brootz,' 'mugrup,' 'blog'—he's up there. Whaddishe, crazy? . . . How come he hasn't got any music? No singing, nothing. Sure, even the band left him. Ha ha ha! There's no band up there! Sure, *they* know he's crazy."

"He's crazy. He's a weirdo. He's on the dope. Yeah. He's on it now. Oh yeah, He's right on it now. Cloud seven."

"How can you tell?"

"You can tell. You can just tell when they're on it. They act sneaky. Yeah. And they have the strength of an *in*sane man. Yeah. Don't go near them. They'll twist your head off an everything. He doesn't know what he's doing. He'll probably stay up there for two days, on the stuff."

Now, it's maybe thirty minutes, and I'm just, I'm just fumpfing all over, I'm stepping on my dick, I dunno where I'm at, man. O.K. And finally I get off and the owner goes,

"Lenny, Christ! We had so many walkouts!"

"I'm hip, man, they were stepping on my feet. Got to be like a herd."

"Well, *Jesus*, I never heard you do that *religious* bit, and those *words* you use!"

"I dunno. You saw me work, man, I don't do the same bit every show, or the same way."

"We'll do something."

O.K. Now, there's walkouts, walkouts, every night walkouts. The chef is confused—the desserts aren't moving.

Now, it's Saturday night, I'm down to the end of the barrel, I'm doing these kind of bits:

"O.K. folks—bob white! Cheep cheep! And now, a duck!"

And dig: the esoteric quality of the humor is further championed by an age barrier. Little old *grandmothers* with crocheted gloves sitting there, eating custard, and spitting it back, with rouge, the whole family—it's like *A Death in the Family*. So the owner decides to introduce me, to cushion it:

"Ladies and Gentlemen, before I bring the star of our show, Lenny Bruce—who incidentally is an ex-G.I., just got back from Iwo Jima—and a hell of a performer, folks, and a great kidder, you know what I mean? It's all a bunch of silliness up here. He kids about the Pope, and ah, the Jewish religion too, and the colored people and the white people—it's all silly, a make-believe world. And, ah, he's, ah, a helluva guy—he's at the Veteran's Hospital now—doing a show for the boys—and he's, ah, and his Mom's out here tonite too, hasn't seen her in a coupla years, she lives here in town—"

He gets walkouts, man. He gets fifty walkouts.

"Boy, they're dropping like flies, tonight. Just blew the whole balcony, it's unusual. Something is different tonight."

O.K. Now, the other clubs in the neighborhood are a Socony gas station and a laundromat that didn't make it. Now, I hang out at the gas station between shows, and get gravel in my shoes. And the conversation is really inspiring.

"Hey, lemme see the grease rack go up again."

"Awright."

"Can I work it?"

"No. You'll break it."

"Can I tie your leather bow-tie?"

"Nope."

"Married?"

"Yeah."

"Ball your old lady alot?"

"Hey! . . . Wanna see a clean toilet?"

"O.K."

Really desperate, right?

"You been to alot of gas stations, right? Ever see a toilet like this?"

"No. It's beautiful."

"Don't lie to me!"

"I wouldn't lie to you."

"It's immaculate, right?"

"Beautiful! Beautiful."

"Eat off the floor, right?"

"Certainly could."

"Wanna sandwich?"

"No!"

Then they've got the machines:

"What are these things for a quarter here, these condums here? You sell alot of them?"

"I dunno."

"Is that a lie, Sold for the Prevention of Disease? Or whaddaya assume they're really sold for . . . You know, I think I saw a condum once, when I was a kid. Aren't they sort of terrible? Sold for the Prevention of Love:

    'Are you wearing anything?'

    'Yeah. I'm wearing an axe on my head.'

Do you wear condums?"

"Ahhh, I dunno."

"I mean, ah, whaddaya do? Do you just have them on all the time? Get up in the morning, 'Well, I'll put a condum on, I'll be ready'? I mean, it just takes any love out of it, it just seems like a planned . . . Gimme some of them."

"Go get em yourself."

"Awright. Wanna chip in? Ah, we'll both wear one,
we'll take a picture."

"Getthehell outta here, you nut!"

I've just lost perspective, that's all. Just lost perspective. Yeah. In another year I'll have about fifteen real
hard-core followers—they'll feel compulsed to support
me, you know, to fly all over. They get the S-O-S's, you
know? Just three people out there, that's all. Just three.
That constitutes a show. As long as I can get booked
for obscenity. Yeah. Over two people, that's an obscene
show.

Oh. MCA sent me to a nice place called Lima, Ohio.
It's really a swinging town. They should all end up that
way. It's a cute little town, you know, and they've got
about eighteen thousand people, and MCA, you know,
they pioneer me, they send me to all these disaster areas:

"Listen, we want someone."

"O.K., send him—he's a trouble-maker. Let him do
Religions, Incorporated there! *They'll* grab him."

So dig. I don't know why the town is there, ever, but
I'm there, and the club—you ready for the name of the
club? *Ciro's.* And the boss keeps telling me,

"You know, they sued us for the name, in '45. Hah
hah! We won, you know. It was in Earl Wilson's
column, did you see it?"

"Oh, yeah, got it in my scrapbook. Who could forget that? Everybody always looks at it and talks
about it, in front of the Brill Building."

And he's one of these guys, he's really hung up on his
old lady, loves his wife. One of those real devoters, you
know? And he keeps telling me, you know,

"She's brilliant! What a mind! She frightens me.
Got such a mind. In this town, she's lost. She thinks
just like a man."

Dig. She was about his third wife, and he married her—

125

she's about the third act to play the club. But she wasn't an act, she was a magician's assistant. You know, with the skinny legs, net stockings that are sewed up so much it looks like varicose veins.

"And now, the egg in the bag! Thank you, Wanda." And now she's like one of these chicks, she doesn't want to give up, she's still got the leopard leotards, and the platform shoes, you know, and she's got this cigarette holder, la da da dum, you know, and you know, tanned face, sagging keester, a real nothing.

And they always *schlep* you into the office. And he's showing me pictures, how the club used to look, you know? And they added on, and on—looks like a fun house. It looks nice inside, but outside it looks like Frank Lloyd Wright is a junkie. He's strung out there, and he's sort of fixed up the place.

And he keeps showing me pictures—you know, of him on a pony, you know—on and on and on.

So now, I'm working, and after the fourth night I start to recognize people. And suddenly I realize they were in the night before. And the night before that. And I suddenly realize that the same people come in every night; but not because they dig me—they're *drunk!* This town's got four hundred people that stay juiced out of their minds—cause they're depressed because they're there. Or they're like people that got hung up in this town, for business, or they're on the lam or something. They don't heckle, you know, they're just loaded. But they don't listen. So I really feel rejected.

And the most depressing thing, you know, is that there's nothing to do in these towns. You go to the park, you see the cannon, and you've had it. The library has the latest Fanny Hurst novel. And the drugstores:

"Don't take the magazines to the *counter!"*
So what can you do? You go to the five and ten, look through that for a while. That's the end of the day.

126

They've got one Chinese restaurant in town, that serves bread and butter, cottage cheese, and fig newtons for dessert. No almond cookies. They give you tea in a real cup. There's no fantasy there.

You know, you always hear about these small towns, you figure, "Well, I'll go on the road, swing, they'll be some wild chicks." So this town, eighteen thousand— *Peyton Place?* It's a *lie!* There's no towns like that. Nothing happens in these towns. And I'm really getting lonesome.

And the waitresses there—nice elderly ladies, cardiac cases with corrective stockings, Ace bandages, and they've all got those handkerchiefs—starched, you know —pinned there. And I'm looking to swing with someone, and they're bringing me in jelly, chicken soup, you know.

Now, I'm there and I'm really bugged. So, one night I come off the floor, and the waitress says to me, "The couple, they would like to meet you."

So, solid, maybe someone will turn me on. So I go over to the table, sit down, maybe sixty-five years old, nice young couple. So dig. They like me cause I did some things about Bruno Hauptmann. They knew some people who knew Hauptmann, and the guy says to me,

"You from New York?"

"Originally."

"Wha'd I tell you! Did I tell you?"

Wife's a real *schtolzer,* short sleeve dress, vaccination as big as a basketball, mole with a hair in it, real Philomena at the wedding. Kind of dress you can see through and you don't want to. So he says,

"I recognized that accent. We're from New York too. I been out here for fifteen years. Yeah. It's a great town, New York, right?"

"It certainly is."

"Yop, really great there. This is my wife. She's not from New York."

127

"Oh! Hmm. That's really something, boy."

"Ever been to San Francisco?"

"Yeah, I worked there."

"There's a great town! Alotta restaurants there!

"Oh, yeah, aren't there. Boy oh boy. And your wife's not from New York and there's alotta restaurants there."

"It's not as good as New York, though!"

"No, you really said something there. It's really not as good. Cause there's more restaurants."

Getting sick by now, you know, waiting for somebody to rescue me, but everybody looks alike! I've got nobody to hang out with. The band, they're the lowest. They bring their lunch in a brown paper bag. And I know, no music, nothing. All they talk about is that they fixed their roof, and this one guy's building his own trailer, you know, that I wish that he'd take the town away in.

Now, all of a sudden, the guy stops talking and he looks at me, and I see sort of a searching hope in his eye. He says,

[lowered voice] "You're Jewish?"

"Yeah."

"What're you doin in a place like this?"

"I'm passing."

"Why don't you come over the house? My wife'll make you a nice dinner, you know, a gedempsteh bliss, you'll eat something."

Usually I never fall into this trap, but I figure, It's something to do. I'll take a bus or something. O.K. Wet cocktail napkin. The Scheckners. Write the address down. Solid. Tomorrow. Seven o'clock. Wonderful. I'll be there.

O.K. I'm staying at the Show Business Hotel—and the show people? One guy runs the movie projector in town, the other guy sells Capezio shoes. Anyway, you know, I read a little, write a little—I just finished a

novel that will come out in installment form in *Playboy*
—so by the time I read, write, maybe it's eight, nine
in the morning before I go to sleep.

O.K. Next day, eight in the morning, the phone rings:

"Hullo?"

"Hello! This is Mr. Sheckner!"

"Who?"

"Mr. Scheckner! The people from last night! From
New York!"

"Ohh. Solid."

"We didn't wake ya, did we?"

"No, I always get up about 12 hours before work.
You know, I need coffee, brush my teeth, get up.
I would've overslept. I'm glad you called me, there,
it's wonderful. What's happening, baby?"

"Listen, why we called you—"

"Yeah, I been wondering when we'd get to that.
Is it any more about New York? Or the restaurants,
right?"

"Na, hah hah! You *meschugenah,* you! Why we
called you, we wanna know what you wanna eat!"

"What?"

"Listen, my wife's gonna get, she might as well
get what ya like!"

"Ohhhhhh. Are you putting me on, man? At this
time of the morning? Chicklets."

"Oh, you *meschugenah* you."

"Yeah, a chicklet and a fig newton."

"Na, na, na, you *luff* you, we wanna know what
you want!"

"Well, anything. Please believe me, I eat anything.
An avocado dip. Anything. A pretzel. Anything.
Some dentyne gum. Your old lady . . . Yeah,
I'll be there. Thank you Mr. Scheckner."

And I get over there, and I do eat anything in the
world, except what they have—liver and brussel sprouts.

That's really a double threat: I don't like like liver and I don't like brussel sprouts. You know. And she's one of these women who cooks it without water, you know? It's like eating paper. So I'm there, and I can't stand liver and I wanna be nice, and I'm eating it and stuffing some in the couch—I'm not going to be over there again, they'll blame it on the kid. The kid'll get rapped.

O.K. Now, they invite some chick over, for me to look at. Real *schlub* with lipstick on her teeth, makeup on her file collar, chipped polish on her nails. And skinny. Did you ever see a chick who looked bad in a knit dress? She looks like a hockey stick with hair on it. And I don't know what it is, but these chicks—I'm really cool, I never come on—they start to get hostile with me. For no reason at all, you know.

"That Hollywood, it's really crazy, right?"

"Well, yeah, it's a wild town. Any town is wild, I guess."

"Well, is that true about Liberace?"

So, then I really start to get vicious.

"Well, whaddaya mean?"

"You know what I mean."

"No, what?"

"Tee hee. That he's a sissy."

"Ohhhh! Oh, yeah! You kidding? But *he's* straight. Eddie Cantor's a big fruit, did you know that?"

"No kidding!"

"Sure. They covered it up in the papers—the B'nai B'rith cooled it. Sure. Rin-Tin-Tin is a junkie, didn't you notice?"

"I told you they're crazy out there. Yona was out there, at Republic."

And now they take you around the house, got to show you around the house. And the tour, the whole function of this tour is to show you how dirty the last people were who lived there. What can you tell people when they take you around the house?

"Yes. That, um, that's really a lovely closet. I like the way the towels are folded. That's pretty hip." And then they have the piano, that nobody plays, with the lace on it, and the wax fruit. And I figured out, the whole function of these pianos is that eight-by-ten picture, that nitwit in the army saluting, you know:

"That's Morty—he's bald now."

Another exposé: One thing you never knew about me. I have a pen name: Ralph Gleason. I'm Ralph Gleason. And you're taking it good. I always thought you'd get pissed off at me for that. In fact I wrote the column for years and then just drifted into this, decided that I'd like to do a little comedy on the side, and you liked me, and I thought I was doing good, so what the hell, a few write-ups don't hurt anybody. And you're taking it good, that's lovely.

I want you to know another thing, too. That I've never been in jail. I've never been arrested. That's all horseshit. What it is, see, I got a publicity agent that's dynamite. And we have nine phoney cops that work for Pinkerton, and we go from town to town, the same bullshit, you know. I get busted, I write the column the next day, and that's where it's at, man.

The last time I was in town the press was very nice to me. So the opening night the press was here, so, I dunno, I must have said a few things that were a little hostile, you know, and then I got a write-up that was sort of vicious. I'll show you. From a fellow, his name is—wait, I got it here. This is yesterday's paper. It's the *Owl* or something. Oh yeah. *The Owl Steps Out*.

Dig. This guy writes a bread-and-butter column. That means like he's afraid to knock cause they'll lose the ads. But he still wanted to be a little vicious, you know? That's the truth. That's weird. In any town I work, guys like Herb Caen always dig me, Ralph Gleason, but I'm the only one that gets bad write-ups in those "What-To-See" magazines. Just, somehow I get real drug with them, you know? So this is a typical example.

> "Bring your anti-knock kit when you come to Fax Number Two this week and next because Lenny Bruce is one comic who doesn't care what he says, as long as he gets a laugh. He has a name for being the most risqué yuk-hustler—"

He must be talking about his old lady

> "in show business."

But finally, so after all of that—I was a little depressed, you know, cause you can't rise above that kind of thing, you know, of being too big for it, but it did, it bothered me—so finally, then, a newspaper of some integrity gave me a good write-up:

> [*shows a Russian newspaper*] "Last night a star was born!"

Yeah. I get bad reviews in every paper, except one with integrity—*The Enquirer*.

Did you see *Time Magazine* this week? With the Shelley Berman thing? They interviewed Shelley—but he sent me a wire, said he didn't say it—they interviewed Shelley Berman, it says, like, ah, "I don't want to be referred to with those sick comics, and Lenny Bruce is the sickest of them all . . . ." And the imagery was really weird. He said that "Lenny Bruce, why his success, that people have a need for him, and they also needed Hitler." So it really cracked me up. Cause it was so *haimish*. Dig that!

Sick humor. I feel that they use the word sick—I think it's lazy writing, you know, for columnists. In other words, if you notice when you read columns you'll see the word "beatnik"—I think they've already got it set in type, and when they're hung for a word they drop that in, "beatnik" "sick"—you know, whatever is fashionable.

I think that a comic that satirizes—it depends where your sense of humor lies—but the general picture of a sick comic is an individual that satirizes handicaps, unfortunates. Joe E. Brown said that he wished that he could be that kind of a mean, you know, comic, but he just can't do that, he's just *corpus christi,* and he doesn't like sick humor.

I don't think he was making reference to me, cause I don't do any, you know, deformity jokes in my act at all.

But I think that the comedy they had *before,* I think, actually was cruel. They actually did cruel comedy. There was the Jew comic, they used to call them; the Wop comic, they used to say; they used to do the blackface, real stereotype Uncle Tom Jim Crow with the curls and the fright wig. They did what they called the German comic, which satirized and made fun of ethnic groups, the way they spoke, and their racial characteristics, which you don't find too much today. I think the comedy of today has more of a liberal viewpoint.

All right. This bit is about MCA, who I talked about the first show. They're a big agency, and they're bringing in an act that's going to knock everybody out—George Andrews really has alot of guts when it comes to bringing in, you know, off-beat acts—a guy who has never played San Francisco, wonderful performer, the wonderful Adolf Hitler.

How did he get started, Adolf Hitler? He was pretty wild. What the hell could he do for an act, right? Just

133

come on, you know, and they go, "Oh, that old crap. You kidding? We heard that story."

Here's the way it happened. We take you back to Bremerhaven.

The agents are in peril—it seems that they have seventy-two hours to find a dictator, and now we hear them talking, two agents:

FIRST AGENT: Ven, ven vill de Cherman people realize it'z no time for ze moralist, for individualists? Do you realize zat ve haf seventy-two hours to find a dictator? Zat Kaiser—I can't believe zat he split—veird. Zis is like a bad dream. He left just like zat, you know. He vill never make it. Vat's he doink?

SECOND AGENT: Selling cars, the *schmuck*. He'll never make it.

FIRST AGENT: Zis is your fault, dot ve didn't haf him on paper, you know. You vent for dot handshake jazz.

SECOND AGENT: I never dug ze kaiser anyvay. He vas a veirdo, mit dot big mustache he had, vas dirty, mit de Monty Voolly bits dere, mit zat hat, mit de dumb phallic zymbol.

FIRST AGENT: Ya, zis is easy for you to talk like zis, but we havn't a dictator, ve haf to find somebody. You know, I took a chance, und called up central casting. You know, it's a freaky business, maybe ve get somebody. Ve try. They're coming in now . . .

Ya, siddown there, vere you vant, fellas, relax. My name is Franz Eiser. I'm ze agent here, und ve're trying to find ze dictator today. Ve have no script, a coupla pages—ve don't know vere de hell ve're going mit ze project ourselves. Ve vanna zee just today how you guys move, zat's all. Just *ad lib* it und do ze bit. Alright? O.K. Ve call up ze first fellow, Ben Visler. Benny, come over here. Zat's it. Just *ad lib*. Ve vanna see how you move today, und maybe ve put a few bucks behind you, you can't tell. Alright? Benny, ah, you look familiar . . . Did I do the Schlitz Playhouse mit you once? No? Doctor Christian? Jean Hersholt? No? O.K. Just sort of do ze bit, alright?

FIRST ACTOR [*Deep, raspy aggressive German*]: Das ist ungespinnert alles gefrimmer, ya!—"

FIRST AGENT: Ah, zat method crap! Get out of here with zat Brando jazz, you kidding mit that? O.K. Paul Schneider. Paul? Do ze bit dere.

SECOND ACTOR [*High, effeminate voice*]: Das ist ungespinn—

FIRST AGENT: Too faggy! Next?

SECOND ACTOR: Das ist ungespinn—

FIRST AGENT: You're a fruit! Now get out of here! Don't bug us no more. Call Bond-Loper and get the hell out of here.

SECOND ACTOR: Thcrew you in the I. J. Farbin building!

FIRST AGENT: Get out of here, you fag! All of you gentlemen, get out of here! Dat's right. Get out! Out, all of you. Ve vill call your agents . . . [*Breaks into tears*] Oh, boy, ve are finished! Zis is your fault, you fink, you! Zis is your fault, you und zat hooker, Anne Frank! Zat you haf destroyed ze Third Reich. Ve haf no dictator! You know vat zis means? Ve are dissolving ze agency—ve are finished! I never vant to look at you again. Zis is *kaput!* I'm going into personal management—I'm going to get a few acts of my own, that's all. I get Bobby Breen, Phil Bredo, dot's vat I need. Sure! Und I don't need you again. Ve are finished, my friend. You haf destroyed ze Third Reich. Ve haf no dictator, und history vill remember you, my friend. Ve are finished!

SECOND AGENT: Hey!

FIRST AGENT: Don't bug me. I don't like you, I don't vant to look at your face any more.

SECOND AGENT: Hey!

FIRST AGENT: You don't understand, do you, ven ve are finished? I don't vant to be bothered mit you.

SECOND AGENT: Hey!

FIRST AGENT: Vat is it?

SECOND AGENT: Don't look now, but dig ze guy on your right dot's painting ze wall.

FIRST AGENT: Vere?

SECOND AGENT: Don't look right avay, he'll think you're doing bits mit him. Extreme right over dere.

FIRST AGENT: Vere?

SECOND AGENT: To your right. Ze guy mit ze mustache und ze hair in front of ze face.

FIRST AGENT: Oh ya . . . Zis is really a veirdo! Look at dot fink mit dot mustache! Hey, you! Frenchy! Put down dot painting. You, ya, mit da hair jazz there. Put down dot painting und step around in front. Yes, you! Ve vanna look at you. Right? Ya. Alright . . . Look at zis face! Is zis an album cover? Hey, vat is your name, my friend?

PAINTER: Adolf Schicklgruber.

FIRST AGENT: You're putting us on.

PAINTER: Hey, come on, don jerk me around, you guys, I got tree garages to paint in Prague today. I gotta finish dem up.

FIRST AGENT: No von is jerking you around, dere. You ever did any show business bits?

PAINTER: Vell, I did a Chaplin impression at a party once. Hey! Don't jerk me around, you guys. My brudder'll punch de hell out ov you!

FIRST AGENT: No one is jerking you around. Ve

136

vanna make you a dictator! You know vat dot means? Ze money you'll make?

PAINTER: I dunno. I make pretty good mit my painting.

FIRST AGENT: Vill you stop mit dis painting? You're gonna maybe make in a minute vat you make mit dis Kemtone crap in your whole life. Stop mit dot dumb painting . . . I like dot first name—Adolf—it's sort ov off beat. I like dot. Gimme a different last name. Adolf vat?

SECOND AGENT: Menjou.

FIRST AGENT: Vill you shut up, you nitvit? Menjou! Alright. Ve need something to, sort of hit people.

SECOND AGENT: Adolf Hit-the-people?

FIRST AGENT: Vill you get the hell out ov here mit zem dumb jokes of yours, you nitvit? . . . Something . . . Adolf Hit— No. Adolf Hit-ler —zat's a vild name, right? A-d-o-l-f H-i-t-l-e-r. Five and six for the marquee—nice und zmall. Dot's nice. Sure. Dot's right. Ve get a little rythym section behind him, it'll swing dere. Jonah Jones, maybe. O.K. Adolf Hitler. Adolf Hitler. Say that.

SECOND AGENT: Adolf Hitler.

FIRST AGENT: I like that.

PAINTER: Vatdehell, ain't I got nuttin to say?

FIRST AGENT: Shutup! You nut, you'll get later. Ve'll fix you up mit some broads. At's all right. A nice big boy like you, mit a mustache? Oh, you freak you! Adolf Hitler. Yes. Ve'll sving mit dat. Alright? Dot's it! Adolf Hitler, tomorrow mein liebchen you vill go over ze Third Reich, call up, maybe, um, call up Leonard Bernstein, ve get some tunes from him. Something very light, a nice opener [sings]: "Goodbye, Denmark, goodbye . . . Poland, how I love ya, How I love ya" . . . Ya. It'll sving. Ya. Call up Cy DeVor, get him something very

137

commercial, ze mohair und ze cufflinks. Alright? Tomorrow, Adolph Hitler, you vill get over ze Third Reich—und ve need von zing more: an armband. Ve didn't do ze armband bit for a vile. Ve need somezing lucky, zat people can identify zemselves mit. Vat's lucky? Somsing, an emblem . . . I got it! Four sevens! Ya. Dot's it. It'll sving. It'll be good. You'll see. Ve'll get him in The Lounge. That'll be it. Tomorrow, Adolph Hitler, ve grow mit ze third Reich!

PAINTER: O.K., I still think you're jerking me around, but vat de hell, I like a buck like anyone else. I'm gonna get them broads?

FIRST AGENT: Yeah, you'll get broads, you won't be able to stand up already. Tomorrow, fix him up mit dirty Bertha. Freak him out. Start him out right. Wear him out. Alright. Tomorrow, Adolf!

PAINTER: O.K. fellas! Vatdehell, I'm gonna get laid—dat's de main ting, right?

FIRST AGENT: Ya, you'll *schtup* your brains out, you freak you. You'll vail, you'll vail! You never had it so good. Do the whole bit—knots in ze cord, anyting mit zem.

PAINTER: Alright, vatdehell, fellas, I'll go along. I'll see ya tomorrow [*departs, gives the fascist salute*].

SECOND AGENT: *Did you see that?*

FIRST AGENT: Vat?

SECOND AGENT: Ze vay he vaved? Adolf!

PAINTER: Vut?

SECOND AGENT: Vave again, sveetheart.

PAINTER: I alvays vaved dis vay.

FIRST AGENT: Who vaves zis way, but a beautiful nut like zis? You can see ze possibilities of zis vave, can't you? It'll catch on—it's a vild vave! It's free form. It's easy. I can see kids doing it. Zese thing

138

come vonce in a tousand years, a vave like dis.
veird! It makes ya feel good! Adolf! Zat's vild! Do
it. Adolf, you ever get hung up for vords, give
zem zis bit, sveetheart!

There's a show in L.A. to help talent. And what they do
on this show is sell automobiles. And then the gaff is
that they're going to help young talent get there. And
they do help a lot of young people in show business de-
velop a lot of traumas. That's how it ends up. And the
poor chicks come on this show, you know, with the
Lerner formulas, you know, the let-out panels, and the
brown-and-white spectator pumps with the whoopee
socks.

And the moderator, she's very chic, with the Lily-Ann
suit, and she always smells from a sour sponge. Real
weird group. So she calls the votes in *a la* Ted Mack:

"Well, let's see, now. The votes are coming in now,
and the bicycle act got 6,000 votes, and the young
fellow who sang *Sorrento* was deported . . . I see
here by your handwriting, young man, that you're
good-natured, you've got a quick temper, and fun-
gus . . . We've got a wonderful show tonight, but
we're going to switch you now to Big Brother, who
has a few words about that new, good car."

"Well, thank you very much, sweetie [*Answering
telephone*]. Well, you want to get into our new
fleet scene, yessir . . . Well, actually I wanna
see the trade-in . . . Well, what are you driving
around now? . . . A '36 Terraplane. They're
bombs. Good roadability—when they turn over
they really stay there, don't they? Yeah, well, I'd
hafta look at it . . . Well, is it clean? . . . Well,
I could let you have, like, about six dollars . . .
Same to you, sir . . . Thank you . . . Same
to your Mommy too . . . Thank you . . . Thank

you sporty . . . Uh huh . . . O.K. buddy, yeah, anytime you wanna, I'd like to meet you down here . . . You're a real nice guy . . . Yeah, ya . . . O.K. . . . Yeah, O.K., sport. Anytime you wanna, you know? That's right, pal . . . Uh huh! Yeah, that's right, buddy-buddy! . . . Come on down, why don't ya! Friend! . . . Thank you! [*hangs up phone*]

"Just alotta nice people calling us up here. But we're not gonna bother you any more with those kinda people, we're gonna switch you over now to Chatsworth with a few words from Fat Boy."

"Well, thanksalot, Buddy boy, this is Fat Boy, heah? Heah heah heah? Folks, we gotta lotta nice cahs out heah in Chatsworth, as ah've said many tahms onna television. We're jus plain peepul, jus lahk yew out theah—morons. Yew know buddi, 'tsa funny thing, about buying yewsed cahs, jus lahk a dayim clock ora watch, know? Yew just don't know what yew got under the hood til you bring it home. But one thing yew can depend on, when yew see a Fat Boy cah goin off this lot, boy, yew see an O.K. sticker onna winshield, and buddi, when yew see an O.K. sticker onna Fat Boy cah, yew know one thing, buddi—theah's an O.K. stickuh onnat winshield!

"Lotta peepul hahd-tawk ya, ya know? Right out heah at Fat Boy's, an we're nice, conveniently located—yew take the Santa Anna Freeway out 101, then 76 through Bakersfield—we're just a day-and-a-half from Civic Center. Just come make a nice pahty out heah. An, it's good cahs, nice peepul. Gotta lotta nice entertainment out heah. We jus finished our Jew-punchin contest, an after that we're gonna burn up the resta them Chaplin fillums just have a good, free, white, Protestant show.

140

"Nice peepul, folks, nice cahs. Here's somma the cahs yew'll be seein, buddi: Here'sa nice little Baker. This cute lil cah just used once, in a suicide pact. Just a lil lipstick around the exhaust pipe. Rub that off with Bab-O. If yew lahk them foreign cahs heah's a nice lil thing, the Fugginsfug, it's a bewtiful lil—this cah was just used in Germany a lil bit durin the wah, takin the peepul back n fo'th to the furnace. Now the motor is good, but the upholstry's a lil shot. But we'll sew that up while we're re-groovin the tires.

"Now, there's been alotta tawk about recession, folks, an ah'll tellya one thing about that recession —it's jus alotta propaganda spread around by alotta unemployed peepul. Awl them peepul hahd-tawkin ya. Jus lahk Uncle Rector used to say— old Uncle Rector, he worked on, he had kinda a dumb job, he worked in a sardine factry. His job was sorta, well yew know before they put the lid on the sardines he used to close awl their eyes. Now that might sound real dumb to yew, but yew wouldn't wanna open up a canna sardines an have awl them fish starin at yew, would yew?

"That's it, folks. Fat Boy's good cahs. But before you go to Fat Boy's, we'd lahk yew to go awl over town. Go evvriwhere, say, 'Buddi, yew been tawkin on the television, now why don't yew put it down theah on papuh? Yew been tawkin, sayin yew slashin prahces—just write it down!' And jus slip it in yo pocket n come back to Fat Boy, and just look up at him lahk some lil ol doll, and say, 'Fat Boy, ah been awl ovuh this daym town but ah *want it!*'

"Just look up in his eyes n say, 'I wan it, Fat Boy!' An he'll really give it to yew! He's been givin
141

it to the public for thirty years! In the same location!"

Sophie Tucker. What could her problem have been? Narcotics? No. You're going to flip.

She's a nymph. A nymphomaniac.

And shock, man. For years the B'Nai B'rith and the Hagzana have been paying off, cooling it, right? And she was very cool. She never fooled around in Lakewood; but like in Dayton, Ohio, she *schtupped* whole yeshiva bands, real *haisser,* and finally they got fed up with it; can't pay off any more, right?

So she belongs to a thing like for alcoholics anonymous, only for celibates, you know. You know, when she gets *hais,* she goes,

"I'm horny! What'll I do! I'm *hais.* I can't help it."

"All right, Sophie, just read a *Popular Mechanics.* We'll be right over."

Now there's a guy in the gig, poor guy, that's all his gig is—in Las Vegas especially. He gets these poor Puerto Rican busboys, and he tells them:

"Manuel? You know what you do to Miss Tucker when she comes off the stage tonight, don't you? We've always been a friend to the Spanish people. I'm sorry it's been three times this week, but you know we have a help problem. And you're all set, aren't you?"

MANUEL [*heavy Puerto Rican accent*]: Look, can you tell me something? Why do I have to *schtup* her, O.K.? Why am I the one to *schtup* her all the time? I can do to her no more, you fink! My legs are chapped, I got cornstarch on them."

"Do you wanna be deported, Manuel? Is that it?"

MANUEL: Come on, I no do to her. Go head, you *fress* her, you like her so much! Get you frien' ——to *hack* her.

142

"Oh, is that nice, now?"

And now, a tribute to the greatest living Polish artist in America today—Florence Zelk. Born in Strasburg, North Dakota, the only son of poor Polish immigrant parents, his father a famous Dixieland drummer, Ben Polack; his mother, who said on a recent interview, "Dankyou veddy moch ladies ant chentlemen. I vuld like to say bud von ting: dot Helen Hayes is a fink! I yam da real Anastasia. She balled da proputty man ta get da paht." His stepfather, Francis Fey, and her half-brother, Patsy Kelly.

Now, Welk. What's behind Welk? A woman—firm, with fantastic measurements: 96, 4, 53; 112 pounds; two feet tall! Grotesque? But a balling chick.

Now, the band has been together for many years. Suddenly he's looking for a new trumpet player. The whole rhythm section, Philly Joe Jones left him, LeRoy Vinegar, Miles—they all split. And we hear Lawrence Welk interviewing a new man for the band—with ten minutes left before show time:

"Awright. Send in da new boy! . . . Huwwow, thonny. How're you? My name is Larry Welk. The agency, Mr. Glazer, told me all about you. You're gonna be perfect boy for my band—you're deaf. Yessir. Ve vent shopping for the boys, ve got all new ties. You like it vit the big horse's head on them there? And ve got nice shoes from Flagg Bros. with the tick soles. And ve got a cricket and a badge. I got the vistle, though.

Now, the rules are: Cooking in the dressing room; Fern does the laundry, fifteen cents a pound, fluff dry; you fold though. That's it. Ve go right on the road. We gotta lotta college dates—mostly industrial colleges—vatsamatter vit you sonny? How come you don't talk to me?"

143

MUSICIAN [*stoned out of his kug*]: Ah, like hello man, ah . . . you know, like, ah . . . alotta cats put you on, Mr. Wig, but, ah . . . you really something else, sweetie, ah . . . really, you know, like . . . like when I laid the scene on some people, I said like I'm gonna make the scene with Welk, you know that cat's busted up, ya know, but, ah . . . I said no matter what, you're the best banjo—or whatever your ax is—you swing . . . that's it, sweetie, swing with your ax . . . you know, like . . . I got Byrd's ax, man, he gave me his ax, you know, like, and you're pretty wild, Mr. Funk, and, ah . . . I really wanna make the scene with you baby, you know . . .

WELK: WHAT THE HELL YOU TALKING ABOUT?

MUSICIAN: I'm, ah . . . I dunno, sweetie, that's my trouble . . . that's my scene, you know, like no one comes through to me, you know . . . like, I'm on *nez*, you know, like, that's *zen* backwards . . . well, you know, sweetie, like everyone's got their own scene, like you got your bubbles, Jim, I got my thing . . . like, ah . . . so, you know, whatever you wanna do, you know, we'll do the thing, you know . . .

WELK: I DUNNO WHAT THE HELL YOU'RE TALKING ABOUT! WHAT THE HELL, YOU A QUEER OR SOMETHING? YOU A GOD-DAMN COMMUNIST OR SOMETHING?

MUSICIAN: Hey . . . don't come on gangbusters' style . . . cause I'll bust you right in the chops, baby, like, don't come on corny, you know, like, you ain't that wild, Polack. You're something else, I swear to god . . . you're really wild, really wild . . .

WELK: WHAT ARE YOU SCRATCHING YOUR GODDAMN FACE FOR?

MUSICIAN: Cause I'm allergic, baby . . . what the hell you yelling at me for, motherfucker, what's all this screechin here . . . look, I wanna tell ya, I jus wanna get a taste . . . can I get some bread in front here?

WELK: You hungry, wanna sandwich?

MUSICIAN: Ahaha . . . haha . . . do I wanna sandwich? . . . haha . . . shit, you're really something else, baby . . . do I wanna sandwich? Yeah, wanna sandwich . . . You kiddin baby? . . . you're a freak, you know that? . . . look out . . .

WELK: Vat are you talking so weird for? Stop acting silly, now, and be nice, cause you're gonna be on the television soon. Now I'm gonna hire you, cause I'm a good judge of character. You're honest boy. I can tell by your eyes—*they're tho thmall!*

MUSICIAN: Hey, I better tell ya pronto . . . ah, so there's no panic here, you dig? . . . I hate to cop out on myself, Mr. Nook, but, ah . . . I better tell you out in front, baby, that . . . I got a monkey on my back, you might as well know that, Mr. Wick and that's it, you know?

WELK: Oh that's all right—we *like* animals on the band. Rocky's got a duck. They'll *play* together.

This is my own observation, that this industry, you know, show business, actually, not from this end, the recording end, not from the motion picture end, but from the cafe scene especially, is the most *un*important part of the world. Actually. Cause this is the only thing that if it doesn't go on, no one is actually inconvenienced, you know. But yet, there's a great segment of cafe performers who continually eulogize, you know, and really get hung up that they're really doing something, you know?

So I figured that one day they'll have a tribunal, and the people will have to answer, you know? So they'll have it on Broadway:

AUTHORITATIVE VOICE: Now, the tribunal has started! You will bring the performers to the fore, state their salary—the money they've been stealing for years—also their names. And the sentences will be meted out. Bring them up here quickly! The first one—your name?

"Frankie Laine."

"How much do you make a week?"

"Eighty-five hundred dollars a week."

"What do you do?"

[*sings "Ghost Riders in the Sky* . . ."]

"Burn his wig, break his face and his fingers, twenty years in jail!"

Pills and Shit: The Drug Scene

Oh! I got busted since I've seen you. I'm going to lay that on you first. I got two arrests. One: illegal use and possession of dar.gerous drugs—which is a lie. They're *not,* they're *friendly.*

Lemme get serious with that for a moment. That's how weird I am: I could never discuss or support anything I'm involved with.

I don't smoke pot at all. I don't dig the high. The reason I don't smoke shit is that it's a hallucinatory high, and I've got enough shit going around in my head; and second, it's a *schlafedicker* high, and I like being *with* you all the time. So therefore I can talk about pot, and champion it.

Marijuana is rejected all over the world. Damned. In England heroin is alright for out-patients, but marijuana? They'll put your ass in jail.

I wonder why that is? The only thing I can think of is DeQuincy—the fact that opium is smoked and marijuana is smoked, and there must be some correlation there. Because it's not a deterrent. In all the codes you'll always see, "Blah-blah-blah with all the narcotics *except* marijuana." So the legislature *doesn't* consider it a narcotic. Who does?

Well, first: I think that there's no *justification* for smoking shit. Alcohol? Alcohol has a medicinal justification. You can drink rock-and-rye for a cold, pernod for getting it up when you can't get it up, blackberry brandy for cramps, and gin for coming around if she didn't come around.

But marijuana? The only reason could be: *To Serve The Devil—Pleasure!* Pleasure, which is a dirty word in a Christian culture. Pleasure is Satan's word.

> CONDEMNING VOICE: What are you doing! You're *enjoying* yourself? Sitting on the couch smoking shit and *enjoying* yourself? When your mother has *bursitis!* And all those people in China are suffering, too!"
>
> GUILTY VOICE: I'm enjoying it a *little* bit, but it's bad shit, anyway. And I got a headache and I'm eating again from it.

If we were to give Man A three glasses of whiskey a day, and Man B were to smoke the necessary amount of marijuana to produce a euphoria like that the alcohol brings, and we do this now for ten years straight, stop them cold one day—Pow!

The guy who juiced will suffer some absence syndromes—he'll need a taste, physically need a taste. The guy that smoked the pot will suffer no discomfort. He is not addicted. Healthwise, the guy who juiced is a little screwed up; and the pot smoker may have a little bronchitis. Maybe.

Since marijuana is not a deterrent, no more than cigarettes, it seems inhumane that they *schlep* people and put them in jail with it.

"Well, maybe marijuana's not *bad* for you, but it's

148

a stepping stone. It leads to heavier drugs—heroin, etc."

Well, that syllogism has to work out this way, though: The heroin addict, the bust-out junkie that started out smoking pot, says to his cell-mate:

"I'm a bust-out junkie. Started out smoking pot, look at me now. By the way, cell-mate, what happened to you? There's blood on your hands. How'd you get to murder those kids in that crap game? Where did it all start?"

"Started with bingo in the Catholic Church."

"I see."

Now lemme tell you something about pot. Pot will be legal in ten years. Why? Because in this audience probably every other one of you knows a law student who smokes pot, who will become a senator, who will legalize it to protect himself.

But then no one will smoke it any more. You'll see.

Do me a favor. I don't want to take a bust. The code reads that *I* talk, *you* smoke, *I* get busted. So don't smoke—drop a few pills, but don't smoke.

Did you see the *Post* reviews? It said that

"His regulars consist of mainlining musicians, call girls and their business managers."

Isn't that a little bit libelous?

I know that Californians are very concerned with the modern. Seven years ago there was a narcotics problem in New York, fifteen years ago in Los Angeles. Now in L.A. it's been like this:

They have a rehabilitation center, and they got this group to attack these narcotic drug addicts. Now, this group is attacking, and getting good at attacking. They

149

mobilize. They get good at it, and better and better and better. First they learn the orthodox way to attack. Then, by hanging out with these deterrents, these felons, they learn *un*orthodox ways. They become bitchy-good attackers—unorthodox, orthodox—and they're wailing their ass off.

Suddenly:

CALIFORNIA LOSING ITS WAR
AGAINST DRUG ADDICTS

There are eighteen hundred empty beds at the rehabilitation center.

"*Schmuck,* you're winning!"

"No, were *losing.* We gotta fill up the beds!"

"You didn't make one win? In fifteen years?"

"No. We're losing, we're losing!"

Well, I assume there's only one junkie left.

Narcotics? Now they've finished with heroin—I think in 1951 there were probably about fifty narcotic officers and seven thousand dope fiends in this state. Today, probably, there are about fifteen thousand narcotics officers and four dope fiends. Fifteen thousand Nalline testing stations, loop-o meters, and they got four dopey junkies left, old-time 1945 hippie.

O.K. One guy works for the county, undercover; the other guy works for the federal heat. O.K. So, finally, finally they went on strike:

> JUNKIE: Look, we don*wanna* use dope any more. We're *tired!*

> AGENT: Come on, now, we're just after the guys who sell it.

> JUNKIE: *Schnook*, don'tya remembuh me? Ya arrested me last week. I'm the undercover guy for the federals.

It's like Sambo, running around the tree. *He* works for the federals, *he* works for the county.

AGENT: Look, we're after the guys who sold it to you. O.K.?

JUNKIE: But *nobody* sold it to me. I bought it from *him,* I told you that . . .

AGENT: Well, will ya just point out one of the guys?

JUNKIE: Don't you *know* him? There's four of us! I told ya that.

AGENT: Just tell us the names of the guys. Co-operate now. Tell us everybody.

JUNKIE [*gives up*]: O.K. He was a Puerto Rican. Drove a green Buick. Hangs out in Forster's.

AGENT: We'll wait for him.

JUNKIE: O.K.

Three days with the investigation:

AGENT: Is that him?

JUNKIE: No, I think it's, hm, ah, I think he was Hawaiian, anyway.

AGENT: O.K. Don't forget. If ycu hear from him—

JUNKIE: O.K. I'll call ya the first thing.

AGENT: O.K.

So now they've finished up that nonsense, and the guy says:

"You mean to tell me that you guy. are gonna screw up our rehabilitation program? If *you're* not using any dope, you certainly *know* some people that need help."

JUNKIE: We don't know anybody. We don't know *anybody. Please. I can't use any more dope.* I don't *like* it any more.

AGENT: Well, you really are selfish. You don't care about anybody but yourself. Do you know we have a center to rehabilitate people with fifteen hundred empty beds?

JUNKIE: I know, I'm shitty that way. I'll try.

I loved that when he got arrested. He was a dope fiend

151

—Bela Lugosi. It was the worst advertisement for rehabilitation: he was a dope fiend for seven years; he cleaned up; and dropped dead.

There're no more narcotic drug addicts, so we're moving now to dangerous drugs. Dangerous drugs—no opiates, nothing to send you to that lethal mania, but the mood elevators, the amphetamines.

The big connections of the dangerous drugs are Squibb and Park-Lilly, Olin Mathison and Merc and Wyeth. Do they know that? Does the legislature know that? I wonder why they're not apprised of that situation. Dangerous drugs—that's the legal phrase—relates to all these medications that are mood elevators, not made for sores or boils. They are made not in Guatemala, but in factories and for a purpose.

Then I said, "These senators, they come from the South. Southerners don't take pills. Nor do Southern doctors prescribe pills." I'll bet you that when all those people were dying of spinal meningitis at Moffitt Field —and heretofore sulpha drugs had worked—you wondered what happened. Guys are dying there:

"They're spitting out the pills!"

"They're *what?* Whatsa matter with you guys? You're *dying* and you're spitting out the sulpha drugs!"

"Look. I'm a Lockheed worker, and I read all about it in the *Herald Express,* about those dangerous drugs. I'm not filling my body fulla those poisons! I got spinal meningitis, I'll get rid of it the natural way—take an enema, I'll sweat and I'll run around. Not gonna take none of that horseshit."

O.K. Now, dangerous drugs. Now, the insanity in that area is that the reason that heroin is *verboten* is that it's no good for people. It destroys the ego, and the only reason we get anything done in this country is that you want to be proud of it and build up to the neighbors. And if the opiate *schleps* all that away, then the guy goes up to the guy who builds a new building and he'll say,

DETACHED HIPPY VOICE: Hey, that's cool.

And that's it. So it's no good. And that's why it's out.

You know what I'd like to investigate? Zig-zag cigarette papers. Yeah. Bring the company up:

DEEP AGGRESSIVE VOICE: Now we have this report, Mr. Zig-zag . . . Certainly it must have seemed unusual to you, that Ziz-zag papers have been in business for sixteen years, and Bugler tobacco has been out of business for five years! . . .

This committee comes to the conclusion . . . that the people are using your Zig-zag cigarette papers, to . . . roll marijuana tobacco in it."

"Oh, shit."

"That's right. Lots of it—rolling it and smoking it."

Dig. The beautiful part about it is that so many neighborhood grocery stores have been kept in business for years—the *schmucks* don't know that, right?

YOUNG VOICE [*trying to sound nonchalant*]: O.K. I'll have Delsey toilet tissues, and, ah, another six cans of soup, and a broom, and, ah . . . some cigarette papers.

OLD JEWISH VOICE: I dunno, ve stay in business so long, it's terrific. All the markets—but ve screw em, we chahge top prices, and the people come in here anyway. They *like* me.

O.K. where does this go on? At a place called Alfie's. Alfy's. Open 24 Hours. Cigarettes, cigars, old Jewish man behind the counter:

YOUNG WISE GUY: Pa?

ANCIENT JEW: Yuh?

WISE GUY: Pa, do you sell many cigarette papers here?

OLD JEW: Uh.

WISE GUY: What do you assume that people are doing with the cigarette papers they're buying?

OLD JEW: De're rollink cigarettes.

WISE GUY: They're rolling cigarettes? In these flamboyant times you assume people are *rolling* cigarettes?

OLD JEW: Uhhh, so vut are you doink mit cigarette papuhs?

WISE GUY: You don't know?

OLD JEW: No.

WISE GUY: They're rolling *pot!*

OLD JEW: Vus?

WISE GUY: Pot.

OLD JEW: *Vus machts du* pop?

WISE GUY: Marijuana, *schmuck!*

OLD JEW: Marijuana? Hey! Uh, agh, *vus?* Hey—
Always talking to some *schmuck* in the back who's not there.

—you heard dot? Marijuana. All dese years I never knew dot. Marijuana. Sig-sag papuhs, marijuana, roll the marijuana, *meschugenah,* marijuana.

Next night an eighty-year-old pensioner walks to the stand:

OLD PENSIONER: "Hullo? Hullo? Solly, in the bek? Hullo? Dingalingalingalinga?"

OLD JEW: Hullo.

PENSIONER: Listen, gimme a peckege Bugler's and some Sig-sag papuhs.

OLD JEW: *Vus?* Sig-sag papuhs? Justa momunt . . . . [*Aside*] Hullo, policeman? Is gecamein a junkie!

154

All right. The kid, six years old, played by George McCready:

"Well, let's see now. I'm all alone in my room, and it's Saturday, and Mother's off in Sausalito freaking off with Juanita, so I'll make an airplane. Yes. What'll I do . . . I'll make, ah, an Me-110, that's a good structure. I'll get the balsa wood . . . cut it out there . . . there we go . . . rub it up . . . Now, I'll get a little airplane glue, rub it on the rug, and, uh, uh, . . . hmmmmmm, I'm getting loaded! . . . Is this possible? Loaded on airplane glue? Maybe it's stuffy in here. I'll call my dog over.

"Felika! Felika, come here, darling, and smell this rag. Smell it! You freaky little doggy . . . smell the rag Felika . . . Felika! Felika! IT WORKED! I'M THE LOUIS PASTEUR OF JUNKIEDOM! I'm out of my skull for a dime!

"Well, there's much work to be done now . . . horse's hooves to melt down, noses to get ready . . ."

CUT TO, the toy store. The owner, Albert Wasserman. The kid walks in:

tinglelingleling!

KID [*affected innocent voice*]: Hello Mr. Shindler. It's a lovely store you've got here . . . Ah, why don't you let me have a nickel's worth of pencils, and a big boy tablet, hm? A Big-Little Book? Some nail polish remover, and, ah, [*voice changes to a driven madness*] *two thousand tubes of airplane glue!*

OWNER [*old Jew*]: Dot's very unusual! Ve haff nefer sold so much airplane glue before. I'm an old man—don't bring no heat on the place! And save me a taste, you know? I vouldn't burn you for no bread, you know?

155

Cut to Paul Cotes, Confidential File:

"This is Paul Cotes, Confidential File, and next to me, ladies and gentlemen of the viewing audience on television, is a young boy who's been sniffing airplane glue. Could be your kid, anybody's kid, whose life has been destroyed by the glue. I hope you can sleep tonight, Mr. LePage. Pretty rotten, a young kid like this. What's your name, sonny?"

"I'm Sharkey, from Palo Alto."

"Well, it's obvious that Sharkey feels a lot of hostility for the adult world. Sharkey, how did it all start, kid? How did you start on this road to ruin? With airplane glue."

"Well, I foist started chippying round wit small stuff—like smellin' sneakuhs, doity lawndry, Mallowmar boxes . . ."

"A little Kraft-Ebbing in there . . . That's very interesting, Sharkey. You've been sniffing it for six months?"

"At'sright."

"Are you hooked?"

"No. I'm stuck."

This *schmuck* here was hooked on morphine suppositories. Like that? Honest to God. If heroin is a monkey on the back, what's a morphine suppository?

When I was in England all these faggots were strung out on sleeping pill suppositories. *Emmis*. So I says to this cat, I says, "Do they really make you sleep, man?"

He says, "Are you kidding? Before you get your *finger* outta your *athth* you're *athleep*, Mary."

That's a beautiful ad:

BEFORE YOU GET YOUR FINGER OUT OF
YOUR ASS—
YOU'RE ASLEEP!
NEBYALTAL

156

"What is *that?* What did he need *that* for?"

"He's *weird,* that's all. He's on it, that's all. He's on it."

"How can you tell?"

"You can tell when they're on it. He's standing on it right now. He *has* to have it. They gotta have it. They kill their mothers for it in the mornings. They get the strength of a madman."

How does he take it?

[*Deep bass voice, with pride*] "I take it in the suppository form."

Haha! I got high just before the show:

[*Urgently*] "Get it up there, Phil!"

"O.K."

"Hurry up! Hurry up! Somebody's coming!"

Now the reason why I take it in the suppository form is that I have found that even with the most literate doctors, it's not the *substance,* it's the *method of administration,* because if this man would take a ton of opiates through a suppository, the imagery is: "If he takes rubicane in the arm, it's monstrous; but the guy takes it in the ass—what can it be? The *tuchus . . .*"

This is a benzedrex inhaler. I know the inventor, who invented amphetamine sulphate, which was originally used for just shrinking the mucus membrane, you know, the air passage, but some fellows found out that you could crush these benzedrine inhalers and—you've done it—and put them in coca-colas, and it would become a cerebral depressant. So, somehow they took out the benzedrine and put in benzedrex.

The old thing—one guy ruined it for the rest.

Now, if you notice, it has a date when it's exhausted. Your nose? No. The inhaler. Smith, Klein and French.

Now it's sort of weird, you know. I put this, and you know, sniff it up there. But it's about a year old, and it's probably exhausted; so I don't know if I just did that, or sticking things in my nose, you know? Or maybe I'm just hooked on smelling my pocket!

Actually, is it lewd? That goes back to taste. You know that it's just not good taste to blow your nose in public or put one of these in your nose in public. And I've never done it in front of anybody. But I just feel like I wanna do it tonight.

For the first time, being recorded on tape, a man sticking a Smith Klein French inhaler in his nose!

"Ladies and gentlemen, we're here at Fax No. Two. A hush is going over the crowd. He's reaching in his pocket. His neck is tightening. Some ladies sitting ringside, traumatically, are sweating. He's taking it out, giggling nervously. Will he stick it up there? Nervous laughs emit from the crowd. He's a degenerate. Two D.A.R. women are throwing up. There go the people from the Mystery Bus Tour."

'We want our $5.75 back!'

"There he goes, folks, he's sniffing!

'Hi, Howard, hi! Zowie! We're really high now, Howard. We certainly are. We've solved the world's problems.' "

And you're only twelve months old, you little bugger!

Exploitation Films present: I WAS A TEEN-AGE REEFER-SMOKING PREGNANT YORTSITE CANDLE. With Sal Mineo and Natalie Wood. See Sal Mineo as the trigger-happy Arty, the kid who knew but one thing—how to *love*, how to *kill!* And see Fatlay Good as Theresa, the girl who knew the other thing, tenderness, and love. And see Lyle Talbot as Gramps, who liked to watch. A picture with a message, and an original Hollywood theme—narcotics.

The film opens as we find Nunzio locked in the bathroom with the stuff, the *baccala*, the marijuana. Cut to the exterior—Youngstown kitchen, there's the wife, you know, the factory-worker wife, the whole bit. He comes home, .

> WIFE [*delighted*]: Put me down, you big nut! Oh, tee hee . . .

That scene, you know? Looking at her,

> HUSBAND [*tenderly*]: Where's our son, where's Ralph?
>
> WIFE [*concerned*]: He's in the bathroom again. And I dunno whatsamatter with him. He's nervous and listless, and he's not bothering with any of his friends, and he's falling off in his studies . . .
>
> HUSBAND: In the bathroom again, eh? Tsk Tsk. Hmmm. . . . [*knocks on the door*] Ralph? What are you doing in there?
>
> RALPH [*sucking in a big drag, then trying to hold it in as he answers*]: Usta minud, I beyout in a minud.
>
> WIFE: He's got asthma.
>
> HUSBAND: Will you stop with that, you nitwit! He's on the stuff!

O.K. Suddenly we hear a knock at the door, a whistle; and he takes the marijuana, throws it in the toilet, rushes to the door—there's no one there! He's thrown it away! It's *gone,* it's *too late!* Beads of perspiration are breaking out on his forehead.

> RALPH: It's gone! There's only one thing left to do—*smoke the toilet!*

Fantasies, Flicks & Sketches

You know, I left Hollywood, but I said, you know, I might as well do some sketches. Then the sketches went into a story, and I started working, and then I came up with a book, you know, that I've been writing, a musical. And this is not the whole thing, but it leads to a crescendo, and it's enough to open up with. So what I'm going to do is sort of tell you about it—sort of like a backers' audition kind of thing, alright?

I'll tell you about the story. It opens up in an F.B.I. office in Washington. There's some guy there, and he's seated, you know, and it's not Hoover's office, it's obviously—you see the White House, the dome in the background, and you've got a big sign above the desk that says T-H-F-I-N-K, which I gave the original to George. And the guy's on the phone, the agent, and he's talking, you know, and he goes

"Yes . . . yes . . . yes . . . Hello Mr. Dulles . . . Yes . . . yes . . . I . . . I realize the importance of it sir, and I'm sorry . . . I don't know how it happened . . . yes . . . I do, and it will be taken care of right away sir."

Click.

"Gimme Fifth Precinct . . . Hello? Listen, which one of you nitwits gave Dulles a speeding ticket? . . . Yes . . . Well, take care of it right away—and find out what happened to that case of tequila that Benelli sent me . . . O.K. And see if you can score for tonight . . . O.K. . . . Solid . . . Later."

O.K. Now he's busy writing at the desk, and the secretary comes in and says, "The phone repair man is here."

He says, "Oh, yeah?" And he's busy, and he goes back to it.

The guy comes in, with the zipper jacket, the tool box, and he picks up the phone, you know, dials 118, repair cable, 104—he's doing that telephone business—and he does a slow take on me.

He says "Ralph Barton! What the hell are you doing there?"

"Shhhh."

"What the hell are you doing? What's this bit? I haven't seen ya since, ah, where did we work together? We worked in Philly! Yeah. What are you doin in a joint like this?"

I say, "Well, I'm—it's a weird bit. About three years ago I was working the Downtown, you know? And, ah, wasn't doing too good, you know, I was working too hip, making the band laugh and all that jazz," (this is my story, you know) "so, ah, so I figured out, I'll try for civil service, you know? So I went down, just for the hell of it—I was loaded— and I made out an application for civil service, for a talent co-ordinator in the South Pacific and Alaska."

He says, "Yeah?"

I say, "Yeah. I made out the test. Now meanwhile, there's another guy, another Ralph Barton"—(that's my name in the play)—"another Ralph Barton who made

161

out an application for the F.B.I. S.S.D., you know? And somehow the papers got screwed up and I ended up here."

So the guy says, "That's pretty wild. Where's the other guy?"

"He's doing choreography in Aniwetok. That's really a bit. Isn't that weird?"

He says, "Well, what happened?"

I says, "The funny bit is that the guy keeps writing letters, protest letters, you know, and The Chief keeps saying, 'That's great! What a sense of humor! Look at this letter! Hahaha.' You know? And it's weird. So finally the guy gets desperate, and he writes a big letter, he calls the Chief a grey-haired pimp."

So the guy says, "Yeah? So what happened?"

"Well, he's in therapy now. But he's getting out next month, and he gets fifteen hundred dollars a month from the medical, he's happy, you know? And I dig the gig here, so we're swinging, you know?"

He says, "What happens if they send you a case?"

"I go! But most of the thing is the S.S.D."

"What is that?"

"Well, it's the security mail department, and I take care of"—dig these speeches—"I take care of these speeches, you know?"

He says, "What kinda speeches are they?"

"Well, the bit is that, if they have any crises, any time there's a crisis, I give these speeches."

And here's some of the crisis speeches. I can't remember them all, but they're really weird. O.K.

"Now they have a crisis. Suppose there's about three or four bombs that don't go off, you know? And there's alotta heat on the White House right away, right? So we come out with this speech. This is a good speech for the President. This is after the fifth bomb hasn't gone off:

162

We've never been, and never will be, a warlike nation. We demand Russia disarm.

He says, "Well, that's pretty wild."

"Now I gotta speech if the other party wins, you know. They're holding all the seats in the Senate and the House of Representatives. Now we give the president a speech where we wanta be a nice guy but still give the other party the shaft, you know?"

POLITICO: Regardless of party, we're all one. One for one common good as Americans. We shall help the other party in every way, to keep from heading to the inevitable path of chaos and depression to which they will lead us.

So the repairman says, "That's pretty wild. Gimme a combination speech. Gimme a speech now for people who want war, people who don't want war, people who are pro-segregation, pro-integration, Little Rock, the whole scene."

"O.K. That's the blanket one. It's called 'Safety First.' This one's a capper. It's a great applause-getter. This is when the president, you know, when you're really hung in a crisis. And he comes out, you know, the president does this speech, that we've had alotta success with:

POLITICO: In this country, regardless of race, color or creed, the color has a right to know it becomes everyone's duty, the duty that has become the right of every man, woman and child, a child that one day will be proud of his heritage, a child that only in these perilous times, when a man-born menace, a horrible bomb, that can only disfigure and defame its creator, a horror, an evil, a bad, a lazy, a lethargic. Lethargy and complacency we cannot fall into. We've got a bomb that can wipe out half the world! If necessary. And we will! To keep our

163

standards, the strength that has come from American unity, that we alone will build for better schools and churches.

Guy says, "That's the wildest!" Now the guy says, "Well, what about if they send you on a case?"

"Well, they got me on a case now. They feel coffee houses are subversive. So I go in and I'm—this agent in North Beach, with the Security Department, got me a job as a comic in this expresso alley, this coffee house, you know. And I dig working, you know—"

He says, "Well, are they hip to what's going on?"

"No. I'm doing the agent bit."

He says, "Well, that's pretty wild. Do I know any of the kids on this show?"

"No. They're all sorta beatniks, you know? But they're nice kids, you know."

He says, "Well, could you get me a gig there? Cause I'm real hung behind fixing phones, man."

"I was wondering about that."

"Well, they're not buying magic acts any more."

He says, "Can you get—"

"Sure. I'll talk to The Chief tomorrow. We'll screw up some more papers, you know. We'll get some—the guy in Aniwetok needs a replacement. So we'll swing."

Guy says, "Alright."

"So you'll meet me there tomorrow night at eight o'clock."

So the guy says to me, "Where's your wife?"

"Oh, ah, we . . ."

"What happened?"

"Oh, we broke up."

"Oh, I'm sorry to hear that."

"Well, you know, that's the scene, you know?"

So we leave on that note—oh yeah: the secretary comes in and we fade into the coffee house, the exterior of the coffee house. It's outside of sort of a brick building, alley-way kind of thing, you know, street lights. And the stage entrance is about, here, and the two chicks (By the way, who are very talented, who I sort of made friends with the last time I was in San Francisco, and I want you to come up. Come on up, sweetheart, and sit down. Sure, cool.) So they are the two girls that work in the coffee house. You know? They're in the show there. But they're not hip to the fact that I am the F.B.I. agent, who's working as the comic.

Now, as the scene opens a classical pianist (Hey Andre, wanna help me out? Yeah. I showed Andre some of the music for the thing). Now, they're there, see? And we hear the classical music coming over the scene. A recital is going on, you know. And you see the signs, for the recital, you know; What's going on tonight?

WHERE ARE WE GOING?

A Reading

by

Carroll Chessman

And then they have all the signs in the coffee house: ZEN, OLE, you know. It'll be a pretty outside thing.

And we hear the music, and I come on, and I'm sort of late for the gig. And, ah (Give it a more—Andre, that's too good. Maybe a corny, what's that song? Da dah? Yeah, but real corny, like, a recital sound) [*Pianist begins hamming up Chopin's C♯ Minor Waltz*]. O.K. The music is coming over, so apparently the show is on, and I come on the scene, the F.B.I. agent posing as the comic, actually a comic with previous cafe background:

AGENT: Say, ah, Felix is on. What time did the show go on?

FIRST GIRL: Nine-thirty. Where's your wife?

SECOND GIRL: Yeah, where's Myrna? This is the first time I've seen you alone.

AGENT: Ah, well, ah, it's a scene we had. We broke up. I've, ah, I've had it with her. That's the last beef I'm ever gonna have with that chick. She's a lunk! But I finally—you won't believe this—but I finally got rid of her. That's it! I'm rid of her.

FIRST GIRL: How'd you do that?

AGENT: She left me.

SECOND GIRL: What happened?

AGENT: Ah, well, it's . . . ah, you're not married, you dunno the scene. She's always accusing me of cheating. That's what *bugged* me. Cause she was always *accusing* me, and I was never guilty.

FIRST GIRL: You never cheated?

AGENT: Well, not when she accused me. And that's what really used to bug me. Because at least if you're guilty you don't mind, you know. Anyway, it was a long time ago when she went to visit her mother in Phoenix. So actually it's her mother's fault. Yeah . . . But I'm better off. As long as I'm gonna be accused of cheating, I might as well go out and do it. That's it! I'm just—but you know the weird bit? I've been married for nine years and actually, I forgot how!

SECOND GIRL: How to do it?

AGENT: No, ah, actually, how to go about asking.

SECOND GIRL: Just ask!

AGENT: Do ya wanna do it?

SECOND GIRL: No.

AGENT: How 'bout you?

FIRST GIRL: No—but thank you anyway.

AGENT: Have you got any friends who wanna do it?

FIRST GIRL: One in Glendale. Oh—but she has to get up early.

AGENT: Yeah, you don't care. You've got each other . . . I think that I, I guess that I'll just get along . . . real fine . . .

Then you bring the lights down, and he sings a thing called "Alone!"

Alone, alone,
Oh joy to be alone.
Yeah, I'm happy alone, don't you see?
I've convinced you—now how about me?
Alone . . . Yeah, but—you're better off all alone.
Yeah, that's it. You can save a buck, when
you're single.

That's what it is—I'm alone, I'll get one of those
bachelor-type apartments, and I'll fix it all up! I'll
get a bullfight poster, and I'll get some of that black
furniture. Did ya ever see that real sharp black
furniture? Real nice, you know? And I'll, and I'll,
I'll get a, I'll get a pearl-white phone, and I'll, I'll
just sit back and relax, and finally, I'll be all alone!
All alone . . .

All alone,
All alone,
Oh what joy to be
All alone, all alone . . .

Yeah. Ah, what the hell. Since ya can't live with
em and ya can't live without em, I'll just live with
alot of em. That's what I'll do! I'll, I'll get me
some sharp chick that—I'll get me a chick that,
that likes to hang out, you know? Somebody that's
not so square. I'll get a chick that maybe, a chick
that likes to drink! . . . Boy, my wife sure used
to look good, standin up against the sink . . .
Yeah . . . It's a drag, I guess, to be alone . . . If
I saw her I'd miss her, but I guess . . . I do miss
her . . . I don't want some sharp talker that can
quote Kerouac and walk with poise . . . I jus
wanna hear my ol lady say, "Get up and fix the
toilet, it's still making noise."

All alone,
All alone,
[*two lines garbled*]

167

Yeah. That's it. Right. Then it goes to:

"Yeah, I guess I'm really getting to be a bring-down.

But it's this *town* that does it. There's so many phonies out here, I never saw so many goddamn phonies in my whole life. That's what it is. If there was at least somebody here you could talk to; but everybody's so—they're all grabbing, running, running . . . Where're you from?"

FIRST GIRL: Lansing.

AGENT: What did you want to leave a nice town like Lansing for? It sounds sorta nice and safe, you know? And small and warm and—what did ya wanna come out here to Phonyville for?

FIRST GIRL: To try to make it in pictures, just like you. To be seen.

AGENT: Ah, you're outta your skull. Who the hell's gonna see ya in a coffee house? Na, that's no reason at all.

FIRST GIRL: There's more to it than that:

[*She sings a musical comedy type number*]:

> In Lansing girls with glasses
> Never got any passes
> made at them.
> Even the so-called nice guys
> Called us four-eyes,
> So we said the hell with them.
> There was no one to love,
> And no one to pet,
> But now with this Don't-Matter Movement—
> We're the queens of the off-beat set!

[*Chorus: the two girls sing together*]

> Thin girls with big feet
> Are now interesting off-beat
> With The Movement—
> Hooray for The Movement!

Curves are not an essenial must
Cause that's just chic
To have no bust
In The Movement—

FIRST GIRL: *Stop!* I used to worry about being over-weight. Because I couldn't get into a sheath dress for the Lansing Country Club, I lost my savoir faire.

SECOND GIRL: But now with The Movement you're very functional with an oversized Viki-Duganesque derriere!

Hooray for The Movement,
Oi veh for The Movement!
We'd love to be wanton women,
Our sin and lust to be flauntin,
But to be a wanton woman,
You need a guy to do the wantin.
[*two lines garbled*]
You got dumpy keesters
And no busts,
Forget Vic Tanny!
Put your trust
In The Movement,
Hallelujah The Movement—

FIRST GIRL: *Stop!* In Lansing, I was just a blob, a vegetating part of a vegetating mass. But now, thanks to The Movement, one hundred and thirty, including I, meet every Tuesday for our Neo-Physical Free Love Functional class.

SECOND GIRL: There are one hundred and thirty students in our Free Love class. If you could just see it! It gives the words "group effort" a new meaning.

FIRST GIRL: Sort of on-the-job training.

SECOND GIRL: In literate circles, it's known as "Freedom From Group Guilt Conscience Pangs."

FIRST GIRL: You know—sort of a group gang pang!
[*lines lost*]
Hooray for The Movement!
Oi Veh for The Movement!
Hooray for The Movement!
Hooray!

Next thing there, it goes to a very funny sketch, but the actors are in Hollywood. No, actually, I'm using these three guys who are. And it's a satire on Forest Lawn. So, it's really far-out humor. I really came on all the way with this one, you know? The guy comes in the office, you know, and they've got this burial, and the guy says

"Well, we have a dirt-saving plan, where we bury you in cement. Wouldn't you like to be part of that new freeway that's going out to Sawtell?"

And on and on. It's real weird.

Now, the sketch—see, this then takes the form of show-within-a-show, where Kobey is the mistress of ceremonies inside. We're now—cut! Cut!

We are now—I've never done theatre—into the interior of the coffee house, and she's on the stage, and she does some real far-out things up there—slides, visual-aid kind of things. And she finishes with that bit and then she makes a speech on existentialism, you know, and she goes back to existentialism, and before that nihilism and dadaism, and then a new threat— "moral canyon-ism." And Kobey is a swinging actress, and she can really get that sort of Allan Zinar-Edna May Oliver combo.

So she finishes with her scene and then in song—ah, the existentialism speech precedes this song, "It Doesn't Matter," which is the theme. It's cut in the middle, the sketch or farce, and then it goes out on "It Doesn't Matter." And you can just sort of get an idea. I told you what the sketch is in the center. (So Andre, in other words, you'll go right through it, see, the sketch. In other words, it's the thing where it's the sketch—well, crazy, you'll swing with it. I know.) I guess you can get a little fuller up on this. Can I have some lights? Yeah, Crazy. O.K.

[*First girl sings*]

> Since we can remember
> There've been sharks and cattle rustlers,
> Folks scufflin for their piece of land.
> Crooked politicians,
> Also Polyander hustlers
> With their pockets filled
> With one another's hands.
> But the [*word lost*]
> The sad thing
> Even sharks who grab the brass ring
> Have the juice,
>> The fix
>> The shmeer
>> The In.
> All the land they can wind up with
> Is a hole, four-by-six!

[*chorus*]

> But it doesn't matter,
> It doesn't matter,
> Ya can't get to heaven
> On a golden ladder;
> Don't feel insecure about the thought of re-
> jection,
> Things could be worse,
> You could wind up—up in *this* section!
> Ha ha! Ha ha ha! Ha! ha!
> While things move,
> Don't get the willies,
> Just think of the pine box
> That handles old billies!

171

It doesn't matter,
It doesn't matter,
[*word lost*] overhead
Shovels, spades!
[*line lost*]
Ha ha ha!
It doesn't matter
[*line lost*]
The most important factor?
To thine own self be true
Don't worry about convictions
Don't worry about disgrace
You'll know it doesn't matter—
When they throw that dirt in your face!
[*Three lines lost*]
[*Tune switches to that of "I've Got the Whole World in My Hands"*]

And you'll know
The whole world,
Will end in the hole;
The whole world
Will end in the hole;
The hole
Is waiting
For you.
Wait-
Ing
For
You.

Alright. Now, since I've got my jacket off, I'm going to do a bit—that jack-it-off bit—see, that came out wrong.

Now, we take you to the town of Transylvania, and Boris does the narrating. Alright. Boris Karloff, Bela

Lugosi. Oh—can you see my wrists stamped? The mark of the *Golem*. The *Dybbuk!* Alright.

NARRATOR [*hushed voice filled with mystery*]: Soon, my friends, the town of Transylvania will be visited by Bela, who's looking for lodgings for the night. Soon Bela will be knocking at the door, and a woman will be answering . . .

tap tap tap tap

OLD WOMAN: [*Harsh, high, rasping voice*]: Who are you young man? I've never seen you before. You're a stranger in Transylvania . . . I said, Who are you? Who are you?

DRACULA [*Hammy, fake-cultured East European*]: Per-r-rmit me to introduce myself. Hahahahaha!

OLD WOMAN [*interested, voice softens*]: Well, you sound pretty wild. Come in! What is your name?

DRACULA: My name, madam, is Count Dr-r-racula. And you see, ve are looking for lodgings for the night. Ve have been fortunate enough to br-r-reak down in your small town of Tr-r-r-ansylvania. Ve are but a small cir-r-rcus tr-r-roop, you see, and ve are ver-ry pleasant people. [*Aside*] It is getting light out, I am getting veak . . . Excuse me madam. There is yoost myself and my friend Igor.

IGOR [*British accent*]: You promised to straighten out the hunch, master, you promised years ago when I came to the laboratory!

DRACULA: Shut up! I'll punch you in the hunch!

POCK!

And don bug me no more! You look gr-r-r-roovy that way. Look at the money ve made on the parties at Fire Island, looking at you . . . Now. Excuse, madam, for the small interr-r-ruption, but ah, ve vould like lodgings, yoost for a vile, you know.

OLD WOMAN [*Pushy*]: Well, I know you show people, and it's usually customary that we get a little money first.

DRACULA: Vell, I'm a little hung for bread now, but, ah, I don't, ah—per-rhaps you'd like to punch Igor in the hunch?

OLD WOMAN [*interested*]: Well, I've never done anything like that before . . .

DRACULA: Yes, there is a whole chapter on this in Kr-r-raft-Ebbing. Or maybe you vant to put on some high leather boots and choke some chickens? You like that? And you can talk dirty to them!

OLD WOMAN: Hahaha! *I'm* not a *freak!* Teeheehee. Oh yes. I remember years ago when Al Donohue was through here. Hahaha. I'll never be the same. No!

DRACULA: Alright. Vat is it you vant?

OLD WOMAN [*shrieking*]: Money! Money! That's what I want!

DRACULA: Alright, alright. Get off my back. Here. Here's ten cents. Now, get out of here . . . Now I vill take my family out of the boxes . . . [*Irritated*] I told you, don't bring your mother! . . . [*Fondly*] Bela Jr. . . .

BELA JR. [*popping out of box*]: Ah, Poppa, Poppa! Poppa, Poppa, Poppa!

DRACULA: Alright, shut up and dr-r-rink your blood. And bite Momma goodnight. You hear me? Don bug us no more! Go to the next room and eat your blackboard and crayons. And pr-r-ractice on sister's neck.

MRS. DRACULA [*nagging Jewish wife*]: Sure, that's a nice vay to talk to the child! Isn't it? Practice on sister's neck! That's all you tink about, you degenerate you! Aghh! I can't stand to look at you any more! Phah! You know vat it means ven a voman can't stand to look at a man any more?

174

Our knot is all gone, Bela. The stake is burned out. You Fancy Dan vit the vaseline on the hair, dirtying up all the pillowcases. Ve are finished now.

DRACULA: Alright! Get off my back, you vitch you! You band rat! Sure, hanging around the Black Hawk, everybody freaked off vit you! And I was nice enough to take you avay from that—ugh! sure, that's appreciation!

MRS. DRACULA: Sure, you vit that vicious tongue, that never brought me any pleasures! No no. It is all over. Ve are finished! I'm going off.

DRACULA: Gɔ ahead. Go off by yourself, you freak! *Now,* you hear? Ve are going into the next room now, and I don't vant to be disturbed.

MRS. DRACULA: Sure, you're going to get high! You're gonna smoke some shit, some of those crazy zigarettes again, and eat up the whole icebox!

DRACULA [*a beaten old Jewish man*]: I'm not getting high—a coupla pills . . . Vy don't you leave me alone?

MRS. DRACULA: Sure, you stupid pimp, you—*phah!* [*to Bela Jr.*] You like vat your daddy does for a living? He sucks people on the neck. Hm hm! You like dat? "Vat is my daddy doing?" "He sucks people's neck, for money." Hm hm! You degenerate, you freak you!

DRACULA: Look, you knew vat I vas ven you mar-r-ried me. Get off my back now. I'm no fr-r-reak.

MRS. DRACULA: Vat is a freak? You degenerate, you're sucking necks! Dot's all you do: "Hello. Vat does your daddy do for living?" "My daddy sucks a neck for a living." Hm hm hm! Dot's nice. Go head vit your friends, suck a neck, you pervert! *Ptu! Phah!*

DRACULA: Ohh, vill you stop? Vill you stop talking this vay in front of the kid?

SUPERINTENDENT [*Tough American voice*]: Mr. Lugosi, I hate ta interrupt ya, but I'm the super here. You gotta knock off this horseshit now. You wanna hear me? I mean, the people just aren't goin for it. I dunno where the hell you people lived before, but ya gotta move. I mean, I don like ta butt in on your personal business, but that suckin people onna neck is *disgusting,* now. I dunno where you people come fr—get your kid off my dog, Mr. Lugosi! God damn! The whole *family's* sick. Come on, son! Get off there! He don't like dat . . . Kid's *weird,* for Chrissake! Stop that, sonny! The dog isn't smiling, he don't like that. Mr. Lugosi, c'mon. I'm gonna give you the deposit back. You gotta get outta here. I mean, you're pushy about it! You never ask people—you're sucking their neck before you even say hello to them! C'mon, get outta here now. Damn fruit, you. You're not kiddin me. I don't want ya to do it to Father McGovern, either, trickin him into the confession booth and getting him onna neck like that, Damn weirdo . . .

I'm going to do a science fiction picture, dig this: It opens up in Atlantis, you know, under the sea, and there're the two heavies, the scientists. One is a hate-crazed skin-diver and the other is a moron physical education major from S.C. who was thrown out for looking over the lockers at the other guys and taking showers with his underwear on. You know these guys, they saved their brown underwear from the army—"It's plenty good! Plenty good, that's all. I'm not pressing anybody."

So that's it, You've got these two weirdos, you know, and they've got this monster they're making. They're working on him, and he's really a horrendous-looking creature. And he's ready for the ascent. You know, they send him up, and he comes up in Coney Island. And he gets up on the beach, and he comes dripping, monstrous out of the water.

"Arghhhhhhhharrrhhhhh."

And all of a sudden these old Jewish ladies see him, and they start whacking him in the face with pocketbooks—

"What the hell is this?"

Kids are punching him, you know, and the sand is too hot for his feet, and he's walking around there, and then a cop gives him a ticket for changing his suit under the boardwalk. So he really gets bugged, you know, and the kids keep punching him, so he feels rejected. So he goes down under the sea, and the scientists say

"Well, did you make it? What was the scene?"

"I bombed."

"You're putting us on."

"Nooo."

"What are you, kidding? You didn't kill?"

"Nooo. They didn't dig me. I dunno what the hell it is."

"Well, did you do all the bits? Did you Arghhhhhhhrghhhhh!?"

"Yeah."

"Did you do Graaaaaaaaagh!?"

"Yeah."

"What'd they say?"

"They said I was doing Jerry Lewis."

"That's weird."

"I dunno . . ."

The other guy says,

"Look, c'mere. We shouldn't have sent him to Coney Island. They're nuts there. Maybe Brighton Beach. It's a little cooler there. That's what it is. He'll flip those people there. Alright?"

177

So they get him weirder, and they give him directions:
"You make a left at the Andrea Doria, come
· up, don't fool with the sea urchins, and make it.
Now split. You ready? O.K. Cool it, and don't bug
anybody."
Now, he comes up, right? Brighton Beach, he comes up:
"Rrrrraaaagh!"
And this old Jewish woman rushes up to him, and she
says
"Are you married? My daughter Sophie . . ."
So he just wigs out, you know. And he's ashamed, now,
to go back. So he hangs around for a while, but finally
he does, and they're waiting.
"Hey, you made it, huh? You swung, I can tell!"
"Noooo."
"Well, what *is* it with you? Cause *we're* not up
there. You doing everything we told you to?"
"Yeah."
"I know what it is. He looks wild, but maybe he's
not thinking horror. He's not projecting himself
. . . Look. Are you really a freak?"
"Yeah! I'm *wild*."
"Cause, don't—you know, alotta guys say they're
freaky, and they put ya on, and they're not really
weirdos, you know?"
"Yeah! I'm a freak! I'm *wild*."
"Cause we're not gonna spend a fortune on pic-
tures and music and the whole bit, you know, if
you're—it's not bad *not* to be a freak, you know.
But *tell* us, if you're a weirdo, you know. That's it."
"No! I'm the wildest! I got chicks—you wouldn't
believe this. Lolita, the whole scene."
"Alright! Alright! You got one more time, that's it."
Now, he comes up—they have a direct cut, and he's on
the subway, standing there, you know. He's so wild-
looking this time. He's got an abalone on his eye, you

know? So these two chicks are there, with the black stockings, the whole bit, you know, and this chick says to her friend, she says:

"Look at him over there. He's got a sensitive face. He's interesting."

So she goes over, she wants to do him in charcoal. So he gets so bugged—they're going about eighty miles an hour—he reaches out the window and he grabs this pole, and that's it: WRAP! CHUNK! WROMP! People screaming, the girder, the whole bit. Everybody's killed, you know, and he made it—Show Business! Finally made the scene. He's just so grooved, you know? So he runs back to the hotel—he finally made it, right?— and he's waiting for the newspapers to come out, you know? Finally the papers come out, he looks:

MAFIA WRECKS TRAIN

A film that will be out soon: here's the opener I've got in my mind:

The mayor, speech. Parade. O.K. Now, here come two *schmuky* cops chasing the gangsters: "Stop, We'll shoot!"

Pow! Pow! The mayor falls down, blam.

O.K. We take you now to—prison break! With Charles Bickford, George E. Stone, Bruce Bennett, Frankie Darrow, Nat Pendleton, the woman across the Bay, Anne Dvorak, Silvia Sidney, and Olivia DeHavilland, who's taking Vincent Price's place in films now.

O.K. Eighteen prison guards hostage in the yard below:

PRISON WARDEN [*harsh, heavy voice over loudspeaker*]: Alright, Dutch! This is the warden! You've got eighteen men down there, prison guards who've served me faithfully. Give up, Dutch, and

179

we will meet any reasonable demands you've got—
except for the light meters. Hear me? Give up!

DUTCH [*hoarse bullfrog sound*]: Yaydeyah! Yah-
dudeyahdudeyah!

WARDEN: Never mind those Louis Armstrong im-
pressions. You'd better give up! You're a rotten,
vicious criminal! You never were any good to your
family and you're your own worst enemy, Dutch,
believe me. *Hab mir gesucht.* Give it up.

DUTCH: Yahdeyah!

WARDEN: Shut up! You goddamn nut you! "Yah-
dayahdada"—*putzo!* [*To the aides gathered
around him*]. I'm sorry I gave him the library card.
That moron . . . I dunno what we're gonna do with
these guys . . . Maybe if we kill about four or five
for an example. [*Picks up telephone*] . . . Tower
C! Kill about twelve down there! . . . The bullets?
Ask my wife . . . Look in the back of my brown
slacks, the bullets are there . . . Come on! Don't
put me on. The ones in the grey shirts—you know
which ones to kill.

FATHER FLOTSKY [*high voice with a thick brogue*]:
Just a moment! Before there's killing, I'd better get
down there.

WARDEN: Not you, Father Flotsky!

FLOTSKY: I'm going down there!

WARDEN: Ah, you don't understand about these
guys. These are monsters! They've got knives and
guns—

FLOTSKY: Son, you seem to forget, don't you, that
I know things stronger than knives and guns—

WARDEN: You mean, ah—

FLOTSKY: That's right! *Jujitsu, that's it!*

WARDEN: You'll be making a mistake, Father
Flotsky.

FLOTSKY: The mistake is mine to make.

180

Now, the handsome, but eccentric prison doctor, Sabu:

SABU [*combination Arab and Negro accent*]: They hate you. You're corrupt. That's why the men hate you and cut you. Don't you know that? That is not the way to kill people. That is why the men cut the men up. My father don't know to do that.

WARDEN: Get outta here, you big pill-head, you! Quit buggin me!

SABU: You jive, motherfucker—

WARDEN: Get outta here with that, "You motherfucker!" So you learned something—now get outta here and stop buggin me. We're gonna start killing them, right now.

O.K. Death Row, first cell:

NEGRO PRISONER [*sings*]: Water boy! . . . Soon Ih'm gwine up ta hebben. Yessuh. That's one thing that's fun to be colored folk—that's all you do, is get up in de mo'nin, and gwine ta hebbin [*sings*]:

> Ah'm gwine ta hebbin, Lord,
> Yes, gwine ta hebbin, Lord,
> Ah'm gwine ta hebbin, Lord.

WHITE PRISONER [*weeping*]: I don't wanna die! I don't wanna die!

NEGRO: Don worry, white boss, it ain't so bad.

WHITE: Whaddayou care, you niggers are *used* ta gettin lynched!

NEGRO: Don worry. We gwine ta hebbin. Fust thing ah'm gwine to do when ah've gwine ta hebbin, is find out what a "gwine" is.

O.K. Some guy's going to the chair:

"So long, Marty. Here's my playin cards, kid. Here's my *mezuzah*, Juan. And there's that door . . . I donwanna go in there . . . I dunno what to do."

"Don't siddown, Martha!"

Alright. Father Flotsky's down in the yard, now.

FLOTSKY: Hello, Dutch. You don't remember Father Flotsky, now, do ya, son? You'd never hurt Father Flotsky. Now, you're not a bad boy, now. Killing six children doesn't make you *all* bad.

DUTCH: Yahdeyah! Yahdeyadedah!

FLOTSKY: Oh, he's disgusting! He's a goddamn nut! They're no good, the lot of them—'Yaddeyahdah" —They're animals! Pour it on— kill them all! They're no good! I'll give them mass confession. But first I gotta bless the motorcycles.

WARDEN [*over loudspeaker*]: You men—the prison guards! Look, I dunno what the hell it is, but Dutch donwanna give up, and I got an election comin up here, and, ah, it's a dog eat dog, you know what I mean. Dutch, c'mon now, don't be crazy. Give up! Ya got two seconds. You gonna listen?

DUTCH: Ah, warden, will you get the shit outta here! I ain't gonna listen ta nobody! Nobody. This whole stinking, rotten prison, nobody!

PINKY [*high effeminate voice over loudspeaker*]: Dutch, lithen to me, bubby.

DUTCH: Who is that?

PINKY: Who ith it? Ith Pinky, the hothpital attendant! Give up, you crazy *vilde* you! You'll make it *life* for uth.

DUTCH: Pinky, sweetheart! I'll give it all up faw you!

PINKY: Woo! Give it up for me? Did you hear that, all you bitcheth in thell-block eleven? Did you hear that warden?

WARDEN: I heard it, ya fruit you!

PINKY: Juth watch it, warden, hmmmmm? Don't overthep your boundth. Are we gonna get our demanth?

WARDEN: Whaddya want? You fag bastard you!

PINKY: A gay bar, and one more thing.

WARDEN: What is it?

PINKY: I wanna be the Avon representative for thith prithon.

Lost Horizons. In this scene the High Lama is giving Ronald Colman the secret of eternal life. The secret of eternal life—everyone's dream, to live forever, in happiness and harmony. The lion and the lamb shall walk together, and the little child shall ball them both.

Now. We hear the High Lama talking:

HIGH LAMA [*barely audible, ancient, ancient voice*]: Well, my son, I've been here in the cave for many years. I'm the High Lama. I'm out of my nut. No, you have never smoked the *lotus lamoga,* have you? It's wonderful . . . My son, I have sat here for many years on this cold stone, suffering from itching sensations, until I found relief with Pazo. Pazo is my *guru,* that I brought in from Patamonza, many years ago when my astral body took off. And, my son, I'm going to give you the secret of eternal life.

COLMAN: My, my, you're wondrous, High Lama! Hm hm! If I were king I couldn't have a fonder wish than to live forever. Tell me something, oh wondrous High Lama, hand me the keys of wisdom: How can I live for eternity?

HIGH LAMA: Well, my son, to live forever, you must never smoke—

Get a load of this old joke, now—

—you must never drink, and most of all, you must never never sleep with any bad women!

COLMAN: Well, tell me something, oh wondrous High Lama, if I never smoke and I never drink

183

and I never sleep with any bad women, will I live forever?

HIGH LAMA: No, my son, but it'll seem like it.

John Graham. I don't know if you remember this guy. He blew up a plane with forty people and his mother. And for this the state sent him to the gas chamber: proving, actually, that the American people are losing their sense of humor. Because, when you think about it just for a minute, anybody who blows up a plane with forty people and their mother can't be all bad. The guy's got like a little thing going there.

But they sent him away. They tried to get a lawyer, couldn't get Otto Kruger, Sidney Blackmer was working on the Scotsborough case.

Now, back to that day at the airport. Was he guilty?

PUBLIC ADDRESS SYSTEM: United Airlines paging passenger Sylvia Green. Will a Sylvia Green report to the United Airlines information desk or ticket counter. Grand concourse now loading gate thirty-one for Hawaii and the Philippines.

GRAHAM: Hurry up, Ma, we'll miss the plane! *C'mon Ma!* Hurry up. Hurry up now! C'mon, you can walk—I don't want those lies again. C'mon, c'mon!

MOTHER [*cracked old voice*]: I dunno why you want me to fly all of a sudden. I dunno I dunno! I'm gonna get claustrophobia closed in up there. I know it!

GRAHAM: Don't worry, Ma, you're gonna get alotta air—hahahaha! O.K. Hurry up! Hurry up! *Throw that cane away,* it's in your mind!

MOTHER: Alright!

GRAHAM: Listen, I gotta game for you to play before you get on the plane.

MOTHER: Games! I love games.

GRAHAM: Shut up! Not so loud, you freak. C'mere. You'll love this. It's wild. C'mere. It's called "Fill Out The Policy." Just write there. O.K. O.K., good. Now, listen, Ma, I got a present for you, and I don't want you to open this up till you get halfway across that shiny sea (and that's all you're gonna get!) Alright. Now, I'll put it in your pocketbook.

MOTHER: I love presents!

GRAHAM: Shut up with that parakeet voice of yours! Alright, now, you'll *love* this.

MOTHER: It's a music box.

GRAHAM: Yeah, you'll get a good sound out of it, uh huh. Plays "Rumania Rumania" and "Hot Nuts" . . . O.K. Ma. Listen, have a good trip, and, ah, don't talk to anybody on that plane.

And now, the take-off: WALLAWANGDANG, WAL-LAWALLAZONGBONGBONGFLINGDINGDING-FLONGDONGBONGBONGFLINGDINGDINGDIN-DINGWOMBOMBINGBINGBINGFLINGALINGAF LINALINGA

GRAHAM: See ya around, ma! Ha ha! If ya believe. WAMWAMWAMWAMFLINFALFINFLINFFLING ANINGAAAAAAAAAAAAAUUUUUUUUMMMMM FLING

GRAHAM: First stop, Armageddon!
FLINAFLINGAFLINGAFLINGJGANINGANINGA-NINGAAAAAAAAAAAAAUUUUUUMMMMMMM

STEWARDESS [*nasal public address system voice*]: Good evening. My name is Stewardess Stevenson. We're cruising—teeheehee!—at four hundred and fifty miles an hour, at sixteen thousand feet above sea level. Your captain is Captain Armstrong, and your copilot is Mr. Noxton. If the passengers would like to look over the left wing of the plane, is the lovely island of Catalina; and to the right— Guam? Hm. Hahaha. Well, well, the ever-chang-

185

ing world. Now. We've got a wonderful trip in store for everyone, and if the passengers want any Chicklets, like, we're out. But I think there's a jelly donut—no, I ate that. There's some Greek cheese that George left—no. I dunno. Anyway, please share the magazines. We've got two *Arizona Highways* and one *Argosy*. Thank you for flying Non-Scheddo Airlines. And now to the controls, with your copilot and your captain!

MMMMMM—uh-uh-uh—MM—uh-uh

COPILOT: Where are we?

PILOT: I dunno, man, I'm so juiced! Whew! That airport bar . . . That guy can make a martini—I'm outta my nut, man. I'm really juiced, baby.

COPILOT: Look, man, you promised you'd cool it. Like, you can't make this scene outta your skull alla time.

PILOT: I know, it's depressing, man. I don't dig height.

COPILOT: Hey!

PILOT: What?

COPILOT: Look. We *gotta* know where we are.

PILOT: Boy, you're really a bug, man. Just enjoy the high, baby, that's all. They're lucky they get anywhere for seventy-nine dollars. Anyway, what does it matter where we are?

COPILOT: Ah, don't start with that existentialism stuff again man, I'm fed up with that philosophizing.

COPILOT: Hey.

PILOT: What?

COPILOT: Hey, I don like ta bug ya, but what's that thing you're always grabbin there?

PILOT: That's the joy stick—moves the wings, the rudder.

COPILOT: You're putting me on.

186

PILOT: No, man, that's really the scene. That's the way it happens.

COPILOT: Is that wild! Where the hell dja pick up on that, Smiling Jack? That's wild. Can I touch it?

PILOT: No. You really ruin things, man. You're not mechanically inclined. Just goof, there. There's some more Jim Beam in the glove compartment . . .

COPILOT: Did ya ball the stewardess yet?

PILOT: No, man. She's really a drag, that chick.

BARRRROOM!

PILOT: What was that?

COPILOT: The back end of the plane just blew off! Hey man! Seventeen people just fell out!

PILOT: Cool it.

COPILOT: Is this weird? There go twenty more! Are we gonna get yelled at!

PILOT: Will you shut up with that! What the hell are we gonna do now? . . . Look.

COPILOT: What?

PILOT: *You* don't say anything, *I* don't say anything. It's our word against their's.

COPILOT: Whatsa matter with you, you nut you! There's twenty people left!

PILOT: Let's dump em.

COPILOT: You're really insane! You can't do a thing like that, you monster! They're awake.

PILOT: I dunno what the hell—

COPILOT: Hey, I got an idea!

PILOT: What?

COPILOT: You remember that guy in the second seat over the wing? The guy who was coming on like he knew alot about planes? He was dropping alotta big words, like "wing" and "propellor"?

PILOT: Yeah?

COPILOT: Why don't ya ask him?

PILOT: No, man, like I don't like to ask anybody

187

for anything. You know, you get indebted to people, you know?

COPILOT: Well, ask him, for me, man. I wanna make it home once more.

PILOT: Well, I dunno, man. Then they're always on your neck for favors, you know.

COPILOT: But, like—

PILOT: *Awright!* Switch on the intercom.

Click

"My name is Stewardess Stevenson—"

PILOT: Will you shut up with that, you nitwit? Everybody knows your name, moron! And stay outta the icebox. And get that guy up here over the wing seat who knows all about planes. And hurry up!

STEWARDESS [*to passenger*]: Sir, would you help us out? They're cranky. Some people fell outta the plane, I dunno what the hell is goin on. I never bother anybody, I can live in an apartment ten years, I dunno my next-door neighbor. I hate to bug ya, but c'mon, help us out, will ya please? I'll give ya half a cheese sandwich. Come on. Will you?

PASSENGER [*suave, superior voice*]: I certainly will. I'll help anyone who's in peril [*whistling nonchalantly*].

COPILOT [*panicking*]: Sir, sir, we're in alotta trouble!

PASSENGER: Oh, really? Hahahaha! That's a little obvious, that you're in a lot of trouble. I would say you're in trouble—everybody fell out of the plane. Hahaha. Yes, that was a beautiful statement. Yes, trouble. Very profound.

PILOT: Well, whaddawe do?

PASSENGER [*lowers voice*]: C'mere. First of all, like, you gonna duke me in on the insurance bread?

188

PILOT: Well, yeah, I'll swing any way, man.

PASSENGER: O.K. Gimme ten in front.

PILOT: We haven't got!

PASSENGER: Well, the watch. Gimme the watch. O.K., I'll take that.

PILOT: Alright. Now, what's the bit?

PASSENGER: Well, it's obvious that you strip the plane of everything. Now, there's about thirty people left out there. You're going to have to ask for volunteers.

PILOT: To what?

PASSENGER: [*whistles*]

COPILOT: What the hell are *you* smoking? What the hell's the matter with you? How you gonna go out and ask people to jump out of a plane? I can't ask people to do a thing like that!

PASSENGER: Let me ask them. I know how to talk to people.

PILOT: Solid. Be my guest, man.

PASSENGER: Good evening, everyone. I've got a surprise—hahaha! Ah, I know that you people have been satiated with many motion pictures where the captain and the copilot and the crews jump out to save the passengers? Well, like, it's not happening. I donwanna bug anybody, but it's time to split. C'mon, anybody. *Any*body! Come on now. Sissies! Whatsa matter—didn't anyone ever ask you to jump out of a plane before? How bout you—the old railroad man. You! The old railroad man. Yeah, yeah, you!

OLD MAN: Please! No! I just got my watch. No!

PASSENGER: Alright with those Gene Lockhart bits, shut up and sit down.

PASSENGER: Hey . . . The six year old kid! Yeah, that *schlub!* He ruined the men's room with the crayons. Is he sleeping? That's cooler. O.K. [*whistling tune that changes to "The Bridge Over the River Kwai"*] Sonny! Sonny, wake up! Wake up now. Wake up! Wake up!

KID [*screaming*]: Where's my mommy? Where's Mommy?

PASSENGER: Right out that door, Sonny. . . .

Balling, Chicks, Fags, Dikes & Divorce

> *"Those* girls!"

That's what the chick will tell you, man.

> "Look, Lenny, if you want those bums, go ahead.
> I mean, if you want those—I'm not that kind of a
> girl—it's alright with me—"

And every chick has got that groove: those girls, those
girls. And I'm dying to find them—where the hell are
they? You look for them, where are they? There's an
elephant's graveyard for hookers and swingers.

> "Those girls those girls those girls"

Or

> "It's gotta mean something to me, Lenny. That's
> all. With *those* bums it's like washing your hands;
> I'm different. To me it's gotta mean something."
> "Well, *schmuck,* it *feels* good! Doesn't *that* mean
> anything?"

Then there's another great classification—the promiscuous virgin:

> "I don't go all the way. That's all—I don't go all
> the way."

And these chicks better be careful. Because when they're gonna go, that may not be the way any more.

You know, I'm gonna make a book up, see. The book on its face will look like it's, you know, one of those very erudite, how-to-make-out, sane-sex-and-marriage kind of things, nut books. But if you follow the instructions in this book, you'll *never* make out at all. Ever. Really constructed so that it's a zero no-score. Sell it for forty-five dollars in plain brown wrapping paper.

Now it says, "Instructions: Always go over to her house for dinner and meet the folks, and don't forget, *compliment*"—and it gives just the dialogue the guy is supposed to use:

> "Oh Mr. Johnson, *boy,* your daughter's got a terrific shape on her! Hah! God bless her, boy, she's got a *body,* I'm tellin you—and your wife has got a nice shape on her, too."

Then when you're out on the date, they like little jokes. Just keep saying,

> "Whaddaya got, the *rag* on?"

Keep saying that. They'll like it. They like people who are frank.

> "Whaddaya got, the *rag* on?"

Keep saying it all night. And then when you're in the car, just ask them in a *nice* way for it, and be cute about it, use euphemisms, *double entendre.* Say

> [*nonchalantly*] "Oh, I wonder if I could get some nookie?"

That's very cute.

> "Oh boy, I wonder who'd gimme some nookie? Boy, I wonder."

And they just think that's so cute, you'll get it right away. Just say extra things, like

> "Boy, would I *appreciate* it! Boy, I'd appreciate

that. I'd tell *everybody* what a nice person you were, too."

"I'll be comfortable on the couch."
Famous last words.

> GIRL: Listen. If you're gonna come up, now, there's no fooling around, you know.
>
> GUY: No, are you kidding? I see that all day. I'm just tired. Too tired to drive home. You live upstairs? Well, what the hell . . .

Sleep on the couch. Those kind of girls that *like* to make you sleep on the couch—and then just rustle lingerie in the next room.

> "Look, I'll sleep on the outside of the mattress, you sleep on the inside. I promise I won't fool around . . . How come you put on toreador pants?"
>
> "They're comfortable."
>
> "That's just a good slap in the face! They're not comfortable. And you can't put your hand under them—that's why you put them on. You're not a *real* toreador."

I think that a lot of marriages went West, you know, they split up, in my generation, because ladies didn't know that guys were different. It's very tough for chicks to realize that, that although we speak the same language—it's like: No guy ever cheated on his wife, ever. But ladies would get hurt and want to leave their husbands because they *thought* the husbands cheated; and they never *did* cheat, because what cheating means, I know, to a lady, means kissing and hugging and liking somebody. You have to at least *like* somebody. With guys that doesn't enter into it. Ladies are one emotion, and guys detached. Not consciously detached, but they just do detach. Like, a lady can't go through a plate glass window and go to bed with you five seconds later. But every guy in this audience is the same—you can *idolize* your wife, just be so crazy about her, be on the way home from work, have a head-on collision with a Greyhound bus, in a *disaster* area. Forty people laying dead on the highway—not even in the hospital, in the *ambulance*—the guy makes a play for the nurse:

> OUTRAGED FEMALE VOICE: How could you *do* that thing at a time like that?
> ASHAMED MALE: I got horny.
> *"What?"*
> "I got hot."
> "How could you be hot when your *foot* was cut off? People were *dead* and *bleeding* to death!"
> [*Apologetic*]: "I dunno."
> "He's an *animal!* He got hot with his foot cut off!"
> "I guess I'm an animal. I dunno."
> "What did you get hot at?"
> "The nurse's uniform, I think."
> "He's a *moron,* that's all, he's just an *animal!* I don't know how you could *think* of it. Your foot was cut off and you could—*ugh,* dis*gust*ing!"

No. Guys detach, it has nothing to do with liking, loving. You put guys on a desert island and they'll do it to mud. *Mud!* So if you caught your husband with mud, if somehow you could get overseas there,

> OUTRAGED FEMALE: *EEEEEEEKKK! Don't talk to me!* That's all. You piece of *shit* you, leave me alone! That's all. Go with your mud, have fun. You want dinner? Get your mud to make dinner for ya.

That's it, so you just can't get angry at them. You can't wanna leave them for that, ever.

Yeah. Guys are carnal, and if chicks really knew that, I think marriages would stay together. Cheating actually is a lady's word. If guys can do it to their fists, they don't

194

cheat on you. They really don't. If they did what ladies call cheating, they wouldn't come back to you. But they do it to their fist, to mud, to barrels.

So if you knew this about guys, would you really feel hurt if you came home and found your husband sitting on your bed with a chicken? Would you really cry, hurt? And wanta leave him? And that's the end of the whole marriage?

WIFE: A chicken! [*crying*] A chicken! In our bed.

HUSBAND: Lemme alone. That's all.

WIFE: *Don't touch me!* You want dinner? Get your chicken to get it, you asshole, you!

In New York its illegal—"seemingly sexual intercourse with a chicken." That's the literal. Now, how could you even fantasize that? Doing it to a chicken. They're too short. How could you kiss a chicken? I can't even imagine that.

FEMALE: Where's your chicken? How come you're alone tonight. Your chicken left town?

HUSBAND: I dunno the chicken. I was drunk. I met her in the yard. Whaddaya want from me? Stop already with the chicken.

"Whenever I cheat on my wife I always tell her. I'm just that kind of a husband. I just, if I cheat on her, I just, I just gotta be truthful, I can't lie, and I always tell her . . ."

Never tell her. Not if you love your wife.

"I just can't help it. I'm honest, and when I chippy on her I just *gotta* tell her—cause I like to *hurt* her:

'Ah, sweetheart, ah, you didn't find this hand-kerchief with lipstick on it and I wanna show it to ya. I wanna confess . . . Ah, I cheated on ya again, and, ah, I always wanna tell you when I cheat on ya, cause I know that you should leave me—and take the eight kids with

195

ya! I wouldn't blame ya. And if ya had a job in the five and ten and supported you and the kids, it would be O.K.' "

Never cop out. *Never ever ever.* Not if you *love* your wife. Cause chicks don't know anything about guys at all. All they know is about Billy Graham—the fantasy, you know, about the kind of Norman Rockwell people that never did exist. No, guys can make it on the highway. But chicks—the climate has to be just right. Guys, *nada.*

In fact, if your old lady walks in on you, deny it. Yeah. Just flat out, and she'll believe it:

HUSBAND: I'm tellin ya, this chick came downstairs with a sign around her neck, "LAY ON TOP OF ME OR I'LL DIE." I didn't know what I was gonna do.

WIFE: Will you get outta here, you dirty liar—and take that tramp with you!

HUSBAND: I'm lyin? Ask Mrs. Slobowski to come down here! This chick came downstairs with a sign around her neck "LAY ON TOP OF ME, I'M A DIABETIC, OR I'LL DROP DEAD." Now what was I gonna do, now?

WIFE: Well . . . keep the door locked and don't let those tramps in here any more.

I'm really convinced that no guy ever leaves a chick. When chicks get cold, they *really* get cold. *Phew!* It's *over.* Really, when it's over with them it's *over.* And guys can never figure that out. They figure there's one more time.

Here's what I figure it is. You always hear chicks say, you know,

"Oh, I wish I could get me a man, you know, someone with some dignity, not this guy I can walk all over, someone who'd be really a man, a *man* . . ."

196

But chicks don't know that guys are like dogs. You know, you take a dog, you beat the shit out of him—POW! POW!—but he'll keep coming back. Ladies are like cats. You yell at a cat *once*—Siamese cat—*phsst!* They're gone.

So that kind of quality that ladies are looking for—they really want a guy to act like a lady.

If you're going to break up with your old lady and you live in a small town, make sure you don't break up at three o'clock in the morning. Because you're screwed—there's nothing to do. You sit in the car all night, parked somewhere. Yeah. So make it about nine in the morning, so you can go to the five and ten, bullshit around, worry her a little, then come back at seven in the night, you know?

The bad break-up is like a long-time break-up. If you're married seven years, you gotta kick for two. Oh yeah, I think if you're married fifteen, eighteen years, then you get divorced, then you must lose your mind. Yeah. They get senile, then, the people. They get whacked out.

There's a certain critical area there, you been married about seven, eight years, where you really throw up for a coupla years. Really, just go throw up.

And if you broke up and you go anywhere alone, there's always *momzas* that ask about your wife. Which is really a hang-up. Especially if you've been married about, well, ten years, say. And you're very tight with your old lady—you'd go everywhere together. And now, you start to go places solo—whether it's a supermarket, laundromat, or a Chinese restaurant:

"Where's the missus?"

"Oh, I got divorced—"

There's an embarrassed silence, while the guy'll identify you—

> "Oh, you're a lovely couple. You should get to-gether. She'll come back to ya."

> "Can I have my stamps? Yeah, I just wanna get the hell outta here."

Chinese restaurant. Some waiter, week after week, for ten years. First time you go in alone, the waiter goes:

> CHINESE VOICE: Where's maw-maw? How come you don't bring maw-maw in? Maw-maw sicka? Ah so, maw-maw velly sick. You better bring maw-maw home some cookies. Tell maw-maw say hello. Tell her say hello to her."

> "I'm divorced."

> *"Ohhhh. You bettuh awf."*

You bettuh awf. Christ, that's really going with the winner. What's he tell *her?*

And what kind of chicks you going to hang out with, if you're over thirty-five? You just can't—I can't—go out with any chick under twenty-five. I really do feel funny. Cause you just, you just know if you met her father, you know, he'd say, *"You're* not going to *marry* her."

So you hang out with chicks that are divorced. But you *never* can go over to their pad. Every chick that I know who's divorced has got a seven-year-old kid. It's really a prop from central casting.

> "Listen, I'd like to have you over the house, but I have a kid—"

> "I know."

I know I'm going to get *schlepped* into the bedroom, right, to look at the kid.

> [*Whisper*] *"Shhhhhhh,* don't wake him up."

> "No, I don't *wanna* wake him up."

He's sweating in his pajamas. Boy, that really kills the image, man.

Or if they don't have a kid they'll have a French poodle
that wants to stay in the bedroom all the time:

"Hey, why don't you let the dog go out?"

"He's a *little* dog. He's not gonna bother anybody."

"I know, I just feel uncomfortable with the dog
here. Has no function. What's he doing here?"

"Looking at us."

"Pervert! Get outta here!" . . . Look, I'm not an
exhibitionist, I can't, the dog is making me uncomfortable."

Sick red eyes, tap dancing on the linoleum. Dumb
French poodles.

If some cat says to ya,

"Look, you goin to Detroit? I want you to call up
this chick, she's a groovy chick, and she's divorced,
and blah blah blah . . ."

Call the chick up.

"Hullo. My name is Lenny Bruce, and John Sal-
stom said say hello to you."

And she sounds really corny on the phone:

AFFECTED VOICE: Oh, yes, I just saw Black Or-
pheus this afternoon—it was a private showing . . .
[*screams at kids in background*] WOULD YOU
LET HIM PLAY WITH THAT? RONNY, PUT
THAT DOWN! [*Soft affected voice again*] Oh yes,
of course . . .

You can see four kids running up and down, grape jelly
on their underwear, and putty, and it's, ahhh, yeah:

"I'd like to have you in, but the whole apartment
house is a mess."

Yeah. Every storey in the place is a mess.

Whenever I hear some guy say,

"You know, I got custody of my kids. Boy, my
wife's a *tramp*, and I got custody!"

Well, the unaware would assume, the unsophisticated,

> "There's a guy who *loves* his kids. He fought his
> wife in court that much to get his kids."

But I know "custody" means "get even." That's all custody means—just get even with your old lady. The only
get even you could have for the chick—cause *they* leave
you—is the kids. That's the only get even. That's the
sweet revenge. Get the kids! Course, you can't be that
obvious with it, you know, just

> "I'm gonna get the kids cause I'm gonna get even
> with you, you shithead you!"

So all the structure and the foundation is,

> "I went over there, the kid's *wet!* I'm not gonna let
> her—the kid's not gonna live like that. Every time
> I go over the kid's *wet!* Kid's wet, kid's wet, and
> that's it. I'm taking that kid away from her, cause
> the kid's wet. And she's havin *guys* over there!
> That tramp!"

> "Whaddaya mean, she's a tramp? She goes in the
> woods and roasts mickeys?"

> "No. She sleeps with guys."

> "That filthy thing."

> "She does it in front of the kids!"

> *"So what?"*

Sounds pretty bizarre, doesn't it: *"So what"*? Well, I'll
tell you. I've had that argument before. It's like, again,
it's:

> Overemphasis of sex and violence on television will
> be a deterrent to your child. Why? In the formative
> years, what he sees now, later on he will do. He will
> ape the actions of the actor.

Good logic. Correct. If so, your kid is better off watching
a stag movie than *King of Kings*. Mine, anyway. Because
I just don't want my kid to kill Christ when he comes
back. And that's what's in *King of Kings*—but tell me
about a stag movie where someone got killed in the

end, or slapped in the mouth, or heard any Communist propaganda. So the sense of values would be, the morals:

"Well, for kids to watch killing—Yes; but *schtupping*—No! Cause if they watch *schtup* pictures, they may do it some day."

[*back to original dialogue with outraged husband*]

"Well, I don't care. I got custody anyway."

"Well, isn't that kinda rough for you? You're a working stiff, you know, just, raising the kid— whattaya got, somebody to babysit while you're working?"

"I have 'em with my parents."

"Well, then you're *really* fulla shit."

Then you're really getting even, man. "I love" would mean at least, "I take, I raise, I pay the dues, I get up in the morning, I make the breakfast, I put her on the bus." But not with grandparents. Your kid is better off with a wife that sleeps with a different guy every *week*, than with grandparents.

Cause no kid six years old is happy in a house that gets dark at seven-thirty. Nor were you. Because old people are always reading. Reading, reading newspapers that have no funnies. And they smell weird. And it's just no fun going in your grandfather's top drawer— opposed to your father's:

KID: What's this?

[*Blowing noises*]

Pow!

KID: Whattaya hittin me for?

FATHER: Cause you know too much already. Get outside. They're balloons. Get out and get some air.

KID: Boy, did I get whacked in the house.

FRIEND: What'd ya get hit for?

KID: Ah, balloons.

FRIEND: They're not balloons.

KID: Yes they are. My father would never lie to me. They're balloons.

FRIEND: You and Hoover and your father are dumb bastards. They're not balloons.

KID: Sure they're balloons. I *think* they're balloons.

Thirty years later. The Surgeon General of the U.S. Army:

"The women that you've seen in these training films, men, the women that you may get these diseases from in Mers-el-Kebir blah-blah-blah . . ."

SOLDIER: Well, that's a very impressive speech, sir, but I just couldn't wear a balloon. I'm sorry.

OFFICER: What's that, Schneider?

SOLDIER: I couldn't wear a balloon.

OFFICER: Look, Schneider, they're *not* balloons!

SOLDIER: Oh yeah, they are. I know what you think they are, but they're really not. They're balloons. My father'll tell ya that—they're balloons.

OFFICER: Look, son, I know what your Dad told you, but they're just not balloons, and you've *got* to wear one.

SOLDIER: I couldn't wear a balloon. I'd feel like an *ass,* sir. It's silly. After the last speech I tried to put one on; but it's silly. That's it—I'd use a guess-what or a maryjane, but I can't wear a balloon.

OFFICER: *They're not balloons!*

SOLDIER: Sure they are. I got a whole box from the last speech. I don't want any. You can have my balloons. It's just dopey. I'd put bubble-gum on, but

"Come to bed, darling."

"Soon as I put my balloon on, dear."

No, I can't do that. That's dumb.

Now if you go back together, the danger time—and here's back to the religion again. There's only one per-

son you're supposed to confess to—not anybody else.
Priests, solid; but not husbands. They have no authority
vested in them to hear any truth. So don't listen to any
of their shit. Cause what happens—guy calls up his old
lady:

> "Hello, Vera? The only reason I called ya, ya left
> some of your crap over here. . . . I dunno, a hand-
> kerchief, a glove, I dunno. . . . Listen, I'm gonna
> come over, we'll shoot the shit, O.K.? See ya. Pay
> the tax bill."

All right. Back together. Kissin time, huggin time, and
bed time. After bed time:

> "Hey Vera, ah, when we were broke up, ah, did
> you make it with alotta guys?"

> "Don't be silly. Outta your mind? Make it with
> anybody else—"

> "Ah, bullshit, man, what the hell, good for the
> goose, good for the gander. We were legally sepa-
> rated. I made it with alotta lotta chicks, you're
> entitled to make it with alotta guys. I'd just like
> to know, for the helluvit. Did ya make it with alotta
> guys?"

> "How'm I gonna—"

> "Ah, *bullshit!* Now, I'm not gonna hit you now,
> I'm not gonna get mad. Just for the helluvit. Who
> did ya make it with?"

Don't tell him. Don't cop out. Never cop out. Don't tell
him—if they've got *pictures,* deny it! Flat out.

> "Ah, you're bullshittin' me. I got pictures here."

> "Where, idiot?"

> "Look at this! You're laying on the couch with
> the guy!"

> "Moron! That's a fag hairdresser."

> "Yeah? What the hell are ya laying on the couch
> with him for?"

"We were seeing who was *taller,* you idiot!"

"I'm sorry . . ."

That's all. Because if you ever do cop out—

"Come on! I'm not gonna get mad. Tell me. I'd just like to know for the hellofit."

See, that's what chicks don't know about guys. It's that entrapment. Maybe it's because their fathers did it to them:

"Just tell me, who? . . . Him? . . . *Phew!* I don't give a shit, but this is, it's a *shocker!* That's, heh, heh, that's the only thing that shocks me. . . . I'm not mad, but that's. . . . what a kick in the *ass* that is! . . . How the hell did ya—you know why, you know why it shocks me, cause you tol' me ya didn't *like* him. You tol' me you didn't want him over the *house,* and then . . . How could you *make* it with him? That fat, disgusting piece of—you *cunt!*

POW!

I always wondered, if you get married again—the only problem with ever getting married again—you have to go to some country, you have to marry somebody who speaks a different language, and doesn't speak any other language. Cause you'd always be afraid, you know, with the second old lady, that you might say something in bed—and your first wife would jump up behind the bed—

EX-WIFE: You said blah-blah! How could you say that to *her*—you said it to *me!*

GUILTY EX-HUSBAND: I just *bullshitted* her. I don't love her. I just said that cause I knew you were behind the bed. That's all.

I know that if Liz were ever to go back to Eddie, and she said, "You know, in the whole time, I never made it with him once," he'd believe. Yeah, I'd believe, man.

204

Cause every guy's a mark. Cause chicks are boss. Just boss boss.

All chicks are boss. Oh yeah. Chicks are boss boss. If you wanna test it out, pick any number in the directory, call up some guy this morning:

MALE: Hullo? Hullo?

FEMALE: Mister, look, I don't know you, but I had a terrible accident here on the highway, and I'm all alone, and as a fellow Christian, do you think you could help me?

Or you could use this approach,

FEMALE: Oh, excuse me, I think I have the wrong number.

MALE: No you haven't, now who's this?

FEMALE: Well, um, I was so confused, and, I had a flat, and, ah, I was gonna call my friend and have him pick me up, my girlfriend.

MALE: Don't worry, *I'll* pick you up!

FEMALE: Well, I don't know where I'm at.

MALE: I'll *find* ya, don't worry.

Out, driving all night, looking, looking, looking. If you only knew the power chicks have . . .

Chicks are always calling you a faggot. Yeah, it's really weird. Chicks are boss. Yeah. Chicks are boss boss. For every Frick, Carnegie, Du Pont, and Big Daddy Mellon, there's always that one chick that he'll pay the dues for.

Yeah, I know that Johnson stands in his underwear for some chick, like a *schmuck,* saying

PLEADING MALE VOICE: Just touch it once? Will ya just touch it *once?* Please, touch it once.

IRRITABLE FEMALE: Look, you want me to touch it when I don't feel like touching it? That's why I don't like to touch it—cause you always tell me to

205

touch it, then, when you *tell* me to touch it, I don't feel like touching it any more.

MALE: I dunno why you don't—

IRRITATED FEMALE: Cause I don't *wanna* touch—I gotta headache.

MALE: You got more goddamn headaches than anyone in the world! You won't touch it once? Everybody says to me, "Let us touch it!" So many people *want* to touch it, too—bust-out hookers that wanna give me the money back. And I go, "No, just my wife touches it, that's all. Cause I love her, I'm not gonna let anyone else touch it." And then I come home and you *don't* wanna touch it.

FEMALE: That's all you got on your mind, is "Touch it once, touch it once."

MALE: Well, I'm gonna let some bust-out hooker touch it!

FEMALE: Go ahead. Have a good time!

MALE [*Pretending nonchalance*]: I will. But I'm gonna give you one more chance. Wanna touch it, it's up to you. Look: I'll go to sleep, and if you wanna touch it, wake me up.

Guys always have that fantasy, right?

WOMAN'S VOICE: I wanna touch it.

MAN'S VOICE: No, no, sweetheart. I'm tired. Lemme go to sleep.

Yeah. What about those chicks? Are there those kind of chicks, man?

We're all the same people man, that's what I dig about' it, man. And it just discourages me that we try so desperately to be unique. Man, we're all the same cats, we're all the same *schmuck*—Johnson, me, you, every *putz* has got that one chick, he's yelling like a real dumdum:

206

"Please touch it once. Touch it once, touch it once."

"You want me to touch it when I don't feel like touching it?"

"Yes."

"You want me to touch it when I don't get any pleasure out of it?"

"Yeah. That's all. I'm a dummy. I'm gonna get it touched. Cause if I wait for you to touch it you'd never touch it."

"I touch it alot."

"No, you don't. You think you touch it alot—you used to touch it alot—but now, it's a favor to touch it. You have a unique way of making your own husband feel like a degenerate for wanting to get laid. Touch it once, touch it once."

"Alright here, I'll touch it."

"No, no, don't do me no favors."

"Touch it once, touch it once. Please touch it once."

"Look, do you want me to touch it when I don't feel like touching it?"

"Yeah."

"Is that true? Just like an animal, huh?"

"Uhuh."

"Is that all you came over here for?"

"That's all, just to do it to ya. That's all. I'm gonna do it, and then I'm gonna go home. I don't wanna sleep over here because I'll have to hide under the sheets in the morning when the maid comes. And you have a cat box. And Rome phone-number pillows, and I don't like em. Yeah, I'm going home. I gonna do it to ya, and that's all. I come over here to do it."

You know, that's another kind of *schmuck:*

"Hey, fix me up with that girl!"

"All right. Here. Do it to him. Right away. Do it to him."

"Hey, fix me up wid her."

"O.K. Do it to *him,* and then do it right away to *him.*"

Any guy freezes with any chick who comes on. I oughta know. If any chick says to me, "Wanta good time, Mistuh?" I run. In fact, I don't think I've ever talked to a strange chick in my life. Ever. Anywhere. Cause you just know they'll yell, they'll call the police. How can you talk to strange chicks, man?

I would never have the nerve to talk to any strange chick—even if she was a really beautiful chick. I'd never have the nerve to hit on her. In a house, somebody introduces us—solid. But guys who can, like, drive past in cars and go "Hello!" even—no.

And the reason I have never had the nerve is that my mother and my aunt, every day they would come home and tell me stories about some guy that was behind the bushes exposing himself. There was a band of dedicated perverts who spent their whole lives in trick positions:

"O.K. Jim? Ready behind the bushes there? O.K., N.G.-7? You've got your position behind the newspaper? You flash, O.K.? WOOHOO! LADY! LOOK AT ME! WOOHOO! HELLO LADY, HELLO!"

Find the *schmuck* in the bush. Yeah. They were all waiting for them. So I said,

"Mama, you've got the market cornered! You oughta film these guys. I mean, it's amazing how they always appear. The elevator doors open up, *'Woohoo! Here we are!'* "

But they had their pocketbooks. They were ready, boy.

208

That dopey big black pocketbook got everybody. With a good parrot scream:

Aghhhhhhh!

Pow!

After all these years I finally figured out that they were bullshit stories. Maybe that was a dopey lie. They were telling me they were good women, every day, right?

You know those guys in the park, the flashers?

"HELLO LADY!"

INTERROGATOR: Come over here, you! I wanna talk to you. What's your story? How come you go, "Hello there!" in the park, but never in the Post Office? All you guys, you're always, consistently, in the park behind a tree: "Hello!" Then running away.

FLASHER: I dunno. Cause I read in the papers somebody did it in the park, and I figured that's where you're supposed to do it.

INTERROGATOR: Hm. How come you go 'Hello there!' when you do that?

FLASHER: I dunro. It's a good opening: 'Hello there!' It's friendly.

INTERROGATOR: Well, do you ever get any acceptance with this, like, '*Hey,* that's *terrific!*'?

FLASHER: Na. It's, ah, it all happens so quick—I just get punched in the mouth and they take me to jail, and that's it.

INTERROGATOR: But you keep on doing it. You must find it sexually stimulating.

FLASHER: No—I'm a celibate.

INTERROGATOR: You're a *what?*

FLASHER: Yeah. It's no sex bit with me. I just, ah, see, I had bad acne when I was a kid, and, ah, you'd be surprised the attention you get with this:

"Look at that guy! He took it out in the park!

And *showed* it to people . . ."

And they make a fuss over you, they put your picture in the paper—it's a hell of a half-hour once a year.

INTERROGATOR: Well, if you don't like to get arrested, why don't you figure out some gimmicks— get a very expensive hat, make believe you're sleeping on a park bench, put the hat on it, see, and then wait for some tramp to go by, he steals the hat and you go

"Hello-o-o-o!"

Then *he'll* get arrested.

FLASHER: You think so?

INTERROGATOR: It's worth a try.

FLASHER: Na, I like to stick to the old ways.

INTERROGATOR: Well, do you mind if I see it?

FLASHER: Na, not a chance, mister!

INTERROGATOR: Just clinically, I would like to see it. I wouldn't touch it.

FLASHER: Well . . . awright.

INTERROGATOR: *Why, what a lovely bunch of lilacs!*

FLASHER: Yeah. I'm the only person who's got flowers there. I was in the Mayo Clinic for that.

INTERROGATOR: They really are beautiful flowers! Well, what the hell would anyone arrest you for showing a beautiful bunch of flowers for?

FLASHER: Well, they never see the flowers, you know, they, ah—

"Hello there!"

and they know what it is and they whap me out, punch me, and take me away.

The point? That the society is perverse: Tonight, if I came to your door, knocked on the door, your mother came out, I reached back and just rapped her in the chops and broke away her teeth so she never kisses

210

your child right again, *maybe,* with the endemic laws in this community, *maybe* I would get three to six months for assault and battery. Maybe. But if I go

"HELLO MA!"

I get a year. That's pretty twisted.

Why will you arrest Paul Newman for exposing himself on a bus?

> DRIVER: Mr. Newman, you've got your joint out! *Ahem.* I mean, ah, we don't wanna cause your family embarrassment and all, but, ah, you can't come on the bus that way any more.
>
> NEWMAN: Aww, I can't come any other way!
>
> DRIVER: Well, that's, um, that's kinda hard. Just put it away, now. Here. Just put that away now.
>
> NEWMAN: Hehehehehe!
>
> DRIVER: Come on now, put it away. Come on. I'm gonna call the studio! . . . Hello? It's Paul. He's got it out again.

[*another movie star*] takes it out:

> "Mr. ——, you've got it out!"
>
> "But it's a divining rod!"

Airplane. Guy is sitting there, sacked out, asleep. Fly open, completely exposed. Alright.

Next aisle. Guy's sitting there, looks over, and he pins it, you know:

> "Stewardess! Can I see you for a moment?"
>
> "Yessir? Gum?"
>
> "No. Ah, um, . . . tellya what, ah . . . Can you give me a pencil and paper, please?"
>
> "Yessir."
>
> "Thankyou.
>
> > 'Dear Sir.
> >
> > > I'm seated across the aisle from you, and your fly is open and you're completely ex-

posed. And I knew this note would avoid any embarrassment.

Yours Truly,
Frank Martin.

P.S.: I love you.' "

Dig what happened to me once. You always hear those stories—you know, of guys being fooled by faggots dressed up as ladies. I was working the Jazz Workshop, across the street from Finocchio's, and it was right after closing, weird, two in the morning, and this chick came up, and she was about six feet tall—really a beautiful chick. She hit on me.

She says, "Look, I'm not the man, I not a hustler, and, ah, I got eyes, I'd like to hang out with ya."

Well, she looked a little too pretty, and faggots have that kind of knack of taking the best from all chicks. And she looked like she had electrolysis. So I was with my friend, we were in a cab, you know, and right away I want to kiss her. You know, Christ!

I say, "Are you a guy?"

She says, "No, I always go through that."

Dig. She's over six feet tall, and dig where she comes from—Texas. So that really allows her any gawkiness.

So I said to her, I said, "Well, it's really bugging me. I think you're a guy."

But I'm not gonna be *that* gauche—"Lift up your dress!" And it really did bug me, you know. So then we get up to the pad—we're staying at the St. Francis, in San Francisco—and she goes to the bathroom, and I said to my friend, I say, "Christ! If that chick is a . . ."

He says, "Well, what's so important?"

I say, "I dunno, man, but I'm gonna flip out." I said, "If she comes out of the bathroom and says something like 'I never take my girdle off,' one of those kinda sticks, you know—"

Sure enough, she comes out in a good black job.

I said, "You're gonna have to take the girdle off, really, cause I can't—I don't care what you do, what you don't do, but, ah, it's gonna be weird. If you need a shave in the morning, it's gonna be forget-it-city."

So finally I split—it just got to be too much for me, the pressure.

Transvestite—that's what Goering was. I love that. Imagine the trouble Hitler had! Isn't that amazing? Goering was a transvestite! And a morphine addict.

In the bunker with him:

GOERING [*Effeminate voice calling down*]: Yoohoo!
HITLER [*Outraged*]: Take that housedress off! Shut up! I've had enough trouble with you people now!"

He really had a cartoon cast—Goebbels, Goering—weird time. That's it.

Poor Hitler. Hitler's alive, you know. He made a deal—he's hiding in the *Police Gazette* office.

Faggots . . . Dig. Isn't the argument against pornography—selling pornography, making it available to the public? That the man is happily married, or he's just a happy cat, and you come along with some matter the predominant appeal of which is to his prurient interest. And what you're doing, you're entrapping him. You're inciting him. Something that the guy wouldn't be thinking of ordinarily—you're getting him horny. You're getting it up, and you're not getting it off, and you're creating a clear and present danger. And it's worthless, and so that's the objection to it. And that's a valid objection.

But when I hear about faggots who get arrested in toilets, I say

"How'd you get arrested in a toilet?"

"Oh, I accosted a peace officer."

213

"Well, that's certainly no concept of *reality*, I mean, you certainly—"

"Well, I didn't know he was a peace officer."

"What do you mean?"

"Well, he didn't have any uniform on."

"Well, he wasn't wearing a costume, was he? He wasn't wearing a low-cut gown—"

What a low-cut gown to a faggot must be is like tight Levis with a padded basket.

"—I mean, he wasn't wearing Levis and leaning up against the urinal like this—sultry—like that, was he? Cause if he was, that's bullshit, then. Cause he was appealing to your prurient interest, then. And entrapping you. You can't do that."

It's a funny thing, all the different stages that we've all gone through. My generation was so—well, me, *phew!* Such hangups about ever being called a faggot that I'm amazed at any guy who can go into a public toilet and do *anything* but *piss and leave!*

Guys who can wash their hands are amazing to me. I just unbutton, *psshhhhht!* up! out!

"Wait, I want to talk to you!"

"Not in here—are you kidding?"

Cause if somebody said

"What are you doing in that toilet?"

"I dunno, ah, uh, heh heh . . ."

"What were you doing in there! Did you make?"

"Yeah, I did, ah . . ."

"Alright. But don't hang around here. O.K."

Old Jewish mothers never know when their sons are faggots. They just miss it somehow. Out-and-out screaming queens—mothers are never hip. I know a guy, lived with his mother for years, a real orthodox Jewish woman, the whole bit. They lived in Brooklyn. And

214

this guy is such a faggot, he's a truckdriver. That's how in he is: he passed through interior decorating, hair-dressing—now he's driving trucks, already. And there's no pretense—no pastels, berets, scarfs; he wears like Lerner dresses. Corrective shoes. Out of it, completely. He lived with his mother for years.

Now, they move to Miami. And I didn't see these people in ten years, so I go look them up, you know. Knock at the door—comes out, he's wearing an Anna Mae Wong dress. So he goes

> HIGH VOICE: "Oh! Lenny! Jutht a minute, I'll go put thomething on."

> "Where are you going, *schmuck?* I know you, man."

> "Talk to my mother."

Dig the mother, how unaware she is:

> [*Heavy Jewish accent*] "Lenny, I'm gonna tell you something about Ronny, you're not gonna believe it."

And I go "Oh, oh, somebody copped out on him."

> "What is it Mrs. Nadel?"

> "You're not gonna believe it—Ronny still didn't get married!"

Oh what a shock that is. Christ, that's beautiful.

> "Whatsa matter with him?"

> MOTHER: I dunno. Maybe he's waiting for the right person. And you know? He ain't got a quarter. He's so good-natured. A night don't go past he don't bring some poor serviceman home, he ain't got a place to sleep.

> "Oh yeah. I don't wanna hear any more about this, Mrs. Nadel."

> MOTHER: But they don't appreciate him. They punch him! They stole his cufflinks!

> "I'm hip. I know, I know."

215

"He loves Halloween!"

"All right, get outta here!"

[*Television star*] took transvestitism to championship bowling, and upset all the dikes that control that field. He has really opened up my eyes. — has been doing swish gag jokes on television for, what is it? Eighteen years? Anyway, since faggots are such conformists, all the young kids, the twelve-year-old, fifteen-year-old faggots, are living up to —, taking their tune from —. And in the most provincial towns people know what faggots look like, from — —: there's a fag.

But there's never been a big dike on television—not one that I could spot. It's hard to spot dikes, cause sometimes we're married to them.

So you can pin a faggot right away; but a butch? Uh uh. Cause there hasn't been that much exposure. So, consequently, in small towns lesbians get away with murder.

I go into a town, see chicks—a real obvious diesel dike with a Bruce Cabot face, Sweet-Orr gown, leather zipper jacket, short hair, no nails, army shoes, really classic—and the people are never hip. The top comment you'll hear is:

"That Mrs. Anderson, she's a real tomboy!"

"Tomboy. I'm hip, man."

"Boy, she can hit a baseball farther than a guy can!"

"Yeah. Uh huh. That's right. What does she do for a living?"

"She's the girlscout master."

"Oh. Cool."

She's a troop-*fresser*.

Now, dike is vernacular for lesbian. Dike is WAKs, WAVEs, policeladies, all those kind of jobs. Oh yeah.

That's a definite dike position. That's a *mensch* job. Now the reason you do a lot of faggot jokes—as opposed to dike jokes—is cause dikes'll really punch the shit out of you. That's all. And it's embarrassing, too, you know. They come in here with rings on all the time. And the only cop-out is: "Ah, you're lucky you're not a man!"

Thank god. And they punch you again.

That's strange—that lesbians have never got any approval. That's an interesting facet to go into. I'm not a dike knocker, I like dikes—that's what Will Rogers once said, "I never met a dike I didn't like."

Somehow queens have always, like, swung; but dikes? Never. No, they never get in anywhere—except trucks.

You know, it's really weird. You've heard, no doubt, that [*movie star*] is a faggot. Course you've heard it. I've heard it, and everything's in the papers:

"— —'s a fag. He's a fruit."

"Yeah, — —'s a fag. A fag."

I started thinking about it. I mean, he doesn't *look* like a faggot to me. Then I find out there's two hookers, who don't know each other—East Coast, West Coast—that balled him. So if he gave up some bread for some trim, well, then he just can't be a faggot.

Double gaited? No. That's some bullshit some faggot made up. I mean, I never did meet any cat who was double gaited. You dig chicks, or you don't, man.

It's very possible that — — is *very* sexual. He's just probably a very horny cat—makes it with guys, chicks, mud, sheep, anything: his fist. He's a real *haisser*—that could be, couldn't it?

Like all of us: me, you, you, you—put us on a desert island for five years, no chicks, you'll ball mud. *Emmis.* You *have,* man. *Knotholes.*

"Are you kidding?—What are you doing next to

217

that tree, you slob you? What are you doing? *Schtupping* a tree!"

"It's *my* tree."

"Your back'll get crooked."

I challenge this audience. I challenge your manhood. I will give you—hear me well (and the owner will back me up)—one thousand dollars. I will pay for the lie-detector test. The daddy of the polygraph is here in this town. His name is Reed. Now if it's good enough for Brinks and Powers, it's good enough for you and me.

You take the lie-detector test. The purpose is to stop casting the first stone: you cannot cast the first stone if you're stoned in front.

I challenge your manhood. Because if "homosexual" means—like the cliche, no such thing as being a *little* pregnant—if faggot means ever involved with a homosexual, active or passive, then I just *know* I'm looking at a room full of fags. Isn't that weird? Whether you were two years old or six years old, any time that scoutmaster or gym coach jacked you off to a Tillie and Mack book, your Uncle Donald wanted to kiss you, or that truck driver that jacked you off when you were hitchhiking on Merrick Road, or you were experimenting and playing doctor—that's it, Jim: you're a sometimes fag.

That's the worst thing you can call us, right? Goddamn, man. It really bugs guys to call them faggot.

We're all whores. How bout that? I sat next to a whore in a plane. She didn't know that—till I told her.

The plane took off, and she went and grabbed my wrist, *boy!* And just squeezed it and started sweating—chick was really scared—squeezed my wrist! Finally, about forty minutes later, *phew!*

And I said, "You know, that shoulda been a great lesson to you. Tell ya why. Because supposing we were in an elevator and I, I grabbed you by the waist. You'd

218

probably call the heat. Cause there was no need for me. But when the need was there, Hey Daddy!

"Yeah. Two dollars, five dollars, any goddamn thing, but get some ass for you Jim and gimme something. You didn't need two dollars—you needed that. But you sold out for the need. Yeah."

So you can't look down your nose at any hookers. Uh uh! No.

Hooker—that's a colloquialism for prostitute—though the word hooker is correct. The word prostitute has been neologized. Too many guys have "prostituted their art." All these men all over the world:

"I'm prostituting myself. I can't work for them. I'm not gonna prostitute myself any longer!"

Now, some Shriner says to the bell captain,

"Son, go get me a one-hundred-dollar prostitute."
"Yessuh."

Ten minutes later a guy comes to the door with a beard. He writes—some *schmuck:*

"Good evening. I'm a prostitute."
"Not for me, you're not. Get outta here. And get the bell captain outta here. He's a bit weird."

But hookers aren't gratifying, cause they won't kiss you on the mouth. They save that for their husbands. That's really weird. I wonder why they won't kiss you? And that's all guys go to whore-houses for—to get kissed and hugged. That's the truth, boy. It's really weird.

A hooker's icebox—a piece of parsley pasted to the side, a black carrot and a bouillon cube. There's never anything to eat in hookers' apartments. They never have anything in their iceboxes.

And Jews are famous—after they ball, they're always *schlepping* to the icebox. Nothing in the icebox:

"Hey, haven't you got anything to eat here?"

"I got, ah, an orchid."

Schmuck eats the orchid.

Religious hookers are good to ball, because the statues always hit you on the head. And the candles are burning . . .

I don't see any chicks that turn me on any more. Here's how I know I'm getting old—I haven't seen any girls that really stimulate me, that look good to me. And it's really corny, but dig what I miss: lipstick and powder. That weird? I like 'em with paint on 'em. To smell like ladies. And if I really get racy, pancake makeup; and a cheap black crepe dress that's low-cut.

Are there any real tits left? Damn your silicone!

"Are they real?"

"I *told* ya they're real!"

"How will I ever know, though?"

"They're real."

"Will you take a lie-detector test that those are your own tits?"

"Yes, I told you I would."

"I can't believe . . . I dunno . . . They're too *real* to be real."

You know, the wonderful elastic phrase in the law, that, you know, applying contemporary community standards —cause there's always a shift in values, of what's decent. And my generation—it's weird—it's not that it's immoral, but I'd be embarrassed at a planned parenthood clock. It would just, *Phew!* I could never make it, ever. And the younger person would say,

"Well, that's bullshit, I mean, you do that, don't you?"

"Yeah, but, it can't be that prepared."

"Well, it's prepared anyway. You *know* you're gonna make it."

"Yeah, but, but but, but *that precise,* you know,
DING, DONG, DING, DONG!

It's just, it's like I'm working in a *whore*house. I
dunno."

And what if it goes off and somebody's over there, you
know:

"Go ahead! We'll eat and sit in the other room."

"No, no. That's alright . . ."

Yeah, it's just, my generation was hung up with that.

Now Scranton, Goldwater, that generation, the over-
forty-five people, and the people who live in the towns
and are only twenty years old but still are the over-forty-
five people, that generation was so concerned about the
absence of sex—when the banner was VIRGIN IS
BEST—that they are truly the most erotic, horny people
in the world.

Dig, you know what a beautiful duo is? German and
Irish. They are winner chicks. That is the most *goyish
goyish*—I'll show you an example.

It's the kind of thing, like—*shicksas.* Well, it's not that
Jewish chicks are lushes, are not attractive, but it's just
that pink-nippled, freckled, *goyisha punim*—that is
hais, boy, that is a rare tribe. And Elizabeth Taylor—
even if I can't *see* the mustache, I know she's got it.
That's all. It's enough. And a mole with the hair in it.
It's just a cooking thing the pharaohs have. O.K.?

That's why I can never get married again—I'm insatia-
ble. Just looking—I won't touch or talk to, but I really
dig looking at chicks. Boy, they're really pretty.

The Dirty-word Concept

If you've ever seen this bit before, I want you to tell me, stop me.

I'm going to piss on you.

Now, I tell you this because some of the ringsiders have objected to it, and it's just fair to warn you, that's all. I don't make any great show of it—I just do it, and that's all. You can't photograph it—it's like rain.

The point of view there is to help you with bad early toilet training. That fact is that you and I have had such bad early toilet training, that the worst sound in the world to all of us is when that toilet-flush noise finishes before you do. I never could go over to your house and say:

"Excuse me, where's the toilet?"

I have to get hung up with that corrupt facade of

"Where's the little boy's room?"

"Oh, you mean the tinkle-dinkle ha-ha room? Where they have just sashays and cough drops and pastels?"

"Yeah. I wanna shit in the cough-drop box."

"Oh, awright."

The *tsi gurnischt* is what puts you into the toilet every time, Jim. And unfortunately, intellectual awareness does you no good.

And you know why we got this—this is really weird—the censorship? It's motivated by bad early toilet training. Every time—

> OLD WOMAN: He made a *sissy!* Call the police."

Yeah.

> OLD WOMAN: Get the policeman up here, he made a *sissy*. He's not gonna make it no more? Get the probation officer. That's all."

So if you're thirty-six years old, you drive down the street, you see the red light in the rear vision mirror—you just crap out:

> COP: You know what you did?
>
> "Yeah. I made a sissy."
>
> COP: *What?*
>
> "I dunno, I . . . What'd I do?"
>
> COP: You made an illegal left turn!
>
> "Oh, damn, I'm pissed with me. I'm no goddamn good, man."

That's it. That's the dues.

Words, boy, they're too much. Forget it. Let's see. I started in show buisness in '50. I won the Arthur Godfrey Show, then I went to the Strand in New York, then, about ten years ago, I went right into the toilet, *Bong!*

But at this time I did, let's see, the Robert Q. Lewis Show, Broadway Open House, Arthur Godfrey and His Friends Show, and the comment of the day was:

> "Lenny, you're gonna go a long way, because you're
> —you're not like those other comics, you don't
> have to resort to filthy toilet jokes. Anybody can
> get a laugh on toilet jokes, but you're clever . . ."

And I started thinking about that. I was proud, but then

223

I started thinking, "How dirty is my toilet?" Yeah. That's sort of strange, that I have to resort to it, or even protest against it, or my bedroom—toilet jokes, bedroom jokes.

Then I would just lay in bed, and I wouldn't even say that word at that time, you know, I'd just think it, you know, then I'd thunder out of the bedroom and dash open the door and

> "*Look* at you, you *dirty, dopey, Commie toilet,* you! And the tub and the hamper—you should know better."

Alright. I'm going to do something you never thought I'd do on stage. I'm going to a bit now that I was arrested for. I'm going to tell you the dirtiest work you've ever heard on stage. It is just *disgusting!*

I'm not going to look at you when I say it, cause this way we won't know who said it. I may blame that cat over there. It's a four-letter word, starts with an 's' and ends with a 't' . . . and . . . just don't take me off the stage, just . . . don't embarrasss my Mom. I'll go quietly.

The word is—Oh, I'm going to *say* it and just get it *done* with. I'm tired of walking the streets.

[*Whispers*] "Snot!"

I can't look at you. But that's the word: snot. I know alot of my friends are thinking now,

> "He's so clever, and then, for a cheap laugh, he says 'snot.' He don't need that, that disgusting character."

But do you know anything about snot? Except that every time you heard it you go *Phah!* Or *Ich!* or *Keeriste!?* Do you think I would just take snot out of left field and use it for the shock value? *Nada.*

Suppose I tell you something about snot, something that was so unique about snot that you'd go:

> "Is that the *truth* about snot?"

"Look, I'm gonna lie to ya? That's *right*. That's about snot."

"How do ya like that! I never knew that."

Cause you never listen, that's why. If you'd listen all the time, then you'd learn about snot. I'll tell you something about snot—no. I know, you're smug:

"We know all we wanna know about snot. We smoked that stuff when we were kids."

Well, I've done some research about snot. How about this about snot: *you can't get snot off a suede jacket!* Take any suede jacket straight from Davega's and throw it in the cleaners and try to run out of the store:

"*Wait! Stop them!* Alright, block the door. *Get them!* Tell the wife to stand over there. . . . Son, is this your jacket?"

"Well, . . . yeah."

"Son, do you know what this is on the sleeve of the jacket?"

"No."

"*You wanna go downtown?!*"

"No."

"Well, what's on the sleeve?"

"Well . . . ah . . . *snot.*"

"Son, you know you can't get snot off suede. It's a killer. Kills velvet too."

"No, I didn't know that. I didn't know that it was snot."

"*You knew that was snot,* son. You can't get snot off suede. It's ruined. You can flake it off, but the black mark will always be there."

"What'll I do?"

"Just snot all over the whole jacket! That's the only thing you can do."

"Do you do that work?"

"No. There's no money in it. Can't get help."

Now, you've seen a lot of snot. You've seen it in back

of radiators in Milner hotels. Looks like bas-relief wood-glue.

Now, I'm going to show you some snot. Just cause I like you—if I *really* like you, boy! Then it's a show. Would Jack Benny or Bob Hope show you any snot? Fake snot, from the magic store, maybe.

O.K. Snot. Snot that fools old Jewish mothers:

[*Jewish accent*] "You blew your nose in the *Playboy Magazine* again?"

Here we go [*blows his nose*]. I did it! And I did it for one reason: to show you how well adjusted I am. Why do I say I'm well adjusted?

Why?

Cause I didn't look later.

Now we see the same man, not well adjusted. See? Slow motion.

A lot of people say to me,

"Lenny, how come you don't look later?"

A lot of people ask me that:

"You never look *once?*"

"Nope! Nope. If you've seen one, you've seen 'em all."

Now I got a handful of snot! That's what I got.

"Which hand has the M&M? Agh! *Snot!*"

I'm going to take it and put it on the piano. Now, when the pianist comes back for the intermission, she'll think it's a note:

"Oh, a request! They haven't forgotten the old tunes. Strange envelope. . . . *Foo!* That's *snot!*"

The hangup is that the word repression—I'll tell you better this way. You know—what is it, on Forty-Eighth Street here, next to the Latin Quarter?—Fun Shops, they call them, those whoopee-cushion stores, the stores that sell unjoyous buzzers, vomit, dog-crap. It's really bizarre. It's fool-your-friend, hurt-your-friend, put a fly in his ice-cube.

"We have a cute little article here, it's, it's fake dog crap."

"*What?*"

"Yeah—fake dog shit—very humorous. Ya see, we take this fake dog crap and we put it on the stairs, see"—

"Now who would buy that?"

"Oh, there's a market for it."

"Well, it doesn't seem very humorous to—"

"Oh yeah—cause you can take it two ways, see? It's *double entendre*. It could be real dog shit or fake dog crap. And then we have this fake vomit—"

"*Now get the hell outta here!* There's no market—"

"I'm tellin' ya there's a market for it. You just donno how it works, see?"

"Well, just don't bring the samples up here, that's all."

"Look. I mean, just picture this. See, here's what happens. The guy comes home, see? The wife puts the fake dog shit on the stairs. The real vomit or the fake vomit or the real dog shit and the fake vomit, see. And he comes home and goes

'*Yippee! Dog shit!*'

And he grabs it and goes

'Ahhh, it's *fake!* Oh, here's some vomit!'

That's fake too, and then he cries his eyes out— and that's the fun. That's after he drinks the fly in the sugar cube."

"Well, I dunno. That's certainly, a weird kind of humor."

If I could just rob fifty words out of your head I could stop the war. Just like that, Jim! It would end. *Pow!*

Fifty words. Semantics. *Pchew! PowPowPow!* Take 'em away.

Hotel—three in the morning—filthy word. Motel—every "well" comedian, as opposed to the "sick" comedian, has given motels such a *schmutz* connotation that I couldn't ask my *grandmother* to go to a motel if I wanted to give her a Gutenburg Bible.

So hotel is dirty and motel is dirty—where's there a clean place to take some lady? A clean word that won't offend anyone.

Trailer!

> GUY: Hey, do you wanna come to my trailer?
> GIRL: All right. There's nothing dirty about trailers. Trailers are hunting and fishing and Salem cigarettes. Yes. Yes, of course I'll come to your trailer. Where is it?
> GUY: Inside my hotel room.

Then it's dirty again, man.

Here's a tip how the word suppression, the dirty words that you swallow, are a deterrent to this community. There is a disease called leukemia. Leukemia, there's no specific cure for. Talking about leukemia certainly would not help it. Here's a disease that's above that. How come? Cause no one talks about it. In fact, when the Community Chest hits on you, do you say,

> "Excuse me, how much of my buck is going to the clap?"

Did you? No, I don't think you did. Why didn't you?

> [*Aggressive male voice*] "Well son, I don't ask about the clap because only bums get it."
> "Oh, I see."
> "And communists!"

And seven million war heroes that must be bums and communists.

"Awright, whaddya wannus to do? Just get some people that's had it not to cop out?—

    ELEANOR ROOSEVELT GAVE LOU
    GEHRIG THE CLAP!"

"O.K., that's good."

"Gave it to Chiang Kai-shek, too. That's why he couldn't get the puttees on."

You see, if you or I ever had it, the doctor would never cop out to us. Lose the account?

"Mrs. Schekner, you got the clap."

Forget it!

"Little discharge, dear, we're gonna give you a little, ah, tell you what, ah, I got a little, ah, vitamin-booster, a little penicillin."

No. She's not hip. No.

I wonder: if I were to work to a Bert Parks kind of audience—he smiles when he defecates—and I were to ask,

"Hey, I wonder how many of the family people out here, how many of the daughters—fifteen-year-olds and older—might have the clap?"

I'm sure there would be a portion of the audience that would want to punch me out.

Wouldn't you assume that the guy who would feel some hostility towards me for verbalizing, just asking that question, if his daughter had the clap—what if his daughter *had* the clap? Is she going to go to her daddy? I doubt it.

And V.D., right up on top—although with Aureomycins you could whack it out in one day. But it stays there.

"Well, you see, leukemia you get in a respectable way, that's all. You know how you get the clap, and, ah . . ."

Because, *doing it,* well, that's about the dirtiest thing we can do. But dig how we have screwed the country. Dig what the good-good culture's done to you.

You only know this if you're about thirty-five or so, and you made at least some of the war, the good war, the war that I was in, from '42 to '45. And you know that if that four-letter word is dirty and doing it is dirty —the good people don't do it, nuns and priests don't do it, and someday we're going to rise above the physical and the carnal, the lustful—well, you agree that it's not the nicest act. In fact, you don't want me to do it to your mother or your sister. You get arrested for doing it in the street. It's a filthy, rotten act.

That's why they don't like Americans anywhere. That's why we have lost the world completely—because we fucked all of heir mothers for chocolate bars. And don't you forget it, Jim. Don't ever forget that.

And if you don't think those kids have heard that since 1942—that bumper crop—those kids that now are twenty-three years old, that's now in control—

"Do you know what happened? Do you know what those Americans did to your poor mother while your poor father threw up his guts in the next room while those soldiers lined up your mother for their stinking eggs and the chocolate bars and their friggin cigarettes? *Those bastards!* What they did with their money over here!"

And that goes from Marseilles, St. Tropez, all the way, Jim, to Constantinople. That's all they've heard, Jim. Those cats over there were duking with their bread.

Now, intellectual awareness does them no good. They know, like, if *I'm* hungry, I'll sell my sister's ass for an egg. It doesn't do any good knowing it: it happened, Jim.

If this society was the least little bit correct, if religion helped it out a little bit, and that act was the least bit the antithesis of what is perverse, and you felt that it was a true Christian act of procreation, if it was sweet hugging and kissing—watch. The fellow comes off the plane:

BRITISH VOICE: Is that the fellow who fucked Mother? Oh, yes! How *are* you? *Damn,* I haven't seen you in *so* long, and you're such a *wonderful* person. You certainly made Mother feel *good.* I certainly would like to *thank* you—that certainly was a nice thing to do. And I understand you gave her some candy besides.

But we don't agree that it's a nice act. It's a filthy, dirty act. In fact, that's what any eighteen-year old chick or thirty-year-old chick will tell you when you take her out:

"You don't *love* me, you just want to *ball* me."

Boy! Listen to that:

GIRL: He was a *nice* guy—he didn't try to fool around with me. But *you* don't love me, you just want to ball me.

GUY: *What?* Of course I love you—I wouldn't want to sleep with you if I didn't love you.

GIRL: No, no. If you loved me you'd drive me to Wisconsin; punch me in the mouth; read the Bible to me all night; you'd borrow money from me. You wouldn't want to ball me. You don't do that to someone you love—you do that to somebody you hate. Really *hate.*

In fact, when you *really* hate them, what's the vernacular we use?

"*Screw you,* mister!"

If you were taught it was a sweet Christian act of pro-creation, it was the nicest thing we can do for each other, you'd use the term correctly, and say

"*Un*screw you, mister."

But the best people in the tribe don't do it.

But you won't admit that—that they think doing it is dirty, filthy. They'll never admit that the clap is here— they'll never admit that their son *has* it. Their son has the clap—where can the son go? Can that boy go to his father? *Bullshit* he can go to his old man. He could never relate to his father. He can't even go to the doctor; he's lucky if he can go to some *schmuck* who sweeps up a drugstore:

"Hey Manny, mop later, can I talk to ya?"

"What is it?"

"I got the clap."

"You? Where'd ya get that?"

"Painting a car, *schmuck!* What's the difference? I got it."

"So whaddaya want from me? Why don't you go to your father? Why don't ya go to a doctor?"

"I can't. Gimme some pills—you work in a drug store."

"Awright. Here."

"Dexedrine spansules . . . Is this good?"

"Yeah, it's all the same horseshit. This is good—keeps you awake, so you know you got it."

"Awright. The reason I want these pills, I got a good job, and I donwanna lay off."

"Oh yeah? Where ya working?"

"The meat-packing plant. Want a couple of steaks?"

"No! Just burn the doorknobs on the way out. Do me a favor—stop kissing my mother goodbye, O.K."

Maybe Jerry Lewis would go on television, and instead of getting hung up with muscular dystrophy, he'd have a Clap-a-thon.

Dear Anne Landers:

This summer I met a boy on vacation, and I fell madly in love with him, even though he admitted he had a boy back home. As a result of our affection I became in a motherly way. I'm all mixed up—I'm only three years old. What'll I do?

232

Dear Knocked Up:
  Call Doctor Mendoza, Tijuana 1-7300.

It's very tough. It's very tough to stop the information.
That's where it's all at. Because the word itself is of no
censequence. What the constitution forbids is any bar
to the communication system. It doesn't want nobody
to abridge the right to say it one time, and one time to
hear it.
  Because the information makes the country strong.
Because a knowledge of syphillis is not an instruction to
get it. Because if you don't have the knowledge of it, and
you just know about the good, and they just let the good
come through, seeping through, what they think is good,
you end up like Hitler. Cause he really got screwed
around like that. He kept saying,
      HITLER: Am I doing all right?
      FIRST AIDE: You're doing *great!* They *love* you.
      HITLER: Don't bullshit, Marty. Someday they don't
      like me—
      FIRST AIDE: They *love* you!
      SECOND AIDE: Don't listen to those liars!
      HITLER: *Kill him!* Who said that?

Now, the daughter that you love, yeah, the daughter that
you love, the daughter that you kill in the back of a taxicab because of a bad curettage—that's how you love
that daughter, because she's a tramp, because she's got
life in her belly and she ain't got a hoop on her finger
that some witch doctor blessed—that's how you love
that daughter. That's that *roch munas* you've got for that
daughter, that she can just talk to her old man just like
that. Snap! When I hear that cat saying,
      "Ah, that tramp! My wife's a tramp, and I got cus-
      tody of my kids."

233

"You're wife's a tramp? Whaddaya mean—sterno, and the woods and all?"

"No, you know what kinda tramp I mean."

"No I don't, man, I dunno what kinda tramp you mean at all."

"She goes to bed with guys."

"Well that's certainly a very Christian act. I can't think of anything nicer to do for any guy."

"Yeah, but she does it in front of the kids."

Well, I am not that well adjusted yet, but you know, man, I would rather your kids see that than you yelling at your old lady or whacking her out. In fact, I guess it really is no deterrent to his growth to see that, no. Isn't that the nicest time? Or is balling just balling? Or is it just that—you just carry around a little aspirin box and make it with that:

"Gimme a little bufferin."

"There it is—a buck and a half."

Chungchungchung! That's it.

The dirty-word concept is beautiful. Postmaster Summerfield is concerned with reporting any pornography and any Tilly and Mack books you have lying around. Right? Now, for your child, who is perhaps in the formative years, for his viewing in the schoolyard are the dirty books, the smut peddlers which Postmaster Summerfield is concerned with—and justly so: these are formative years. But how about some other films that he's not concerned with?

Psycho, for example. If your kid's going to see a dirty movie, and be affected by it, then you must assume he'll be affected by *Psycho.* We have Anthony Perkins, a psychotic misogynist who kills a beautiful chick, Janet Leigh. No reason at all, man. Method: stabbing in the shower, blood down the drain. Method of disposal of body: wrapping it in the shower curtain, *schlepping* it to the swamp, doing her in. For no purpose, man—death, destruction.

Now, the stag movie, the dirty movie—the sixteen millimeter reduction print that you drag from lodge hall to lodge hall, the dirty movie that the Kefauver committee would destroy and then recreate for private parties. Let's inspect the subject matter. What are they doing, that couple?

I can't think of anybody getting killed in that picture. I can't see anyone getting slapped in the mouth, rapped around. Is there any hostility in that film? No. Just a lot of hugging and kissing. And the first time one instrument of death appeared—that pillow that might have smothered the chick—it went under her ass, and that was the end of the picture.

Please tell me what the hell the couple is doing that's that rank, vicious, rotten. The only thing I find offensive in that film is that from an art concept, cinematically, it's a bore. Yeah, those *schtup* pictures—forget it, man. No idea of the sensual, there's no music track, you know. But as far as hurting your child—what are they doing, that couple?

No. It's vicious and rotten and dirty—that you've bred a generation of faggots and misogynists, lady-haters and homosexuals.

Well, it's part of our culture that we teach our children: "These are your eyes, your nose, your mouth—and your *ga-ga*." Part of the guilt for the dirty I'm sure relates back to several hundred thousands of years ago—when everybody was giving up something for the Lord—and how guys would cap each other and wait around, and put it up on the bulletin board, and one guy said,

> "I love the Lord better'n anybody in the tribe. I'm giving up nine rivers for the Lord. Write it down. How about you?"

"Seventeen rivers, ten farms. That's for the Lord. How about you?"

"Well, today I'm gonna be the best man in the tribe cause I'm giving up seventy-eight rivers, fifty-five farms, ten sheep, six oxen, and a mountain for the Lord."

And St. Paul just watched these people, and after everyone had chucked in, and the best man in the tribe had stated he was best man by giving it almost all away, St. Paul said,

"Wait a minute! Before you give out the prize for the best man in the tribe, I'm going to give up something for the Lord you'll all remember: *F-U-C-K NO MORE PAUL!* That's it!"

"Hey, Paul, are you bullshittin or somtin? You're givin at up? Faw how long?"

"I'm giving it up for ever and ever!"

"Just to prove a point, huh? Well, that's *ridiculous.* He's, ah . . ."

"The best man in the tribe."

Why?

"Cause I don't do it, that's why. You who do it—second best. And you who *talk* about it—*we'll bust your ass.* Celibacy is the way."

It's the clean way, it's the best way. So all the *schtuppers* . . . turn into *fressers!* Ha ha! Didn't figure on that! That would really be weird.

Now. You'd assume that in a society that says, "Alright, this is clean; this is dirty"—that in the entertainment capital of that society, the entertainment capital of the world, Las Vegas, that the attraction would be the most austere. What's the attraction at Las Vegas?

"Well, at the Stardust we have the Passion Play."

"Correct; then they're consistent. What follows the Passion Play?"

"Well, I think they're having a Monet exhibit, then Eugene Ormandy and the New York City ballet. It's a very spiritual type of show."

Is that the attraction that all the purists support in Las Vegas? No. What's the attraction? Tits and ass.

"I beg your pardon?"

"Ah, tits and ass, that's what the attraction is."

"Just tits and ass?"

"Oh, no. An Apache team and tits and ass."

"Well, that's about all I actually go to see—the Apache team. And that's just one hotel. What's the second biggest attraction?"

"More tits and ass."

"Get off it! The third?"

"Tits and ass, and more ass, and tits, and ass and tits and ass and tits and ass."

"Do you mean to tell me that *Life* magazine would devote three full pages to tits and ass?"

"Yes. Right next to the article by Billy Graham and Norman Vincent Peale. *Life* and *Look* and *Nugget* and *Rogue* and *Dude* and *Cavalier* and *Swank* and *Gent* and *Pageant* (the Legion of Decency's *Playboy*) and millions of other stroke books—the antecedent to *Playboy, National Geographic* with the African chicks—oh yes, they're stroke books."

It takes the seriousness out of everything if you can imagine Kennedy in back of the bathroom door whacking it to Miss July once in a while. I stroke it once in a while; I assume he does.

"Ah, well, that may be the truth, but you just can't put TITS AND ASS NITELY up on the marquee outside on the strip."

"Why not?"

"Why not! Cause it'd *dirty* and *vulgar*, that's why not!"

237

"Titties are dirty and vulgar? Well, they're not to me. I like to hug 'em and kiss 'em."

"No, you're not going to bait me. It's not the titties, it's the words, the way you relate."

"I don't believe you. I believe to you it's the titty that's dirty. Cause I'll change the words to TUCH-USES AND NAY-NAYS NITELY.

"Hmmmm. That's a little better."

"Well, you're not anti-semitic. That's point one for you. But how about making it very austere—Lat-in: GLUTIUS MAXIMUS AND PECTORALIS MAJORS NITELY."

"Now that's *clean!*"

"To you, *schmuck,* but it's dirty to the Latins. And the fact that you're an illiterate doesn't get you off the hook."

"Well, I don't care what you say, you just can't put TITS AND ASS up there. You have to have some-thing a little, ah—LA NOVELLE VOGUE! LA PARISIENNE!"

"Ah, the Follies! Lou Walters! French tits and ass. Class with ass."

"I'll buy that. Unless I can have something patri-otic—how about THE MOST AMERICAN GIRLS IN THE WORLD?"

"American tits and ass—Grandma Moses' tits and Norman Rockwell's ass: draw my ass and win a Buick. My ass you can draw; you can draw my ass! My ass you can draw."

That's why the *word* isn't dirty—the *titties* are dirty. Oh yeah. The titties are *filthy*. That's why you can't have a marquee reading

TITS AND ASS NITELY

Uh um. Cause the titties are dirty and vulgar. And if we deny that—then it's all a lie.

Here's how the titties work. If the titty is bloodied and maimed, it's clean. But if the titty is pretty, it's filthy.

There's a time and place for the titty. That's why you never see any obscenity photos that are atrocity photos. Um Um. Any titty that's cut off and distended, that's good.

Yeah, its really weird.

Eleanor Roosevelt had nice tits. She really did. A friend of mine saw them and said they were terrific. That's not disrespectful; in fact, she would have liked that, I think. Yeah. He walked into the bedroom and she was fixing—

GUY: Excuse me.

ELE: That's all right. You were looking at my tits, weren't you?

GUY: Well, I wasn't looking *at* them, I was looking at everything—the wall, and everything—

ELE: That's all right. You can look at them.

GUY: Uh, they're O.K.

ELE: People say they're the nicest tits ever. Ever ever ever.

GUY: They really are nice tits. Could I touch them?

ELE: No. no. Nope. Cause alot of people want to touch them and then they'd touch them too much. That's all. Just look at them. Just look at them and say they're nice tits.

GUY: Awright—they're nice tits. In fact, I'm gonna tell my friends how nice they are. Heh heh. And what a terrific person you are for showing them to me.

Touch it once, touch it once.

What's "it"? That's what I got busted for: "It". "It" is Clara Bow. But I cannot be superstitious with that, the *double entendre*. Because to me your titties are no joke. They're pretty and they're not humorous to me. It's not a hahaha. That elbow-nudging sly-innuendo hahaha you-know-what-it-means, that Jack Paar with his cool, Alexander King the junkie Mark Twain—your Uncle Willie, who I would never let baby-sit for me. *He's* a nice moralist—when you're eleven years old he's always grabbing your sister:

"What a *nice* little tickle-ikle-ikle!"

"Yeah, I'm hip, you tickle-ikle-ikle."

Obscenity Busts and Trials

I want to read this, cause I like it. This is an arrest report. And employee's report, that's what they call it.

Subject: Obscene show.

Sir:

On the above date and time I attended a Lenny Bruce show at the above location, in the company of policewoman Corlene Schnell, 100643—

in case you ever should see her—

During the half-hour show Bruce used the following words on several occasions:

> bullshit
> shit
> motherfucker
> penis
> asshole.

These words were clearly understood by both policewoman Schnell and myself. The substance of Bruce's dissertation was primarily based on denouncing religions, God, and the police in general, in that order.

Sir:

At the above time and date I attended the entire show of Lenny Bruce with policewoman Schnell.

During this show the following words were used repetitively:

> shit
> bullshit
> motherfucker
> fuck
> asshole.

He had stories regarding unnatural acts with animals, including the Lone Ranger and Tonto, and his horse. The substance of Bruce's shows was a degrading dissertation on the subject of the Jewish religion, God, and the acts of the courts in the United States.

O.K. There's one really great thing in here. Oh yeah. Since this time six teams of officers in this division have viewed the Bruce show, and have submitted 15.7 reports. Some of the other obscene words used by Lenny Bruce are as follows:

> bullshit
> ass
> asshole
> tits
> penis
> pricks
> cocks
> cunts.

He also referred to comic-book characters as dikes and fags.

Now the thing I like about this is that—now this is the last report—and the last report, I can tell that the guy started to listen to me work, cause he says:

> Bruce's show in general made fun of his past experiences with law enforcement and the courts. He also makes fun of all religions and many people that are currently in the news.

On October 23, 1962, at approximately 10 P.M., Sgt.

Klein and Detectives Frawley and Shire attended location of suspects act. Suspect's act primarily centered around sexual activities of various sorts. In one anecdote the suspect described an individual as a, uh, c-o- . .

Alright.

a term used to indicate the act of oral copulation.

Boy it's weird how he heard just that.

Various descriptive words such as "bastard" "asshole" "goddamn" were interjected at various times during the performance.

O.K.

On October 24, 1962 at approximately 10 P.M., Sergeants Block and Klein attended suspect Bruce's show. As a result of what transpired on the previous dates mentioned, District Attorney Hecht was contacted and requested to attend the show for expert advice, which he did. On this date suspect Bruce's act was similar in content to those performances previously mentioned. At one period suspect started complaining to the person controlling the stage lights that they were too bright, and after a brief period during which the lights were not dimmed, suspect looked up to the control booth and hollered, "Where is that dwarf motherfucker?" He subsequently bent over to the first table and said, "He thinks I'm kidding." In one of his anecdotes relating to New York policemen dressed up as women to apprehend mashers he stated, "This would never stop a real rape artist because some of those cops really have nice asses."

Now I didn't say that. See, they're really taking this out of context. What I said, I said—dig how *they hear:* Here's what I said: "There are many transvestites posing as policemen." There's a big difference. [*At this point someone in the audience tells Bruce that the cops are*

243

attending this show] Oh, really? Well, I hope they got a big van. You're all going.

Alright. I said it would be really bizarre if they were dedicated rapists, and it didn't matter, and then all that that they heard. O.K.

On previous dates as well as this date the audience consisted of approximately 50 to 60 patrons. Many of them were females, both young and old. After the completion of the suspect's show on this date the undersigned deputies conferred with District Attorney Hecht who had viewed the show. Deputies were advised that there was sufficient evidence at the time to warrant the issuance of a complaint.

And they arrested me and handcuffed me and took me away in the patrol wagon.

Now, uh, I don't want to get arrested any more. I don't like it. I was arrested in San Francisco—see, I was reading the minutes, that's how I happened to use the term coc—um, the Company C.O. Here's how it happened. In San Francisco I was doing some *ad lib* and I talked about the first time I worked the town, and—you always can tell when there's a bust. Oh, it was really strange when I got arrested here. About twenty minutes before I was arrested I saw the peace officers. I recognized them. I'd never seen them before, but I knew they were peace officers. I really did. I always can spot them. They never need haircuts, and, there's never any hostility, they're just, ah, looking at it.

Now, I figured they're there to see me work—you know, they're enjoying it, and laughing. All of a sudden I see one guy make a move, like, checkmate! One guy stands at the door. Now I'm about to get finished working, I figure he's going to go to the men's room, and oh, oh! I see that guy's making a left, then he's coming up on the stage.

I say, "Oh, I'm getting busted."

He comes up on the stage—and it's on *tape,* it's *beautiful!* You hear the heat busting me. It's too much. It's the most dramatic tape you'll ever hear in your whole life, man. You hear:

STRONG VOICE: All right, folks, that's all. We're vice officers. That's the end of the show. O.K., Lenny, come on.

O.K. Then you hear a little voice going

"I don't have any I.D."

Look. Heat on my left . . . heat on my right. . . . Mmmmmm. . . . How do I know that you're heat? Well, I've never seen anybody sit that way. Hah! That's sort of strange. Now why would the heat be there?

I was arrested for obscenity in San Francisco for using a ten-letter word which is sort of chic. I'm not going to repeat the word tonite. It starts with a "c." They said it was vernacular for a favorite homosexual practice—which is weird, cause I don't relate that word to homosexuals. It relates to any contemporary woman I know or would know or would love or would marry. But they got hung up with faggotry. Alright.

Well, the whole scene was that Dirty Lenny, Dirty Lenny said a dirty word. And I got busted for it, and *schlepped* away in a patrol wagon.

Now when I took the bust, I finished the show—I said that word, you know, the ten-letter word—and the heat comes over and says,

"Ah, Lenny, my name is Sgt. Blah-blah-blah. You know that word you said?"

"I said alotta words out there."

"No. *That* word."

"Oh. Yeah?"

"Well, Lenny, that's against the law. I'm gonna hafta take ya down."

"O.K. That's cool."

245

"It's against the law to say it and to do it."

"But I didn't *do* it, man."

"I know, but, uh, I just have to tell you that."

"O.K."

Now. I get into the wagon. And the one heat is cool. He said, You broke the law, and the specifics, and that's all. Now the other guy:

"You know that word you used? I gotta wife and kids—"

"I don't wanna hear that crap *at all,* man. I don't want to get involved emotionally with this."

"Whaddaya mean you don't wanna hear that crap?"

"I don't wanna hear any of that shit, man, that's all. I don't wanna get involved with personalities. Unless you're that kind of husband that is that loving that he shields his wife from every taboo derogatory phrase. Or are you the kind of husband that maybe just keeps his old lady knocked up and chained to the kitchen and *never* brings her a flower and *does* raise his hand to her and *does* rap her out? But if I say 'shit' in front of her you'll punch me in the mouth—*that* kind of chivalry, man? . . . Did your wife ever do that to you?"

BAM! Then it got very sticky.

"Never!"

"You ever say the word?"

"No."

"Never said it? Honest to God never said it?"

"Never!"

"How long you married?"

"Eighteen years."

"Did you ever chippy on your wife?"

"Never!"

"Never *one* time in *eighteen years?* You never chippied on your old lady?"

"Never!"

"Then goddamnit I love you! Cause you're the kind of husband I would like to have been, cause you're a spiritual guy. But if you're lying, you're going to spend some dead time in purgatory, man. 'Let ye cast the first stone.' "

You know, we really got into it, *into* it.

Now, get into court, take fingerprints. The judge? A tough outside *verbissener. Tough-o.* Right? He comes in:

"Blah-blah-blah. Siddown."

Swear the heat in.

"What did he say?"

"Your Honor, he said blah-blah-blah.

The judge:

"He said *blah-blah-blah?!*"

Then the guy really *yentaed* it up:

"That's right. I couldn't believe it. Up on the stage, in front of women and a mixed audience, he said *blah-blah-blah.*"

The judge:

"This I never heard, blah-blah-blah. He said *blah-blah-blah?*"

"He said *blah-blah-blah!* I'm not going to lie to ya."

It's in the minutes—"I'm not gonna lie to ya." Alright. The D.A.:

"The guy said blah-blah-blah. Look at him. He's *smug.* He's not gonna repent. He's *glad* he said blah-blah-blah!"

Then I dug something: they sort of *liked* saying blah-blah-blah. Because they said it a few extra times. They really got *so* involved, saying blah-blah-blah. The bailiff is yelling, "What'd he say?"

"Shut up, you blah-blah-blah."

They were *yelling* it in the court.

"He said blah-blah-blah."

"Blah-blah-blah!"

"Goddamn! It's *good* to say blah-blah-blah."

"That blah-blah-blah!"

O.K. Now, we're into the second day of it, and the judge kept *schlepping* me out about his grandchildren, his grandchildren. What if his grandchildren? And I said, *boy,* am I *that much* of a despot? Is he sincere about his grandchildren? How would I know, how could I find out? The only way would be to entrap him. Cause if he would get that much out of line, then that kisses off the grandchildren.

We're both from the same tribe, so I know what kind of chick to get. Boy, that's one thing the *goyim* got, are chicks, man, *winner* chicks! So I say, Let's see, what chick do I know? I know one chick who is really perfect for the part—a combination kindergarten teacher and hooker. Yeah.

Now, I tell her, Sweetie, look, do me a favor. I want to entrap the judge. And we talked it over. And so I said, You gotta be very cool, you can't come on with him; he'll freeze right away. Be very cool. Meet in the elevator of the courthouse. Have a heart attack, a slight one, cause all Jews identify with sickness.

And she goes into the elevator: "OH!" *Thunk.*

He runs over, "What's the matter with you?" Rubs her wrist, gives her the dopey Jewish doctor speech:

> "Look, you're a young girl, your body is like an automobile. If you give it too much gas, and the clutch—"

That crappy dumb parallel. Alright.

But to get him to a pad is very tricky. Drive drive drive drive drive. If she said she had to change clothes, he would freeze. Cause he'd wait in the car. To change a bandage—that's legit. He can watch her take a bandage, nothing dirty about a bandage. But a bandage may make it less than sensual.

Sup-hose! Perfect. A little vericosity. *"Oi,* got sup-hose?" And he's digging her. How do we get her over to the sack? Another heart attack.

"OH!" *Boom.*

He runs over.

"What's the matter, *another* heart attack?"

"Oh, Judge, I'm just so embarrassed, I'm just in from Oklahoma—"

It's horny enough to be white, but Oklahoma, it's such an *ofay,* the Jews'll go blind if they look at her.

"—I'm in from Oklahaoma. I was doin a benefit for the crippled Catholic Jewish war children from the Ronald Reagan post, in memory of Ward Bond. And you've been so good to me—"

And she kisses his hand, very dry, very respectable, except a little wet at the end.

Now the second heart attack had one deft move—a pop-off bra, toreador pants, *Pow!*

Now we have to record all this, see? How to record it? Six months previous, a genius operation, a tape recorder set inside the throat: no wires, one small goiter scar.

Now the damnation.

CHICK: Judge?

JUDGE: Uh.

CHICK: I wanna tell you something, but I'm afraid that, oh, that you're gonna think that I'm, oh, perverse.

JUDGE: Look, who's to say vuts normal? It's what?

CHICK: Well, I—do you know why I was attracted to you?

JUDGE: Why?

CHICK: You remind me of my grandfather.

JUDGE: That makes you *hais, meschugenah,* you like that, right?

CHICK: Yeah, and I would, it would sorta knock me out if you would sort of enjoy the phantasy with me, and imagine I was your granddaughter.

JUDGE: Alright, *meschugenah,* you like that? What'll I say?

CHICK: Just, "*Zug* me, Zeda."

JUDGE: *Vuss?*

CHICK: Tell me I'm only six years old.

JUDGE: Alright. You're six years old.

CHICK: Do you like giving it to your grand-daughter?

JUDGE: Do I? *Take it, Zeda! Give it to me, tochter! That's it, take it; sock it to me, give it to me, you Litvak Lolita!*

That's all. Play that back in court:

TAPE RECORDING: *Give it to me Zeda. Rip me Zeda. Sock it to me Zeda. Give it to me you Litvak Lolita.*

That's the end of the lower court. That just blows it right there.

For four days the testimony in the court in San Francisco we heard

"He did a man and a woman who were involved in a perverse act. He accompanied himself on the drum."

A perverse act. The fifth day I brought a tape in. They didn't know I was taping the shows at the time. And this is the "perverse act" they heard:

[*To be accompanied by cymbals and drums*]

    Tooooooooo
        is a preposition
    To is a preposition
    Commmmmme
        is a verb!

To is a preposition,
Come is a verb.
To is a preposition,
Come is a verb the verb intransitive.
To
Come
To come.
I've heard these two words my whole adult life and
as a kid when I thought I was sleeping.
Tooooo
Commmme
Tooooo
Commmme.
It's been like a big drum solo:
[*drums rolling and cymbals flaring in a crescendo of excitement*]
To come to come, come too come too, to come
to come uh uh uh uh uh um um um um um uh
uh uh uh uh—TO COME! TO COME! TO
COME!
Did you come?
Did you come good?
Did you come good?
Did you come?
Good.
Did you come?
Good.
To
Come
To
Come—
Didyoucomegood?didyoucomegooddidyou
comegood?
Recitative:
I come better with you sweetheart than with any-

251

one in the whole goddamn world. I really come so good with you—after being married for twenty-two years—goddamn I sure do love you! I really came so good with you—but I come too quick, don't I? That's cause I love you so much.

Goddamnit! Do you know that with everybody else I'm the best baller in the whole world? But with you, I'm always apologizing. If you just wouldn't say anything—just don't say, "Don't come!" That's what it is.

Don't come in me
don't comeinme
don'tcomeinme mimme.
Don't comeinme mimme mimme.
Don't comeinme mimme mimme
Don't comeinme mimme mimme
Mimme.

Comeinme
Comeinme
Comeinmecomeinmecomeinme—
COMEinme!

Don't comeinme mimme
don't comeinme—
unless you want to kill me.

Recitative:
My sister bled to death in the back of a taxicab, with a bad curettage. Because she had a baby in her belly. She was a tramp—my father said she was a tramp. That's why she bled to death in the back of that taxicab—cause she couldn't come home with a baby in her belly. A tramp with life in her stomach—so don't come in me, unless you want to kill me.

I can't come, don't ask me!
I can't come—

252

                              Cause you don't love me.
I love you but I just can't
come when I'm loaded!
                              Cause you don't love me—
                              That's why you can't come.
I love you! Will you get
off my ass? I'm just loaded.
I shouldn't juice and ball at
the same time.
                              Cause you don't love me.
I love you but I just can't
come when I'm loaded!
Now will you get off it?
                              Cause you don't love me.
Awright! Awright. You want me to tell you why?
I'm gonna tell you the truth: You know why we
never had any kids? Cause I can't come, cause
it's DIRTY! All that bullshit in the books, but
it ain't in that Sunday book, because the good
people don't come. And I'm gonna rise above
the physical, the carnal—don't you think I'm
ashamed of coming? It's filthy and rotten. And
I'm just sorry they blamed it on you. That's why
we never had any kids; but they blamed it on
you and kept you in bed with those dumb tem-
perature charts. So if you want any kids you
better get a different old man. But I sure do
love you. But I just can't help it—intellectual
awareness does me no good. I know its not dirty
but it is dirty. You know what I mean? God
damn it! Oh shit! Maybe we oughta adopt some
kid from some bum who can come.
If anyone in this room finds that verb intransitive,
to come, obscene vile vulgar—if it's really a hangup
to hear it and you think I'm the rankest for saying it—

you probably can't come. And then you really are shitty —disposition-wise.

I bet a lot of censors can't come. They wouldn't be going to the movies so much if they could come. How can you come and go to the movies? Weird.

Although it's against the law, there are people who *are* promiscuous who *aren't* married and involve themselves in liaisons. Now, what happens to that cat? Can he cop out to the chick, and say, "I can't come"?

> "No, I'm not gonna tell her, listen to all that bull-shit. What'll I do? . . . I'll fake coming!—

A horny hoax! Ha!

> "That's what I'll do. I'll just go,
> > 'OH GOD! OH GOD!'
> That'll do it."

Now, I wasn't hip—I never got arrested before—so I thought, "Gee, I'll get a chance to pick the jury!" What a groove *that* was. Because I have looked at you for the last twelve years and have talked about everything wild there is to talk about, and I can *clock* you, I can *pin* you, and I know what you will have some *sympatico* with.

So here we come to picking the jury, and here comes one lady, a Roman Catholic and, I know, a deterrent to me. As a juror she would make me pay dues. But I had alot of conflict about rejecting her—I'm ashamed of the prejudice I have within me, so I say,

> "Oh, well, frig it, put her on. Maybe she was Gene O'Neill's mother, man."

Sure enough—

> "Would you people on the jury be prejudiced if you hear any words blah-blah-blah?"
> "No, no."

254

The first word came up and this lady *flushes*. She went *whoosh!* Just *red,* man.

I said, "Oh oh! Did her!" She just did a turn-around every time that word got said; she just gets *redder* and *redder.* And I say, "What's she got on her forehead? *Dirt?* What's today? *Wednesday?* Oh oh! That's gonna be a lotta dues."

But my attorney says, "Well, Christ! She's not gonna *lie!* She's not gonna say that that word got her horny, is she? She's not gonna say that it aroused her sexually?"

I said, "She might lie for the Lord."

Yeah. Cause it's not even lying—I'm a despot, a nut, a lunatic! Because what mattered was, The Despot Must Be Destroyed:

> "Yon are the murderers. I am pure and good.
> There are the murderers, those *dirty murderers.*
> I must rid the community of the murderers. I will
> *murder* the murderers!"

Bang. The deed is done.

> "Where are the murderers?"
> "We just murdered them."
> "Thank God!"

And sure enough, when she went out, she was the hangup. She was the hangup. And I knew the questions were going to go down, and they did go down that way. First thing,

> *"He's guilty!"*

She didn't want to hear *anything.* So two seniors in college—one of them's a beautiful cat—he says,

> "Well, look. The judge says that he shall not make
> his characters speak falsely. If they are refined,
> they'll be refined, etc."

They argue, argue, argue. But I won out! Because, as I knew, this lady was a drunk. I says to my attorney, "No, it's cool. Cause they'll lock her up three hours; she's gotta have a taste; she'll split!"

I was saved by Old Overholt.

Oh! I must tell you. *Webster's Third Unabridged*—not the *Dictionary of American Slang,* but I mean the public school dictionary—has the word "bullshit" in it, in your public school. And it says, "bullshit: nonsense." It has p-r-i-c-k in it. It says, "a disagreeable person." It has "shit" in it—"inferior." It has "pissed off"—"angry."

And Webster is current usage—contemporary community standards. "Fuck you" doesn't mean "intercourse you." It did mean that, maybe way back then, but the U.S. Supreme Court demands that you apply a contemporary community standard and give the words a contemporary meaning. Because if you get *literal* literal, you subvert the purpose of the law by taking one fragment of it and screwing up with it.

Those words are now liberated from shame. They're in the dictionary now, finally. And the reason they came to the dictionary, finally, was through continual usage. Enough guys said to their wives

   "YOU CUNT!"

POW!

And that's why it's in the dictionary now: c-u-n-t.

Alright. This is a part of the public records, so it's not obscene.

County of L.A. Sheriff's Department. Complaint report. Violation 311.6: speaking obscene words in a public place. October 24, 1962. Troubador Theatre. 11:40 P.M. Lenny Bruce.

Suspect was placed under arrest at above time and location for the violation as listed as the result of the following investigation. On October 17, at approximately 11:30 P.M., Sgt. Block and Detective Hoga attended the location to view a show featuring suspect. In the course of the suspect's narration, he uttered obscene and offensive words including a reference to his ex-wife as being the type that became upset when he entered the bathroom while she was *fressing* the maid. The word *fressing,* in Yiddish, means eating. To eat a person—

And I never did say this—

—to eat a person is a reference to committing an act of oral copulation upon that person. Throughout his narration suspect interjected the words s-c-h-m-u-c-k and (quote) p-u-t-s—(poots?)—which are Yiddish and mean penis. Suspect also used the word s-n-t-f, a Yiddish word meaning sexual intercourse. (Sntf?) S-n-t-f. Also during narration by suspect the terms asshole, jack-off, tits and ass—

Ah, that's a very strange narration.

Dig. This last arrest—two weeks ago—I was arrested by a *Yiddish undercover agent.* Isn't that a slap in the face? *Emmis.* Somebody wrote the thing up. Dig this:

Sick comic Lenny Bruce, out on bail on a narcotics charge, was arrested by a Yiddish undercover agent who had been placed in the club several nights running to determine if Bruce's constant use of Yiddish terms was a cover for profanity. The officer said it was. Lenny asked the judge if he could bring his aunt to court to cross-examine the officer to determine how fluent the officer was in Yiddish.

Dig what I got arrested for saying: *schmuck.* And the word *schmuck*—well, I was arrested by an *illiterate* undercover agent. The word *schmuck* is a German word and it means, literally—and I'm sure you'd insist on the literal meaning, not hearsay—it means a man's decoration, in German, as a boutonniere or lapel watch. The Yiddish dictionary, the Harcoff dictionary: *schmuck,* "a yard, a fool." So there we have the literal and the colloquial. I don't think any Jew ever neologized and said,

"You're acting just like a man's penis!"

Did you? No. It's

"We drove in from Yonkers. Who did all the driving?

Me, like a *schmuck.*"

Now, "Me, like a *schmuck*" doesn't mean "Me *like* a *schmuck*"—unless you're a faggot Indian:

"Ho white man! Me like a *schmuck.*"

"Well, if you do, don't bring it in here."

"You no like a *schmuck,* eh?"

"Well, once in a while."

Oh, we were in the cell together this morning. That was *beautiful!* As soon as we got busted, some *schmuck* said,

"Ah, the gestapo!"

I said, "Shut up. Just do me a favor, *don't.* No *tumler,* alright?"

"No, I'm *with* you!"

"You're *not* with me, Daddy, you're looking to thwart authority, I don't know what your *schtuck* is, but cool it. Get outta here." "No, no!"

This *schmuck* just *wants* to get arrested, man—he starts really picking on the heat.

I said, "Look. Hey," to the cop, "lemme get in the car. Cool, cause the whole scene's embarrassing, alright?"

And sure enough the *schmuck* ends up in the car with me. I see this body hurtling towards me—

"I'm *with* you, I'm *with* you!"

"I'm hip, you're with me."

"Well, Christ, I did it for *you.*"

"No, you *didn't* do it for me—get off, ya nut! Lemme alone."

258

Now, we got that cat—oh, that beautiful bartender—
—George saw a quick chance for a little front-page-o,
so he got very brave, and refused to show his draft
card.

"I refuse!"

"What?"

"Anything."

He got *schlepped* away. Alright. So then Alan walked in.

"Hello."

"Who are you?"

"I'm the proprietor."

"Oh. Come to jail."

Bang-bang-bang. Alright, *schlepped* away.

Now, as soon as we get in the cell I start to get bad.

[*singing*] "Water boy. Yes, I'm gwine up ta hebbin."

I swear to God. Now, I got a very ludicrous sense of
humor. Now, there's a guy in the cell next to us and
he says, "Got any matches?"

[*tough voice*] "Fo fi' dollars. I'll give you a match
for fi' dollars. An' I'm gonna take over dis cell, and
you're gonna get the crap whacked outta ya, ya
hear dat?"

So I said, "I wish I had one of those matches that
makes a snake."

Alan says, "You're really cruel."

"I wouldn't *really* do it, dopey."

Now, in New York, no jury trial. Yeah, strange. They
has a three-judge bench, cause it's a misdemeanor. Colored judge, Irish judge, English judge. Alright.

Now, Dorothy Kilgallen testified on my behalf, and
Nat Hentoff, someone from *Newsweek,* and several
others. Now. Dorothy Kilgallen on the stand in my
behalf. O.K. The obvious question the prosecution's
going to ask:

259

"Miss Kilgallen, do you use the word motherfucker in your column?"

"No, I don't use the word motherfucker in my column."

"Why not?"

"Because it's not my language, it's Lenny Bruce's language."

"Well, do you feel that your column has suffered from the lack of that language?"

"No."

"Why should *he* be allowed to use it?"

"Well, because he's doing a scene, and he shouldn't be made to put refined words in the mouths of vulgar people, and a theatre's a theatre, and he never uses the words as a sexual reference to appeal to the prurient interest."

Now comes the real issue. The whole trial is about a statement I made relating to the president's assassination. Now, listen in context to what they consider obscene: I said that when the president was killed and the governor got it and Jacqueline Kennedy [*crawled onto the back of the car*], the pictures that I saw in *Time* magazine distorted that event. I think the guy got a medal when he climbed up into the car for shielding her.

Well, it's a conclusion on my part, naturally, but the caption that *Time* magazine put under it—that she was going to get help—is a distortion. Especially the last picture—that she was helping him, the Secret Service agent, aboard. No. She was leaving, and he was pushing her back. She wasn't helping the guy aboard at all.

Now why I found this repugnant, though not unlawful, is that I have a daughter, and if her husband were to get shot and she were to panic, like all of us would do, she would feel *guilty,* cause of that Good Woman that stayed. And it seems dishonest to set up an image like

that, to enshrine her, like, "These are the *good* people—
they stay." And really they *don't* stay, and—bullshit.

Now, "haul ass to save her ass" is about the only
thing that smacks of, ah, Anglo-Saxon. But the judge
said to Richard Gilman of *Newsweek*—this is an exact
quote:

> "Do you think that the use of this filth, disgusting
> language, is necessary to get over this questionable
> point of view?"

So, the judge was saying, in effect, that the *point of
view* was the hangup with him.

Now dig. There's a colored judge on the bench. Now
I kept hinting that it was a Negro colloquialism, and
there's the Negro judge, sitting in back. So now they
call Nat Hentoff:

> "Mr. Hentoff. The word 'motherfucker.' Do you
> use it?"

"No."

"Have you heard it used?"

"Yes, many times."

And he said that he'd heard it as a term of endearment.

"Where?"

"I've heard it in penthouses as well as the gutter."

Now we go to Alan Morrison, the Editor of *Ebony*
magazine, who had seen me do the show in question:

> "Have you ever heard the word motherfucker?"

"Many times."

"Have you used it?"

"Yes."

"Where?"

"My house."

Now the Negro judge is sitting in back going, "Hm,
well, hm hm, *ahem*." *Beautiful*. You know, he really
looked dignified. I really have great respect for the
bench.

But it would be a beautiful musical curtain line: The three judges just about to exit, and one turns to the other at the end and says,

"See you later, motherfucker."

Busts II: Causes and Consequences

The police are here, so be careful you don't spill the heroin out of its paper. The first thing, I come in, the waitress hit on me, *"They're here!* There's five of them here!" How do you like that? There's five guys who never kissed any ladies or choked children!

Don't you know that *Nixon* even comes to see me? They're here because they *dig* me, man.

What's the opposite of paranoia? I really had that thing going—I always twist it around that they *like* me! It's really sick. They *like* me, *schmuck,* and they're doing that for *me.*

But I'm paranoid enough. I got arrested so many times this year—my fly is open, I'm on dope, *everything.*

After a while ya get so many arrests, ya think "Geez, *everybody* can't be wrong." But they are. It's like paranoids—classic paranoia is like, the communists are always chasing you and the Mafia. It'd be beautiful if we'd find out years from today that the Mafia really was chasing these people. There was no paranoia at all.

You may wonder what happens. Yeah, you figure: All the publicity—he feeds on that. Well, I'd say that since the beginning of these arrests, my money and career have dropped seventy per cent. Yeah.

Classic illustration. Here's what happened: I got arrested in San Francisco. And I was in court, and these photographers were taking my picture. After about a half hour it got to be a bore, you know, so I said, "That's enough, man." But they kept clicking, so I started to implore them, and then I went and stood behind the flag—for asylum. Alright, jerks the flag out. Then I got really drug.

> "When sick comic Lenny Bruce came to court in Los Angeles the other afternoon in connection with his narcotics rap, the photographers and newsreel and T.V. cameramen waited for him. Bruce fooled everyone by painting four-letter words all over his face so no one could take his picture."

Actually I put a tissue towel on my face. I mean, *come on!* They took my picture for two hours. I got *bored* with it.

Very interesting—in the court here, the guys stood *behind the judge* and took my picture.

So then I started running a little, trotting, trotting around the courthouse. L. A. is too much. They're beautiful. In the newsreel they dubbed sound to them chasing me—*da da dum da da dum da da dum dum dum*. Now, I'm running, running, and running, twice around the courthouse, and I'm really getting exhausted. So I wheel around, and as I wheel around, this guy's about five feet from me, he falls, and I hear a guy go, "I got it!"

O.K., now, a couple hours later, I'm arrested for assault and battery and sued for one hundred thousand dollars. You know, this cat, I never touched him. Then I started thinking, I said, You know, I gotta figure a defense—cause when you've been arrested this many times, well, they just *know* that you're wrong.

I'm just so *weary* of being arrested. Yeah, it's just, *phew!* Boy. In the first place, it's whacked me out financially—I don't have any money left. I had to sell my pad. And it keeps me from even working.

Captain McDermott came in here [*Gate of Horn*]:
"Who's the owner here?"
"I'm Alan Ribback."
"Well, I wanna tell you that if this guy Lenny Bruce ever uses any four-letter words or talks against religion, I'm going to pinch *everybody* in this place, do you understand?"
"I'm not against any religion."
"Well, maybe I'm talking to the wrong guy. Who hired Lenny Bruce?"
"I did."
"Well, I dunno why you hired him, you've had alotta good people here; but this guy mocks religion. I'm speaking as a Catholic. And I'm telling you that your license is in danger. And if he mocks the Pope again I'm going to pinch everybody in this place. Do you understand?"
"Yes, I understand."

I just hope that the Messiahs return in time. Because I get this second bust, and the Curran Theatre, that seats three thousand people, and's always filled—all of a sudden it's eight hours before showtime, and the booker says, "We've sold six hundred tickets."
"Oh, Christ!"
"Well, you've had two narcotics arrests, you've had six obscenity arrests, an assault—hm. Who'd go to see a dirty-talking dope fiend? You wanna pay for the house? *Give away* tickets."

That's the next step—I get arrested and the *whole audience* gets *schlepped* in. For viewing a lewd show.

Dig, it would be so beautiful. If I had a real *verbissener* audience that really doesn't like me at all, and on top of it they get *arrested:*

> "Ah, now, lemme get this straight, now, Mrs. Dolan. The man said 'cocksucker' and you stayed there for forty-five minutes? He said 'motherfucker'—we got the tape there—and you stayed there for another fifty minutes? Is that right? Well, I think that thirty days on the farm aren't gonna hurt you at all."

My generation saw a few of the freaks in the carnivals—you know, Zip and Pip the Onion-Head Boys, the Mongoloid, the Chinless, the Alligator Woman. Our kids won't see any of those freaks, at least only a few of them. It's a shame.

But we will see a few of them. Yeah. Thank God for the Catholic Church—those thalidomide babies will grow up to have a good time with Barnum and Bailey. So they'll still see Zip and Pip and Flip and Mip.

Yeah. That's what I *really* got busted for. That's what I always get busted for. And it's really strange. I know that the peace officer that busts me really doesn't even realize that, that that's what he's busting me for.

The reason I got busted—arrested—is I picked on the wrong god. If I had picked on the god whose replica is in the whoopee cushion store—the Tiki god, the Hawaiian god, those idiots, their dumb god—I would've been cool. If I would've picked on the god whose belly is slashed—he's a bank. Chinese, those idiots, their yellow god. But I picked on the Western god—the cute god, the In-god, the Kennedy-god—and that's where I screwed up.

Now the weird thing, and it really does annoy me, is that there are people who are that unsophisticated as to assume that the peace officers are the ones that arrested me. *You're* the ones that arrested me, not the peace officers. Oh yeah, you are. We're the lawmakers.

Like, the police officer doesn't get up in the morning and say,

> "Let's see, what'll I do today, who'll I arrest? Ah, I think I'll arrest Lenny Bruce, and . . ."

No. He gets the report. Protocol, that's the scene, man. No. Here's what happened. There were people that walked out of the club. They were offended, and they went through the proper channels. They didn't take a brick and throw it through a window; they made a complaint and then the complaint was answered by the peace officer, and then the peace officer *schlepped* me away. There's no hostility at all. No. They're very cool about it. Didn't involve personalities.

That's one thing, though. With all these arrests, I always feel like an American officer in a Japanese prison camp. Oh yeah. Never any shame connected with my arrests. That's my feeling. I've brainwashed myself.

But here's how it ends. One day I'm going to get an order to appear in court: "Oh, shit, what is it this time?" But when I get there the courtroom will be all decorated, dig, with balloons and streamers and confetti, and when I walk in they'll all jump up and yell *"Surprise!"* And there'll be all the cops that busted me, and the judges and DA's who tried me, and they'll say,

> "Lenny, this is a surprise party for you. We're giving you a party because even after everything that happened you never lost respect for the law."

Spotting Heat, and Understanding Judges and Lawyers

Last night I pinned the heat, I see them. They were sitting over there, see. All of a sudden—I'm working, I'm into about twenty-five minutes of the show—*Chung! Pow!* I see the heat. The minute I see them, I like them. Yeah. One guy's laughing. Now, all of a sudden the one heat got a little bigger, and he took a cigar out. Then I knew he was completely out of it. Yeah.

Over there's sitting some guy, a real strung-out junkie, *schlafed* out. The guy's nodding, sleeping. So I'm thinking, "Who's he gonna bust first, me or him?"

How do I know heat? I'll tell you how I know heat. I am the capper capper capper at pinning people. Well, cause I really love you, that's why, goddamn it. And I've been looking at you for so long.

Here's peace officers: Number one, they never need a haircut. That's the first thing. You spot them, hair always cut good. Now, we see two guys together. They're still on the gig, so the attitude, the position of sitting is never sloppy posture. They're cool, never hostile. They're detached—sort of with you and without you.

The reason you can spot cop cops is like: all accountants look alike cause they follow the stereotype of the accountant—the lawyer, the engineer, he looks like a, cause he's supposed to look like a. O.K. Policemen—plainclothes policemen—first place, they're two guys working. We see two guys walking, and they're working at it. They have ties on and they're dressed. They're two guys together. Yeah, that's heat. They're not arrogant, no. And they have a feeling of belonging anywhere. It's amazing. Any—I don't care—any club, nightclub they've never been in, they just go. *Pchung!* Done. That's all.

Now, I feel no hostility towards heat. I just know that you've got a job to do.

Yeah. The next time you see the policeman in a demonstration, look at him. Look at him and then you realize that he's about my age, and he dies for less than four hundred dollars a month. And he's doing your gig and he's a second-class citizen. And everybody sees him and says, "That *shithead,* look at him!" And he's lonesome. Yeah, it's a lot of dues.

I found out that it's sort of masquerade time when you go into court. The attorney will say, "Get a haircut, and get a blue suit—get a haircut and a blue suit and get rid of those shoes."

That's so that the jurors are not confused, so that that day in court they can pick out the felon—you know, the one in the blue suit. Cause that day the man in blue is bereft of gun and badge. No bullets. *He's* got on the *brown* suit. Judge has got on his black robes, and it's masquerade time.

Judges have said to me, "I've never heard such disgusting language in my life!"

269

About two years ago, I would say, "Ah, he's fulla shit!"

But I believe him today. Cause I've found out two things. One, the paranoia is just ignorance. Because two years ago I thought that the judges were lying, and that they were persecuting me, which is illegal prosecution. Then I find out that—I listen to the language in the court—and the judge doesn't *hear* those words.

For a while I had lost perspective—until I started listening to the prosecution's arguments. And now that I listen, really listen to the prosecution—not listen for their finish and then stop talking—listen to their *point of view,* I see that there is a *different culture.* It has different values and a different set of standards.

How did this happen? The judge in New York said he'd never heard such filthy and disgusting language before. That judge has been on the bench for twenty-five years—what kind of a world does he live in?

The whole world dresses in blue suits. The judge really believes that all of us have blue suits. That's it—we lie to them continually. Everyone has a haircut—the biggest bum in the world has a haircut and a blue suit and is *charming.* And the language in the courts: "I pray you." That's it. You don't say, "Shithead, get off it!" Uh uh. People talk different in front of judges. We talk different to librarians, judges, nurses, our kids.

The judges don't really know what it's like, because everyone comes before the judge with a mask on. So in a situation where the people are resisting and angry, the judge figures, *"Jesus! He's absolutely nuts!"* He really doesn't know how it is.

And peace officers just to a little bit lesser degree. If you think that people talk that way to peace officers —"Fuck you, Johnny!"—they don't. They don't talk that way in front of them. And I've questioned enough of them to realize that they live in a bit of a different world. Peace officers, when they hear the words, they don't hear them colloquially. They hear, "Pissed off," they don't hear "Urinate from afar."

The halls of justice. That's the only place you see the justice, is in the halls. "Oh, how they beat me—they rubber-hosed and Sam Levined me in their back rooms." Lemme tell you about police brutality—a lie, a definite lie. Bullshit. You hear about it, but you never see it. And I'm perceptive—I've been in the jails in Europe—one half of one quarter of one percent is true. And, I check every story out and I say

"Did it happen to you?"

"No, but this frienda mine—"

Ahh, bullshit! And if it's happened to you I want you to tell me about how it did happen, cause I've really asked thousands of guys already.

But now, the motivation for that lie—where would it stem from? A guy gets busted for exposing himself or shoplifting. Now, comes to court, guy figures,

"Everybody'll put me down when I get outta jail; but if I can get out and say,

'*They beat the shit outta me!* They punched me around—but I was a Bogart, a Garfield —*I didn't sell out! I didn't give em one name!*' "

Names? The *schmuck* was arrested for *exposing* himself!

"I want the names of udder guys who exposed themselves!"

"I'll never sell out! I would take *twenty years* in prison before I would ever give em one of your names and let you do a *month!*"

Is that bullshit? I would give names upon names of those yet *unborn,* before I would do any time for you. Unless you knew the Maf or some bunch of *schtarkers*

—then I'd give my life for you. They'd take mine if I didn't.

In the court, the judge, you'd assume, is very concerned with the Supreme Court. In the lower courts—*nada*. He's concerned with the spectators—his wife, his sisters, daughter, I don't know. That's why judges continually say, "Approach the bench!"

So you approach the bench:

> JUDGE: You *asshole,* you're not gonna steamroll *this* court!

I wrote a lot of notes to the judges that got me contempt. And I didn't mean it for contempt, cause I'm not contemptuous of anyone I don't know. But I had like a report: "You're taking this case too lightly."

Before I *got* there. So I said, "Hey, man," in this letter I told him,

> "that ain't the way it is. I'm not. This has cast a leper's stain that St. Francis could never kiss away. And as far as lowering the standards of the community—San Francisco, which supports more faggot bars, Turkish bathhouses hung up with vag-lub charges, and Fisherman's Wharf, that shares tenancy with a rock washed with the tears of Christ and women left behind—no, man, I don't know how I could lower those standards."

I, one time, was my own counsel. That's all. That's when I got the year.

I didn't realize what an attorney goes through.

Here's what he's doing. See, I'm used to working to just one audience. He's working to the jury, then getting it into the record, working to the judge, and his client. Four people, four levels he's working on.

And a guilty—*Wow!* The few guilties I've got, I've

watched the attorneys, and I know they never get used to that. It's heavy dues for an attorney—
"GUILTY!"
—and the attorney's ears blanch. That's right.

So when you've got a client with the kind of a guilty that *Ruby* got—I'm sure *that* sentence—*Whew!* Can you imagine sitting there

> [*deep threatening voice*]: *ALL RIGHT RUBY, YOU'RE GONNA RIDE THE LIGHTNING!*

Whew! BARUNG! *Jesus!*

And Belli's screaming in the back of the room

> "Don't worry, Jack!"
> "Ouuuuuu, fug it . . ."
> "It's alright, Jack! I'm with you!"
> "Ouuuuuughagh, whathefug, ouugh . . ."
> "Come on, Jack!"

He's talking, trying to make some sense to him there—and I was just praying that when he walked through that crowd, that just by some miracle, maybe, that some cat from *Winterset,* Margo would come with mud and blood on him

> "I'm Oswald, ya prick! Ya thought ya got me—"

POWPOWPOWPOW! Thunk.

> "Oswald?! Wattayou, kidding? He was dead!"
> "Na, they screwed up! Dallas fucks up *everything,* man. He had a tag, and he got a guy who had leukemia, he got out of the hospital, he got in, I dunno, some shit, and he lost his hair in there, that's all."

Oh yeah. That would really be embarrassing.

The Law

I figure, when it started, they said, "Well, we're gonna have to have some rules"—that's how the law starts, out of that fact.

"Let's see. I tell you what we'll do. We'll have a vote. We'll sleep in area A, is that cool?"

"O.K., good."

"We'll eat in area B. Good?"

"Good."

"We'll throw a crap in area C. Good?"

"Good."

Simple rules. So, everything went along pretty cool, you know, everybody's very happy. One night everybody was sleeping, one guy woke up, *Pow!* He got a faceful of crap, and he said:

"Hey, what's the deal, here, I thought we had a rule: Eat, Sleep, and Crap, and I was sleeping and I got a faceful of crap."

So they said,

"Well, ah, the rule was substantive—"

See, that's what the Fourteenth Amendment is. It regulates the rights, but it doesn't *do* anything about it. It just says, That's where it's at.

"We'll have to do something to enforce the provisions, to give it some teeth. Here's the deal: If everybody throws any crap on us while we're sleeping, they get thrown in the craphouse. Agreed?"

"Well, everybody?"

"Yeah."

"But what if it's my mother?"

"No, you don't understand. Your mother would be the fact. That has nothing to do with it. It's just the rule, Eat, Sleep and Crap. Anybody throws any crap on us they get thrown in the craphouse. Your mother doesn't enter into it at all. Everybody gets thrown in the craphouse—priests, rabbis, they'll all go. Agreed?"

"O.K., agreed."

O.K. Now, it's going along very cool, guy's sleeping, *Pow!* Gets a faceful of crap. Now he wakes up and sees he's all alone, and he looks, and everybody's giving a big party. He says,

"Hey, what's the deal? I thought we had a rule, Eat, Sleep and Crap, and you just threw a faceful of crap on me."

They said,

"Oh, this is a religious holiday, and we told you many times that if you're going to live your indecent life and sleep all day, you deserve to have crap thrown on you while you're sleeping."

And the guy says,

"Bullshit. The rule's the rule."

And this guy started to separate the church and the state, right down the middle, Pow! Here's the church rule, and here's the federal rule. O.K., everything's going along cool, one guy says,

275

"Hey, wait a minute. Though we made the rule, how're we gonna get somebody to throw somebody in the craphouse?

We need somebody to enforce it—law enforcement."

Now they put this sign up on the wall, "WANTED, LAW ENFORCEMENT." Guys applied for the job:

"Look. Here's our problem, see, we're trying to get some sleep and people keep throwing crap on us. Now we want somebody to throw them right in the craphouse. And I'm delegated to do the hiring here, and, ah, here's what the job is.

"You see, they won't go in the craphouse by themselves. And we all agreed on the rule, now, and we firmed it up, so there's nobody gets out of it, everybody's vulnerable, we're gonna throw them right in the craphouse.

"But ya see, I can't do it cause I do business with these assholes, and it looks bad for me, you know, ah . . . so I want somebody to do it for me, you know? So I tell you what: Here's a stick and a gun and *you* do it—but wait til I'm out of the room. And, whenever it happens, see, I'll wait back here and I'll watch, you know, and you make sure you kick 'em in the ass and throw 'em in there.

"Now, ycu'll hear me say alotta times that it takes a certain kind of mentality to do that work, you know, and all that bullshit, you know, but you understand, it's all horseshit and you just kick em in the ass and make sure it's done."

So what happens? Now comes the riot, or the marches —everybody's wailing, screaming. And you got a guy there, who's standing with a short-sleeved shirt on and a stick in his hand, and the people are yelling, "Gestapo! Gestapo!" at him:

"Gestapo? You asshole, I'm the *mailman!"*

That's another big problem. People can't separate the authority and the people who have the authority vested in them. I think you see that a lot in the demonstrations. Cause actually the people are demonstrating not against Vietnam—they're demonstrating against the police department. Actually, against policemen. Because they have that concept—that the law and the law enforcement are one.

What it is, I think, is that people really want to beat the devil. And I think that started with the early, early missionaries, you know. That's why the people never could really separate the authority and the people with the authority vested in them. Cause, you know, with the savages, you know, the missionary would teach them the religion, and after the speech the savage would go:

> SAVAGE: Well, are you God?
>
> MISSIONARY: Well, noooo, but, ah, heh heh, ah, what the hell, you know, just, ah, we never mind that—I do you a favor, you do me a favor, that's all.

So that's where it's at. And I think that's a hangup in our country right now.

Cause you always hear that kind of a story, about the peace officer who pulled a speeder over, and the speeder turned out to be the governor. And he had the audacity to give him a ticket. So the fact that people repeat that story so much, that means that people don't believe that the governor could ever get a ticket. So then it's just the degree of the law that the governor could break. That means he could kick you in the ass or anything.

But that's bullshit. It's really not that way. Cause everybody's vulnerable. Yeah. Everybody's ass is up for grabs. And it's really a groovy system.

Now, the problem I had, of understanding the law, was because of the language in the law, and the fact that instead of taking each word and finding out the case that the word related to, once in a while I got lazy and I would apply common sense. And then I got really screwed up.

Really got to separate the judicial the executive and the legislature. And the most dangerous department, just the department itself, is the police, the district attorney—not the man, but the department. It's very dangerous for him. And the whole reason for the constitution was that, there was like one king. He was the execution, everything.

And the king's men got outta line, they got crazy all the time. So you've got to keep them in check—that is what the veto system is. See, at that time the Anglican Church were really ballbreakers. That was one of the words they used then, ballbreakers. Ballbreakers means backbreakers. The Anglican Church caused us discomfort—they didn't really break your balls, but they hurt them. It's not literal.

The Anglican Church were really ballbreakers. They would stop us on the way home from our meetings—the Protestants—and say,

> HEAT: Where're ya going? Whatta ya got under that cloak?
>
> PROTESTANT: It's mine. And you can't stop me without a warrant.
>
> HEAT: Bullshit. Whattaya got under your cloak? You got a Bible under there?
>
> PROTESTANT: You can't search me.
>
> HEAT: No—unless you make a furtive move. [*Aside*] If he scratches his ass he's dead. *Aha! A Bible!* O.K., book him and take him down.
>
> PROTESTANT: Look, when're you people gonna stop this crap, now?

HEAT: When are you gonna stop with your dopey meetings?

So they had more meetings. The guys said, "Let's get outta here. Let's go to a different country. Let's go to a place where we can be safe in our houses, from unreasonable searches and seizures, where the only people that can stop us are those with that warrant."

Now "probable cause" means, certainly not the probable cause to go without a warrant. They made it this safe, that if you have a warrant, then you've got the probable cause to get the warrant, then you can bust the guy in his own house; but not otherwise. And the reason for that safety valve is that judges are brighter than peace officers—for one reason—they've had more exposure. So you stand a better chance of being safe in your house if the peace officer first has to go to the magistrate.

Here's how it works: *Lagen Tfillin* is a Jewish orthodox rite. Here's how that works: you take a leather string—mostly rabbis use it—and they tie it around their arm, as if one were a narcotic addict. A very devout scene. You can imagine: some old Jew on the second story there, he's tying his arm up, *dovining,* and he's got a glass of tea. Puts a spoon in the tea, stirring it up—and a narcotics agent from Oklahoma who never saw a Jew in his life, would just knock the door down and drag that old Jew into jail *Pow!* like that.

But if he had to go to a magistrate first, it's quite possible that the magistrate would say, "Well, what section of town is it? Delancey St.? Houston St.? Well, maybe it's a Jewish religious rite. You better check this guy first before you *schlep* him down."

Yeah, the king was everything, so they said,
    "How we'll do it now, we'll really make it safe,

we vote on the rule, Eat Sleep and Crap, that'll be the law, constant. Then, if anybody busts us for breaking the rule, they have to go first, to the judge, the judge has to look up the book, and then we'll make a round-robin."

But what's happening is that the crime rate, see, has disappeared, and the task force that we hired is getting bigger and bigger and bigger—there's never any lay-off in the police department. The welfare is up, and it's getting so, just so there's no work left.

Here's what I figure happened to the crime rate. First—the basic need to steal is like, for coal, you know, you're hungry. All right. So now the economy is up, so that went disappear-o. O.K. now the second need to break the law was for some sort of status, some virility. O.K. the fact that now we give these people analysis, that went disappear-o. O.K. now the second need to be sick. Now there's just nothing left.

But the law is a beautiful thing. The people who attack the law don't really understand it. You know what it's like? It's like the Supreme Court, that's the daddy and it runs the store because it knows how. All the state courts and the civil courts, they're just the clerks, and the daddy says,

> "Now you just sweep the floor and unpack the stock and that's it. I don't want you to place any orders or change the displays—and keep your hands out of the register."

But the minute he turns his back all the clerks think they know how to run it better, and they start changing everything and ordering the wrong things and it's a mess. The Supreme Court's the Big Daddy, it knows what is, but the little guys keep trying to run the store.

What Is Obscene?

Right now there's some bullshit with obscenity. There's an obscenity circus that's been going on now for about five years. And I really can't believe that it's not settled.

There's a Los Angeles ordinance now, 1961, that this guy got busted behind, when the judge said, *"I* don't need any art critics. I *know* what's obscene." But the judge didn't know, in that local court, that that wasn't the question the guy was asking. He was saying, this ordinance is unconstitutional because it doesn't have "knowingly" in it. And that's the principle of the whole American law system—the *intent*.

"So how could I *know* it, *schmuck,* when these people told me on the book jacket that this is *art?"* So the lower court said *bullshit* and the Supreme Court said *bullshit* to the lower court, and that's when *I* started getting into trouble.

Because from '61 on came the argument between petulant lower court judges and the Supreme Co⸱⸱ spoiled rotten D.A.'s. The city attorney i⸱ ⸱ —every time he'd lose in Washi⸱⸱⸱

kicked when he got home. Just bitching, bitching, bitching:

"*Frig* the Supreme Court!"

They're going to do it their way.

Now, the state really has given me an excellent education—you know, continual prosecution and defense. Now, what is obscene? Obscenity—I'll hip you to something—it's the prurient interest. If I do a show about eating garbage, or dead children, or necrophilia, and you say

"That's the most dis*gusting*—"

No, that's not obscene. It's disgusting, distasteful—but not obscene.

Or if I do a show and I talk about what sluts the Voodoo ritualists' wives are, or if I say that about the Pope's mother, or rabbis, etc.—that's not obscene. If I do a show blaspheming Voodoo:

"Voodoo is fulla crap!"

"Well, he's not right, and he's blasphemous."

But if I blaspheme the Voodoos, the Catholics or the Patamonza Yoganondas, that is *not* obscene.

If I say, "Shit in your fist and squeeze it!" Not obscene for two reasons.

One, because of a new ruling in the Supreme Court that if it describes narcotics, the word shit is not obscene. In other words, if you shit in your pants and smoke it—you're cool. That's in the picture *The Connection.*

And also, because to be obscene, I must stimulate you sexually. That's what obscene is—the prurient interest: if I get you horny. That's it.

Now, as far as me, if you get horny with me—well, that's good: the witness there would be very interesting:

"What did he say that was horny?"

"Well, whenever I hear the old *glutius maximus,* it gets me this rod on, heh, heh . . ."

That's why the obscenity laws are very embarrassing to the judicial system. Because of the latest decisions, you hear the judges say, "You're taking the teeth out of the law. How can we administer justice?" And the problem is that there's no such thing as First Amendment punishment, just protection.

So, Nico Jacobellis, he owned a theatre and he showed *The Lovers,* a film. In the film there was a guy kissing a lady in bed, and his head disappeared off the screen —towards the foot of the bed. So they said that the film was obscene for what went *off* the screen!

Yeah. And it went up to the U.S. Supreme Court, and the Supreme Court repeated a lot of things they said in a case called Roth. Sam Roth was the guy who sold dirty books in the mail, and the circulars he used were obscene. So he did some time—he got a guilty. Now, the first time, this was in '57, they said,

> "You, Roth, you are obscene, and obscene talk hasn't got the protection of the First Amendment. Therefore you're gonna do some time. Your material is utterly without redeeming social factors— patently offensive, appeals to the prurient interest"—

The prurient interest is like the steel interest. What's wrong with appealing to the prurient interest? We appeal to the *killing* interest.

You know, I got to do some reading, and I found out that the Catholic Church had the best, clearest definition for obscenity. It makes the Supreme Court decision vague. Dig:

> "For the matter to be obscene the intrinsic bent of the work must be to the prurient interest."

Now that's where the Supreme Court stays. T gets vague. But dig the Catholic Church

283

"To put it more concretely, the genital apparatus
must be in a position to unite sexually."

Now you want a clearer definition than that? That's
beautiful. How can anyone say that's vague and indefi-
nite? And dig, they really got cute with it:

"And the words 'vulgar' and 'disgusting' shall not
apply, since human liberties are at stake."

Alright. Now after that they say, that

"the test shall not apply if the person is sluggish."

I really like that. Cracked me up.

If you check the records, there's not one citizen who
bought a dirty book. Every case has been initiated by
the police department.

You know, the literal view of the law is that what's
obscene is *dirty* screwing and *fancy* screwing. If a guy
can tear off a piece of ass with class, then he's cool; but
if the author depicts factory workers who are not experts
with stag shows, then it's obscene, which is just nonsense.

Tract Home Chippy, for example, would be the trite
pulp book. *Tract Home Chippy.* The good book, they've
accepted then, is D. H. Lawrence, *Lady Chatterly's
Lover.* All right. Now, it's really absurd. You've got two
books. You've got *Lady Chatterly's Lover,* and we've
got here, *Tract Home Chippy.*

Now we got two couples in each book. D. H. Lawrence's couple, they're not married, but he knows how
to handle the scene. Nothing patently offensive: there's
silk sheets, *lebesraum*—I mean the guy knows how to
go about it.

Let's go to *Tract Home Chippy.* They're factory
workers. They're both virgins. I mean, page after page
and this guy doesn't know how to do *anything.* Never
did it before. He's ripping the clothes, conveying of

284

semen before the penetration, didn't wear a contraceptive—it was *disgusting!*

Let's go back to D. H. Lawrence. This guy can really tear up a piece of ass—the third broad he's on already.

mean this book was really *stimulating*—you felt like going out, getting a broad . . .

That's what it is, it's absurd:

> "So, in the opinion of this court, we punish untalented artists."

Which could never be, man.

That's what I always figured the law was for—to protect ladies. Not against vulgar sounds, certainly not; but to protect ladies against horny guys. They knew that some guy would come from the country, who had no exposure, unsophisticated. So the legislature said,

> "Well, this guy would come from the country and he might go to the city and see a very horny show or read a horny book, and *he'll* get horny, and then he'll rape somebody who *didn't* read the book, or see the show."

So they said, Well, we must have some laws to restrict the behavior, to cool the people out.

But as far as *disgusting* is concerned—the reason we left England was just for that right, to be disgusting. If there're any immigrants out here, by the way, who are thinking of becoming citizens, then you might be offended by some of the statements made by Jesuits or rabbis, concerning their gods, that would deny your gods. That's not against the law in this country. Or you Chinese people who might hear your god referred to as "A fat slob, the Buddha"—but that's our right.

In fact, that's why we left England years ago—because we couldn't bitch about the church, the Anglican

Church, we Protestants. And we had underground meetings.

> "I'm tired of this shit, let's get somewhere else, let's go to a different country where we can have our meetings and be Protestants. Let's go somewhere else so we can be disgusting. And do disgusting shows. No one can stop us—flaunt it in their faces."
>
> "*How* disgusting?"
>
> "Well, go in front of a synagogue and sing about pork."
>
> "*That* disgusting? What about the Moslems?"
>
> "Fuck 'em. The Jews too, and the vegetarians. Cause that's our right—to be disgusting.

Prurient interest. That's it. To the immigrant: If, after the show, and taken as a whole, there's no redeeming social factor to this show, but if the show does appeal to your prurient interest, if you're sitting there with a hard-on after I get off, then I should get busted. That's the way it is, that's the way it goes.

But if you're *disgusted,* well, that's your ass, that's my right, because I'll sing about pork, and wail about it.

Oh. Back to obscenity. The law relates, and justly so, that I should be allowed the poetic license of theatre. Legit theatre is not censured that way. So this is my theatre, my platform, and, of course, when all the facade is *schlepped* away—that word that I said, if that word stimulated you sexually, well, you're in a lot of *trouble,* Jim.

And I'm sure your father will be quite unhappy.

The Good-Good Culture

Paul Malloy, who's sort of Christ in concrete, he's got a thing going, it's "Decent-Indecent"—you know, "What is God?" And Good is God is Danny Thomas. So, I want to show you some pictures of tramps.

[*Holding up a pin-up nudie photo*]

These are bums. This is an indecent woman. The Paul Malloy culture would call this lady indecent.

Ohhhh, no! Are you kidding? *Indecent?* How can that sweet, pink-nippled, blue-eyed, *goyisha punim* be indecent? Are you kidding? Indecent? God *damn* Paul Malloy, man. I *love* that lady. And she's religious—see the beads? That's how the sisters look before they take the vows. They take one last picture, and that's it.

Now, lemme hip you to something. Lemme tell you something. If you believe that there is a god, a god that made your body, and yet you think that you can do anything with that body that's dirty, then the fault lies with the manufacturer. *Emmis.*

If I could be that Roman Chriswell, and this was the second day of Christianity, and I could predict:

"Hear ye, Christians! Hold on to a bit of Rome. Because we come from an anthropomorphic society, we can touch our God, and you have this Christian god of yours that made your body. Do you believe this phantasy, Christians? That God made your body?

"I believe that two thousand years hence you will arrest my daughter's daughter's daughter's daughter for having her titty out in the subway. And you will ban bikinis and tell six-year-old little girls to 'Cover up! Cover up!'

"You say, 'Nay, Nay, God made the body!' But I believe you will deny this and you will say that the body is *dirty*."

And then the guilt will lie with the manufacturer. And then you have to *schlep* God into court with Belle Barth.

And that really offended me in court, when they swore on the Bible, man, and they went blah-blah-blah-blah. And I said, *Whew!* Look at them! What's their story? How can they *lie?* How can they look me in the face and say that God's the creator when they *don't* believe that God created the body?

You know why they don't believe that God created the body? Cause they qualify the creativity. They stop it above the kneecaps—and they don't resume it till it passes above the Adam's apple. Thereby giving it lewd connotation.

My concept? You can't do *anything* with anybody's body to make it dirty to me. Six people, eight people, one person—you can do only one thing to make it dirty: kill it. Hiroshima was dirty. Chessman was dirty.

For years I've been buying *Playboy, Nugget, Rogue, Dude, Gent,* all those other stroke books. I buy those books for one reason: to look at the chicks, man. I

288

don't need a Nelson Algren short story for rationalization.

Last year Paul Malloy was hung up with Hugh Hefner,
the owner of *Playboy* magazine. The column went something like this. He said,

> "Hugh Hefner, the publisher of *Playboy* magazine,
> sent me an invitation to the Playboy Club. I
> wouldn't show my kids the pictures of the half-nude
> bunnies that Hugh Hefner sent to my home."

But this lady here is not obscene to me at all. And I
damn anyone who will say that my mother's body or
my daughter's body or my sister's body is dirty. No.

You tell me about this god of yours that made this
body—but then you qualify it. You tell little children
to cover up. You make it dirty. The dirty body. Well,
I'm going to tell you something: this is the most decent-
looking chick I've seen since I've been in town.

You know, in the backs of those "Fun Shops" you'll see
guys looking through racks and racks of pictures of
ladies' nay-nays wrapped in cellophane. All those pictures. Those guys looking through the racks there. One
eight-by-ten nude photostudy of a chick that's held
together by an aluminum hymen—that staple that the
guy will try to peer around. Wonder why a guy spends
all that bread—two bucks, six bucks, eight bucks—to
look at ladies' nay-nays? And some of these guys aren't
satisfied with looking at the flicks, and will violate your
daughter in a vacant lot.

How is it—and the records are there for you to view
—that *consistently,* the sex-maniacs that violate your
daughters, *murder* them after they violate them? And
have good religious backgrounds, consistently. Is it a
little possible that these guys came from that kind of a

family where the father might have been that moralist who went on public record to say,

"I wouldn't show my kids any picture of any half-nude tramps! No tramp runs around my house naked!"

And everybody covers up and the kid goes

"Christ! What can that look like? *How erotic can it be?* How erotic that my father's such a nut with that telling my sister to cover up—and she's only six years old—that he would go on public record to make such an issue of it? Well, I'm gonna *see* what that looks like some day, and if it's as dirty as my old man says it is, I'm gonna *kill* it."

Give me your next sex maniac, and every time out I'll show you:

"We don't understand! He had a good religious background!"

I'm hip he did, man. Yeah. And he's gonna pay the dues for it.

Tramp tramp tramp. You know how you can spot the real tramps in the Paul Malloy culture? Real tramps have babies in the bellies and no rings on their fingers, and they get their just desserts by bleeding to death in the backs of taxicabs.

Tramp tramp tramp the boys are marching.

Now, if you were from a different culture you'd say,

"This guy Paul Malloy is a 'Christian'? I wonder what these Christians were like? Let's see . . . Christ—what's his story?"

"Well, ah, if he was here the Russians would watch their asses. He was pretty good with a bowie knife. He'd start on the Russians, then he'd get Castro and he'd punch him out."

"That was his stick—violence and getting even.

That's what he's noted for."

Phew! What kind of a Christian is this guy Paul Malloy? What kind of a Christian would say, "Are we gonna forget that Hiss was a convicted criminal? Are we gonna forget that Hiss did forty-four months in the joint?" Certainly no good Christian would forget that. Then he goes on. Now he's talking about murderers. Why Must We Coddle Our Killers? He says he's not against rehabilitation—if the guy spends the rest of his life in jail.

Do you know why they took the prayers out of the public schools? Not only don't we forgive those who trespass against us; but we stick a hot poker up their ass so they never can forget it. We make them pay the dues, dues, dues. These people take the most perverse part of Christianity, and they make it a hate-you god, a suffer-suffer god.

I'll tell you who the real Christian of the year is— Jimmy Hoffa. I mean that sincerely. Um hm. Jimmy Hoffa is sure more of a Christian than Bobby Kennedy. Why? Cause Jimmy Hoffa hired ex-convicts, as Christ would have—I *assume* Christ would have hired ex-convicts. Unless he's that Paul Malloy Christ that makes you suffer and repent.

> "The only medicine that's good for you is iodine, cause it burns you, sinner. Keep douching with CN, or lysol that hasn't been diluted."

Ouuuuhhh!

I tell you, when Jehovah does return, you know, they're going to look back at this whole generation and say, "It's just *fiends, beasts!*" That's what we are.

Do you know that, well, let's see, in about a half-hour, some guy will be walking to his doom? How can we do that? How can we have people in prison for thirty years? Open the doors! It's *enough.*

291

There's a clergyman, he's willing to be the hangman in Australia—no one else would do it. He couldn't get a brown suit, though. But rabbis and priests get seventy-five bucks a throw. Could Christ walk with anybody in Death Row?

"Yes, my son, you must be brave."

Sure, *schmuck*—you're splitting, he's sitting.

No, I guess I'm pretty much of an atheist. Yeah. Believe believe believe. I'd have to all the way believe. I can't half-way believe. So if Adam and Eve doesn't make it, the "it" starts to fall apart. And then I say, "What color is god?"

"He's yellow."

"Oh, he's not yellow, he's black."

He's all gods. He's black, yellow, green and blue. That's right. He's a Maryjane god. He's any kind of god you want him to be, god, that's what he is. He's an anthropomorphic god. He's got eyes ears nose—he's, ah, *black!* He's Kasavubu, Lumumba . . . but I know that he's yellow . . . he's Jewish, black and yellow . . . he's, well, he's part Irish, and Jewish, and black . . . he's a pumpkin god, he's a halloween god, he's a good sweet loving god who'll make me burn in hell for my sins and blaspheming, he's that kind of god, too. He's a god you can make deals with:

"God, I promise if you do this—gimme one chance!—if you do this I'll never do that again, alright? I didn't jerk off for a year, now. I'll be good I'llbegoodI'llbegood. I'll be good honest I'll be good I'llbegoodgod."

And he's a god that you can exploit and make work for you, and get you respect in the community, and get St. Jude working for you, and all those other Catholic priests, Jewish—Eddie Cantor, putz-o exploiter, George E. Jessel and Kiss-it-off Santas. Yeah. He's a god that'll look at this culture and say, *"Whew!* What were they *doing,* man? They've got people in prison for thirty-five years!"

How can we be out here tonight, man? How can one Pope go in or out, or president, knowing that that jam has been on some guy for thirty-five years? That's terrible, man. Let him up, just a little bit. Let him out *one* time. Because when that guy went to the joint political conditions were different, economic conditions were different—he wouldn't have gone to the joint today. *Whew!* Boy. There's a guy who hasn't been kissed or hugged for thirty-five years. That's really enough, man.

Whew! All the things they've done in his name. Um umm. That's why he stuck around so long. Like any commercial art form. . . .

Now I really honest-to-god feel that way—there's never from a moral sense, right or wrong. It's just *my* right and *my* wrong. That doesn't make it empirical—not at all.

Somebody told me that we're using monkey glands on people to rejuvenate them. Then somebody coming back from Mexico told me that they're using *human* glands. Yes!

I said, "Well, where do they get them?"

Guy says, "From live people, people that are dying, and, uh, it's very expensive."

So I said, "What does it cost?"

"About a thousand dollars."

Oh yeah. A lot of people are dying, you know, the hospitals:

"Oh yeah, he's almost dead—that's alright."

Sure. You're gonna see. When there's more demand—

the first thing—the state insane asylums are going to be emptied out, quick! All died very quickly.

See, our moral concept is, What's accepted, what we will agree upon. That's what the moral concept is. If we agree that killing a few will save the most, then it'll be O.K. So if it comes right down to it, if we want to live a little longer—the sophisticated class, the gentry, will cook with it first:

[*whisper*] "Listen, I know a place, ya go . . ."
And with the first government control, then they'll have the farms—raising people:

"That's a good liver, good heart . . ."
You'll accept it. When it comes right down to the you-go-bye-bye:

> "These people don't know anything. They're raised for that purpose."
> "Yeah? You're sure?"
> "I'm telling you. They *like* that."
> "O.K. But I wanna paper saying that he gave it up, ah . . . *Oh I can't take the guy's liver and his heart and his balls! All that stuff?*"
> "*Sure.* Are you kidding me? He's better off without it. He gets it the next time, don't you know that?"

> "It's the work of the devil, to stick any chimpanzee's kidney in your kidneys, to use dead men's eyes. If I'm cockeyed, I gotta big back, the Lord meant it that way."

The Romans, they said, "We are moral and we are right. But we have one group that is against everything good. They are called Christians. And we take them and throw them to the lions. Because they deserve it, man. That's the only way to look at it, you know. Our legislature believes this is correct and we throw them to the lions."

Yeah, the Romans really had the Christians pegged—
they worked their asses off:

"Here we are in Rome. Now, before you come
around with your liberal horseshit about these
Christians and all their bullshit, get close to them
a little, will ya? Don't listen to all this shit you read
in the newspapers, first look at the record. It speaks
for itself. We have fifteen gods in Rome, and we
paid for every one of them, and they belong to
us. They're our gods. We got everything working
here, the Christians wanna come in, Johnny-come-
lately, and take it all away.

"Did you ever get close to one of these people?
I mean, soap and water don't cost much, does it?
They dress in rags! They stink to high heaven! Half
of them are on welfare.

"I don't know if you've ever talked to these
Christians—you people live up on the plateau
don't know what it's like. You get down here, and
get near them—they stink to high heaven. They all
got diseases. Every Christian's got leprosy, and
they don't believe in birth control—give them a
condom and they'll knock you on your ass! They
got a million kids and no way to support.

"And you say to them, 'Hey! Look at our gods.
We paid for them. Where's your god?'

"Then you get some horseshit: 'You can't see
'em'—that's all they will tell ya. They haven't got
none, that's all! They can't afford none.

"How would you like it if the Christians set
up headquarters in Rome, hey? That's why we
must segregate—with lions."

Now, as rough as segregation gets, boy—lion-eating, forget it! You know, there's a big difference between being
schlepped away from a lunch counter—yeah, I'd rather

be refused the right to service than be served as refuse, anytime.

No right or wrong. My right, your wrong—but as far as anything that you can graph it with, you know, it keeps changing.

I weigh one hundred and fifty pounds. Today this is right. Twenty years ago it was wrong—I was on the bench in an ad, a guy was kicking sand in my face, POW!
"Hey skinny!"
Right? And a *schtarker* came along and grabbed my chick, "C'mon baby, let's get outta here."

And I was left alone on the beach, with a beach ball. It's hard to ball a beach ball. The air keeps coming out.

Now, the real hangup is that intellectual awareness does you no good. That's why I have no faith in analysis. Pills are the answer: cured syphilis, it'll cure schizos. And the two big problems, alcoholism and narcotics, they back off. So they have a very embarrassing record. I think that Catholicism is as correct and cheaper and has more drama involved. That catharsis scene. Because understanding the problem doesn't help you. Doesn't help me.

I understand that intellectually—that a woman that sleeps with a different guy every week is a better Christian than the virgin. Because she has the capacity to kiss and hug fifty guys a year. And that's what that act is—kissing and hugging. You can't do it to anyone you're mad at. If you're just a bit bugged with them, you can't make it.

So that chick who's got that much love for all her fellowman that she can make it with fifty guys a year—that's intellectually; but emotionally, I don't want to be the fifty-first guy. Cause I learned my lesson early, man. The people told me, "This is the way it is, Virgin is Good, Virgin is Good." Yeah, that's really weird.

This conflict, you know, like you talk to the average guy:
"Isn't that a pretty chick?"
"Yeah, she's beautiful."
"What's her beauty—to you?"
"Well, ah, she's got a pretty face, nutty jugs . . ."
"Well, ah, would you marry a woman like that?"
"Of course."
"You'd like her for your wife?"
"Sure!"
"Would you let your *wife* dress that way?"
"No no no!"
"Why not?"
"Cause she got her jugs stickin out, man."
"What'd you dig her for in the first place?"
"Cause her jugs were stickin out."
"But you don't want her to dress that way."
"No, no!"
So that's where the conflict is—we want for a wife a combination kindergarten teacher and a hooker.

We're all taught a what-should-be culture. Which means. a lot of *bull*shit. *Emmis.* Because instead of being taught, *This is what is*—that's a beautiful truth, what man always has been—we're taught the fantasy, man. But if we were taught This Is What Is, I think we'd be less screwed up.

You know, if we could just *shape up*, man, and *admit,* the jails would start to empty out. If you would admit that perhaps you've always loved yourself above all, that you have sold your country out and will continually, that *you* are first, that you are above flag—

It's—well, you see, the trouble with the Paul Malloy culture, it teaches Cast the First Stone, consistently. You see, you may know that you're not the Good Man, you're maybe a little weak; but you know that the Good Man does exist, and the part of Good that doesn't relate to you relates to that other guy.

Did you see those flicks in *Time* magazine? They had three dirty pictures about that whole incident [*Kennedy assassination*]. A guy got a medal for—what? For risking his life—that was part of the medal. The first picture I saw, when she went out of the car, he shielded her, protected her. But I believe the one real action that did happen was that he did place her back in the car. I think that was part of the medal.

Now in *Time* magazine I see some different captions. Now the conclusion that I've formed was denied by *Time* magazine, which said that she was going to get help. Now, I challenge them: to which checkpoint would she go? Where's her experience? "Oh, yes, when he shot I knew and I went right off the car to get help, so I could bring back the help." No. I think that's bullshit.

Now, why did the guy get the medal? Certainly not the last caption, that he's being helped aboard. That's bullshit. Yeah.

Why this is a dirty picture to me, and offensive, is because it sets up a lie, that she was going to get help, and that she was helping him aboard. Because when your daughters, if their husbands get shot, and they haul ass to save their asses, they'll feel shitty, and low, because they're not like that good Mrs. Kennedy who stayed there. And *fuck it,* she *didn't* stay there! That's a *lie* they keep telling people, to keep living up to bullshit that never did exist. Because the people who believe that bullshit are foremen of the juries that put you away. And indict:

"Goddamn it, *I'd* never sell my country out!"
"You ever been tested?"

"No, but I'm just not the kind of guy that would. I know it. I'd *never* sell my country out. Powers is a fink. That's why I'm gonna cast the first stone: he's no good. He's a wrong guy, bad apple. If *I* get on the jury, *I'll burn his ass.* And he's going away for a long time. That's it, no bullshit. I've got the secrets right here. *I'm* a loyal American. No, *I'd* never sell my country out.

"They got the other guy? They got his *pants* down? But I don't give a goddamn *what* they do to him, I'd never sell—What're they putting a funnel in his ass for? Can't put a funnel in his ass! Geneva Conference! Tell 'em to take the funnel out— they can't do that . . . What're they heating up that lead for?

"You're not getting these secrets from me! Forget that with those tricks!

"They wouldn't put hot lead into that funnel that's in that guy's ass, now, would they? For a few dumb secrets! Would they? Would they? . . . they are . . . well, that's *ridiculous!*

"Oh, the secrets? *Surprise!* Here they are, buddy. I, ah, I mean, I got *more* secrets, too, you wouldn't even believe! These are bullshit secrets. I'll *make up* shit. I'll give you the president and the White House!

"I just don't want to get hot lead in my ass, that's all. It's just, ah—*Fuck you! You take the hot lead enema!* Are you kidding? I just don't like hot lead in my ass, that's all. Yeah. Had it once, didn't agree with me.

"We got a *million* secrets! What the hell's six hundred secrets, for Chrissakes?"

That's it, Jim. Any of you people can take the hot lead enema, then you can damn Powers, or that Peeping

299

Tom, or that tramp there. But until then, Jim, *hab roch munas,* get off his back, have some pity, Jim.

This is a publication called *Variety.* For many years Frank Sinatra has projected a very virile image. I've always suspected this, but I've never gone into it. Now Sinatra goes to be a producer. Albert Maltz is a screenwriter. Now, you know the old American cliche: "If you've paid for your crime, then no man can be tried twice." I'm sure everyone agrees with that. You pay your dues, end.

Alright. Albert Maltz has been suspected of being a communist. He pleaded the Fifth and got into a whole *tumler,* and for this, he has been censured as far as writing is concerned. Now I'll tell you now, I would never plead any Fifth. Communism? Forget it. It's an archaic form of government that never can work.

But Sinatra hired this guy to write "The Execution of Private Slovak," and then chickened out and bombed out. Dig. This is Sinatra:

"In view of the reaction of my family, my friends, and the American public—"

I don't know what family he's talking about, and I don't know what American public he's talking about, but he instructed his attorneys to make a settlement with Albert Maltz and inform him that he will not write "The Execution of Private Slovak." And he goes on and on. He says:

"But the American public has indicated it feels the morality of hiring Albert Maltz is a more crucial matter, and I will accept this majority."

Well, I don't know if you know it or not, but Lawford's old lady is Kennedy's sister, and Kennedy, naturally, probably was the moral factor, probably put a lot of pressure—not directly: Joe Kennedy probably called up Cardinal Stritch, who in turn called Spellman, who in turn probably called Carmine DeSapio, who called Vito Genovese, and then to Sinatra, and *bandam!* You know?

But this time Sinatra had enough money to afford some integrity. That's what I feel. I feel that this is not a man, a guy who balls a million chicks and gets juiced out of his kug.

You know who was a man? Christ was a man. I don't want that decadent, debauched picture for the American public. I don't want a swinger, I want a down person, who's concerned with issues, who would have the *chutzpah* to stand by Maltz: I hired him, later, man. Not have the *kohach* to whack out some guy in the toilet in the Riviera.

It's like the faggots who were busted, deviates. They're schoolteachers. So the Hearst paper wants to know how come, that these faggots—they're convicted, but now they're teaching school again—how come the school board didn't chuck em off?

Well, there's two schools of thought. One, perhaps, that they're good teachers, that's why they're still teaching, and there's been no incident reported yet where a kid came home and said,

> "Today in school I learned five minutes of geography and ten minutes of cocksucking."

Now, if you're the parent that says, "Well, no, that's not the factor. Even though they paid their debt to society, my child is in imminent danger of being attacked by these people—after all, they have a record for this, and who knows? In the heat of passion they may do it again."

Alright. If that's the argument—"I was a Jew lived in dread fear of Christian schoolteachers. They're well-known for their missionary ways. Who knows? In the heat of passion they may pervert my child, stick a St. Christopher medal in his hand."

You see, I can always relate back to theology. Christ forgave, and if you say you're Christians, then *you* forgive. And then Albert Maltz, Dalton Trumbo, Ring Lardner Jr., who were Communist writers—And I believe in judicial law. If you break my law, I want you to pay your dues. And they did, they did a year in the joint in '48; but that's all—they spent their time.

Now if you want to keep stringing them out and not forgive them, you're *pagans*. But if you *are* pagans, I don't care, man, but just be *consistent*. Say, "We're *not* Christians, we're gonna persecute an ex-con, we're gonna lean on the flag and the Bible, we're gonna take those writers tomorrow and put them up against the wall and shoot them—"

But Ronald Reagan has to pull the trigger. No one else, my friend.

You believe in a law, solid. But once the cat pays his dues, that's enough. Let them alone, man.

That's what everyone is always offended with, just hypocrisy. That's why you've never been bugged once in your life by cannibals. Cause they never said they were vegetarians. "We *fress* people, man, that's our stick." And they were consistent with it. Yeah, so . . .

This poem was written by Thomas Merton, and, it's a groovy poem, and it really says a lot to me:

> My name is Adolf Eichmann.
> The Jews came every day
> to vat they thought vould be
> fun in the showers.
> The mothers vere quite ingenious.

They vould take the children
and hide them in
bundles of clothing.
Ve found the children,
scrubbed them,
put them in the chambers,
and sealed them in.
I vatched through the portholes
as they would doven and chant
   "Hey, mein Liebe, heyyyy."
Ve took off their clean Jewish love-rings,
removed their teeth and hair—
for strategic defense.
I made soap out of them,
I made soap out of all of them;
and they hung me,
in full view of the prison yard.
People say,
   "Adolf Eichmann should have been hung!"
Nein.
Nein, if you recognize the whoredom
in all of you,
that you would have done the same,
if you dared know yourselves.
My defense?
I vas a soldier.
People laugh
  "Ha ha! This is no defense,
   that you are a soldier."
This is trite.
I vas a soldier,
a good soldier.
I saw the end of a conscientious day's effort.
I saw all the work that I did.
I, Adolf Eichmann,
vatched through the portholes.

I saw every Jew burned
und turned into soap.
Do you people think yourselves better
because you burned your enemies
at long distances
with missiles?
Without ever seeing what you'd done to them?
Hiroshima . . . *Auf Wiedersehen* . . .

* * *

Chronicle

May, 1959, *The New York Times*
"The newest and in some ways most scarifyingly funny proponent of significance . . . to be found in a night-club these days is Lenny Bruce, a sort of abstract-expressionist stand-up comedian paid $1750 a week to vent his outrage. on the clientele. . . ."

June, 1960, *The Reporter*
"The question is how far Bruce will go in further exposing his most enthusiastic audiences . . . to themselves. He has only begun to operate. . . ."

September 29, 1961: BUSTED FOR POSSESSION OF NARCOTICS, Philadelphia.
October 4, 1961: BUSTED FOR OBSCENITY, Jazz Workshop, San Francisco.
September, 1962: BANNED IN AUSTRALIA.
October 6, 1962: BUSTED FOR POSSESSION OF NARCOTICS, Los Angeles.
October 24, 1962: BUSTED FOR OBSCENITY, Troubador Theatre, Hollywood.

December, 1962: BUSTED FOR OBSCENITY, Gate of Horn, Chicago.
January, 1963: BUSTED FOR POSSESSION OF NARCOTICS, Los Angeles.
April, 1963: BARRED FROM ENTERING ENGLAND, London.

March, 1964, *The New York Post*
"Bruce stands up against all limitations on the flesh and spirit, and someday they are going to crush him for it."

April, 1964: BUSTED FOR OBSCENITY, Cafe Au Go-Go, New York City.
October, 1965: DECLARED A LEGALLY BANKRUPT PAUPER, San Francisco.

November, 1965, *Esquire*
"I saw his act . . . in Chicago. . . . He looked nervous and shaky . . . wretched, broken. . . . You thought of Dorothy Parker, who, when she saw Scott Fitzgerald's sodden and too-youthful corpse, murmured, 'The poor son of a bitch.' "

August 3, 1966; DEAD. Los Angeles.

Epilogue

Lenny Bruce did not die of an O.D.; he was murdered. Murdered by the same people and for the same reasons protesters are getting their heads cracked open in Oakland and New York and Milwaukee and Washington, D.C. and on college campuses—because Bruce's words and gestures said too clearly just what people are saying now in words not so beautiful or piercing and in gestures much more meaningful: that America proposes Christian Love and Democratic Goodness, and dispenses death and hate and corruption and lies. And if you say this too loudly in the USA, you'll get a bust on the head or a bust on some Big Lie, like the lie that Bruce was "sick," like the lie that he was obscene, like the lie that he was an addict.

Bruce wouldn't have liked that paragraph. Despite his philosophy of facing up to "what is" instead of swallowing the legends of "what should be," he never faced the ultimate truth of what is in America. He never faced the facts of what is with the police, the government, the courts and the judges that busted and murdered him. He was afraid to—it's hard to split completely from the Biggest Daddy of them all, the Establishment. Bruce couldn't do that—he couldn't even mouth the words to approach that. He satirized anything else viciously and beautifully—the whole spectrum of the lies and the hate of America—but he never really laid into cops, courts or the government. He picked at them occasionally—he had to—after all, everything he was saying drove to that point. But he could never really make the final break. Instead, he apologized for the agents of his persecution.

But this doesn't change where Bruce was at. And when you know where Bruce was at, most of the stuff that's been written about him becomes, to say the least, irrelevant: the early, nasty attacks published in the same magazines and newspapers that later, after Bruce had been silenced, turned around and praised him; the carpings by those who couldn't bring themselves to go all the way for a crude, uneducated hipster; the soppy obituaries and post-obituaries by journalists, newspapers and magazines that never helped Bruce at all when he was alive. Bruce was a subtle and complex artist; but even the smartest literary criticisms and peans for him are irrelevant. Polishing trenchant phrases for elite reviews to draw astonished gasps from admirers in the cultural establishment isn't where Bruce was at at all. Bruce was an artist, but he was dedicated to *what* he was saying, not the fact that *he* was saying it. So from where he was at, Bruce didn't like the Establishment's self-appreciating culture, even when it was saying how great Lenny Bruce was. For himself, Bruce preferred jazzmen and hipsters and people who were where he was at.

Bruce wasn't an activist, but anyone who says that he digs Bruce and prints it in the *Times* or *Time* or the *Examiner* or the *Star,* anyone who says he digs Bruce and goes to work for Dow Chemical or IBM or the Peace Corps, doesn't comprehend. The only people who really dig Lenny Bruce are the people who are doing the same thing Bruce did—cutting loose, turning on, turning away, trying to turn America around.

308

Index of Bits

I. BLACKS

II. JEWS

III. RELIGIONS INC.; CATHOLICISM; CHRIST & MOSES; AND THE LONE RANGER

IV. POLITICS

VII. PILLS AND SHIT: THE DRUG SCENE

VIII. FANTASIES, FLICKS & SKETCHES

IX. BALLING, CHICKS, FAGS, DIKES & DIVORCE

X. THE DIRTY-WORD CONCEPT

XI. OBSCENITY BUSTS AND TRIALS

XII. BUSTS II: CAUSES AND CONSEQUENCES

XIII.   SPOTTING HEAT, AND UNDER-STANDING JUDGES AND LAWYERS

XIV.   THE LAW

XV. WHAT IS OBSCENE?

XVI. THE GOOD-GOOD CULTURE